Going for the Mail

A History of Door County Post Offices

By James B. Hale

1996

Published by the Brown County Historical Society
Green Bay, Wisconsin

Art Direction by Jeremy Ness of Kiar Designs, Ltd.

P.O. Box 8085, Green Bay, Wisconsin 54308-8085
(414) 465-2446

ISBN 0-9641499-3-1
Library of Congress Catalog Card Number: 95-83803

Printed in the U.S.A.

Table of Contents

Preface

This book is part encyclopedia, part anthology, part narrative and part almanac. It pulls together the scattered bits and pieces of information I have been able to find over twenty-odd years of reading histories, searching newspaper files, talking to postal historians and interviewing Door County residents. The information herein is not presented as a complete or totally accurate history. Sources are too scattered, too sketchy and sometimes too inconsistent in details to allow a claim of completeness. I have tried to be as accurate as the facts permit, but interpretation occasionally has been necessary.

Few historical projects can be carried on alone, and mine is no exception. Since beginning a study of Door County post offices in 1968, I have received information and advice given freely and enthusiastically by many people. I am especially grateful for funding received for this project from the Cliff and Clara Herlache Heritage Foundation and the Door County Historical Society.

Individuals and organizations who have been most helpful over the years are Stanley Greene, Conan Bryant Eaton, Arden Robertson, Orville Schopf, Edward Allen III, Frank Moertl, Carl Kannewurf, Kubet Luchterhand, John Enigl, William Robinson, Charles Peirce, Arthur Van Vlissingen, Ann Thorp, Harry Chaudoir, Frederic Cassidy, Joan LeClair, Thomas Pinney Sr., Alan Patera, Merwin Leet, Frank Tachovsky, Harry Chaudoir, Bill Meindl, the *Door County Advocate* staff, the Door County Library staff, Wisconsin Postal History Society members, Door County Museum, Peninsula Genealogical Society, Library of the State Historical Society of Wisconsin, and postmasters of Door County.

Some of the material included here appeared earlier in *Badger Postal History* (journal of the Wisconsin Postal History Society) and the *Door County Almanack* #3. Data on postmasters given with each individual office history are from various publications of the U.S. Post Office Department or Postal Service located in the National Archives, Washington, DC.

Finally, I can do no better than to quote Conan Bryant Eaton, who offered a statement in his book *Death's Door - Pursuit of a Legend* written by A.C. Wheeler in an 1861 history of Milwaukee:

"In presenting this book...the Author asks no indulgence; his object, he must be permitted to say is a good one, and those who do not admire the execution have the same privilege to grumble that he had to write."

In this sentiment I heartily concur.

-James B. Hale

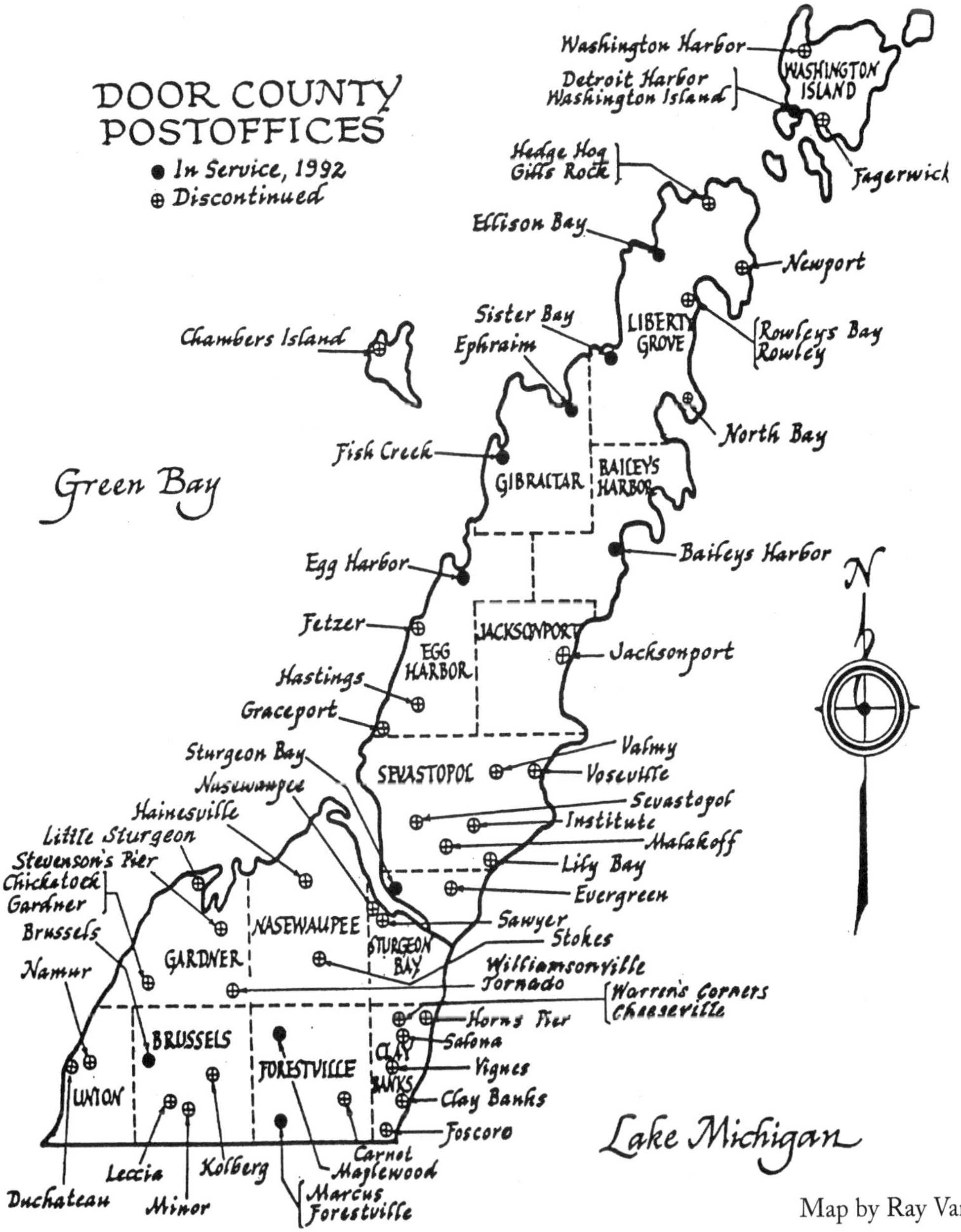

Map by Ray Van Handel Sr.

Introduction

In February of 1867, a settler near Little Sturgeon in Door County wrote a letter back to his family in Pennsylvania:

> *Dear Sister Annie,*
>
> *I am waiting for your answer to my letters, but will write again anyway. Alfred and I are trying to finish clearing timber so we will have enough ground to plant this spring. His hip bothers him considerable so the work is slow. I am fine. How are things at home? Write soon. It is always good to hear from you.*
>
> *Your Bro., John*

A similar thirst for news of friends, family and old homes was characteristic of our pioneer forebears in this country. Door County was no exception. Here, as elsewhere, the only method of long-distance communication was by mail. Thus, wherever there were people far from home, there was a demand for service from the United States Post Office Department.

The post office always has been a great social institution, although it is seldom recognized in that context. People have an inherent need to communicate with each other, and the post office helps to satisfy that need.

Before the days of telephones, radio and television, the mails were a major source of information on happenings elsewhere in the world. The local post office itself in the early times, and to a considerable extent today, was a community center where people gathered to find out what delights or sorrows might arrive in their mail, or to swap gossip with their neighbors.

This eager anticipation of the daily mail was as true in Door County as elsewhere. Elsie Anclam, daughter of a Baileys Harbor postmaster, wrote about how it was at the turn of the century:

> *In the autumn of 1892 my parents, Mr. and Mrs. John Anclam, came to Baileys Harbor where they purchased the store of Augusta Wohltman. The following spring they moved into the large white building, to operate the general store and post office until 1914...*
>
> *The post office cabinet occupied a corner of the store and when the mail arrived, late in winter due to snow-bound roads, the crowd gathered around, making considerable noise, sometimes unnerving the postmaster trying desperately to sort the mail. The mail, in those days, was carried by wagon in summer; it was known as the 'stage.' In winter a sleigh was used with a coal stove supplying the heat...("Childhood at Baileys Harbor,"* The Peninsula *7:24-25, 1963)*

"Going for the mail" in most small towns is still an important part of life.

Postal history, as a subject for amateur historians, is a combination of local history and philately. The Wisconsin Postal History Society, for example, is a group of about 200 people, mostly from Wisconsin, who share an interest in all things related to the past and present of mail services in the state. The Society is affiliated with the local history program of the State Historical Society of Wisconsin and with the Wisconsin Federation of Stamp Clubs. A main activity of the membership is the acquiring of old envelopes (called "covers" by collectors) and postcards that bear the postmarks and other postal markings used during the life of each post office. Another major activity is a series of research bulletins on various aspects of postal history from Wisconsin's territorial years to today's electronic mail systems.

Postal history can be studied and collected world-wide, by state or county, by a single post office, by topic, by stamp issue, or any other aspect that interests you. Wisconsin's first post office was established at Green Bay in 1821, and there have been more than 3,700 offices in existence in the state at one time or another. Only about 800 are operating today. Thus, there is a large body of information potentially available to both the local historian and the stamp collector.

To understand how postal services have operated, it is necessary to know the names, locations and dates of operations of post offices; types of stamps, postmarks and other markings applied to mail in transit; mail transport routes and methods (rail, truck, RFD, stages, air, etc.); post office personnel and their dates of service; and derivation of post office names. Such information can come from many sources - U.S. government publications, especially of the Post Office Department and Postal Service, the U.S. National Archives in Washington, DC, state and local history societies, philatelic libraries, old books of local history (Wisconsin county histories of 1870-1920 vintage are especially helpful), newspaper archives, interviews with older local residents, and other collectors and historians. The Laurie Room at the Door County Library in Sturgeon Bay has many important materials for postal historians.

Sometimes post office-related items come along when you least expect them. At a craft show I found a walnut savings bank accessed by the door of a lock-box once used in the Ephraim post office. Another unexpected example was the promotional button for the 1988 Maifest celebration at Jacksonport which featured an old photograph of the Jacksonport post office. I learned of the existence of a recording of a 1954 radio interview on Door County's rural mail delivery system (transcribed later in this book) through a casual conversation with a neighbor. It is a charge to one's ingenuity to keep ferreting out facts from the many available sources.

The more exploring of the past one does, the more unanswered questions arise. That is why the search for better answers remains fascinating. The unknowns become a challenge, and it is a great satisfaction when, little by little, pieces fall into place as some unexpected historical fact comes to light.

The U.S. Mail in Door County - An Overview

The United States Post Office Department did not officially come to Door County until June 22, 1854, when the first regular office opened at Washington Harbor on the north end of Washington Island. Before that time, the mails were irregular and undependable. Settlements were few and were confined to the shores of Lake Michigan and Green Bay.

H.R. Holand wrote of the people on Rock Island in the early 1840s that

> *Their chief handicap was their distance from any post office through which to learn the news of the outside world. The most accessible one (and the one with better connections to the east than Green Bay) was at Chicago, 300 miles away. Mail intended for the settlement was usually directed as follows: 'H.D. Miner, Rock Island, care of Williams, Chicago, Illinois.' On his occasional visits to the metropolis, Job Luther would get the little bundle of Rock Island letters and newspapers, often many months old.* (History of Door County, *Vol. I:466, 1917)*

In 1854 the county itself was only three years old, having been set off from Brown County by the state legislature in 1851. The original Door County also included present-day Kewaunee County, but in 1852 the legislature reduced Door to its present size and established Kewaunee as a separate county.

There were no roads inland. The nearest post office was at Green Bay, where the first post office in what is now Wisconsin had been established in 1821. However, a trip to Green Bay was not easy, since it involved a 100-mile journey by boat in the summer or on foot over the ice in winter.

By the 1850s, and before Washington Harbor had a post office, the fishermen on Washington and Rock Islands were having mail brought to them from Green Bay in the summer months by the fish buyers who made weekly trips by boat. In the winter, however, the people who stayed on the islands were left to their own devices. They chose H.D. Miner, son of the first Protestant missionary among the Indians in Wisconsin, to make an occasional trip to Green Bay on the ice. When the ice was in good condition, he made the round trip to Green Bay twice a month. Mr. Miner also carried mail from Washington Island twelve miles north to St. Martin's Island in Michigan. He was hired to do this by the St. Martin's residents for 25¢ per letter or paper.

In the fall of 1856, the first road was cut through the woods from Sturgeon Bay to Egg Harbor, and in the following winter another road was opened from Sturgeon Bay south to Green Bay by way of Little Sturgeon Bay. This made more frequent communications possible between the county and the rest of the state. The resulting demand for postal service was soon followed by the establishment of more post offices and the hiring of private contractors to carry the mails between post offices. Sturgeon Bay in 1855 and Fish Creek in 1858 were the county's second and third offices. By 1862, thirteen offices were operating in the county.

The *Door County Advocate* devoted much comment on the location of contract mail routes. The major routes in the 1860s were from Green Bay to Sturgeon Bay, from Kewaunee to Sturgeon Bay, and from Sturgeon Bay north. In the early 1870s, more routes were added as more post offices were established. The *Advocate* on January 26, 1871, announced the Postmaster General's request for bids on Door County mail routes to be in effect from July 1, 1871 through June 30, 1874, as follows:

> *No. 13363. From Little Sturgeon Bay to Brussels, eight miles and back, twice a week. Leave Little Sturgeon Bay Monday and Friday at 11 a.m. Arrive at Brussels at 2 p.m. Leave Brussels Monday and Friday at 3 p.m. Arrive at Little Sturgeon by 6 p.m. Proposals for three-times-aweek service invited.*
>
> *No. 13364. From Ephraim to North Bay, 10 miles and back, once a week. Bidders will propose suitable schedule of departures and arrivals.*
>
> *No. 13365. From Ephraim to Washington Harbor, twenty-six miles and back, once a week, from December 1 to April 30 each year. Bidders will propose suitable schedule of departures and arrivals.*
>
> *No. 13366. From Washington Harbor to Green Bay, eighty miles and back, once a week, in steamboats from May 1 to November 30 each year, by a schedule to be arranged.*
>
> *Information about sending in bids can be obtained from any postmaster.*

In 1873, more mail routes were put up for bids, including Baileys Harbor to Egg Harbor and back once a week; Baileys Harbor by Jacksonport to Sturgeon Bay and back twice a week; Ephraim by Fish Creek and Egg Harbor to Sturgeon Bay and back twice a week; Sturgeon Bay by Warren's Corners, Clay Banks, Foscoro, Ahnapee and Alaska to Kewaunee and back once a week; Green Bay by Bay Settlement, Wequiock, Dyckesville, Namur, Duchateau and Brussels to Sturgeon Bay and back once a week.

The year 1858 was a vintage one, with offices opening at Fish Creek on August 26, Nasewaupee (on the west side of Sturgeon Bay) on September 4, Marcus (later to become Forestville) on September 16, and Chickatock (later renamed Gardner) on October 27. Little Sturgeon and Baileys Harbor opened in 1860, followed by Egg Harbor and Ephraim in 1861, and Brussels, Duchateau (in the Town of Union) and Clay Banks in 1862. Of these thirteen, six no longer exist - Washington Harbor, Nasewaupee, Gardner, Little Sturgeon, Duchateau, and Clay Banks.

The early days of the county's postal services were not without their problems. A tragic one was described in the *Door County Advocate* of July 5, 1862:

> *LOSS OF A MAIL AND SUPPOSED SUICIDE OF THE MAIL CARRIER.—The mail for Door County, which left Green Bay on Monday morning last, and which should have reached Sturgeon Bay the following day, (Tuesday) at*

noon, was lost on the route through the woods, under very distressing circumstances. We have been unable to gather particulars in full, but at the time of going to press, learn that the mail was carried by the contractor, Mr. D.H. Hubbard, of Fort Howard, who was carrying it on horseback. It appears that after leaving Sugar Creek post office, somewhere between there and Little Sturgeon Bay, he fell from his horse, and on recovering from the insensibility, arising it is supposed from the fall, found the horse and mail gone. Mr. Hubbard at once started in pursuit, but failing to find either mail or horse, returned to Sugar Creek, where he was heard to say that he should 'go again in search of the mail, and if he couldn't find it, they would not find him alive,' or words to that effect. It would seem that he failed to find either horse or mail bag, as the report has reached us from several persons that his body was found hanging from a tree, in the woods between Little Sturgeon Bay and Sugar Creek, but beyond this we cannot learn any particulars as to who found the body, the exact spot where it was found, or what further has transpired in relation to the unfortunate event. Up to this time Saturday noon, the mail-bag had not been recovered.

The details of this intriguing event probably will never be learned, since it was never mentioned again in the pages of the *Advocate*. Another interesting aspect of the story is that there never was a post office named Sugar Creek in the county. Duchateau post office was located near the upstream end of Sugar Creek and was probably better known to the local residents by the latter name than by the former, a situation not uncommon at other small, rural post offices.

Weather was a constant problem, with winter snows and summer mud a regular impediment to the mail carriers. The *Advocate* of December 24, 1863, reported a typical example:

A heavy snow storm commenced raging here on Saturday night last, and it has been snowing and blowing all the week since and still continues. The lumbermen say it is two and a half feet deep in the woods on a level, while here in the village and on the roads and in the clearings the high wind has drifted the snow into banks of from four to ten feet deep. We understand that the mail for Green Bay, which left here on Monday morning, did not reach there until Wednesday. The return mail has not yet arrived, now two days behind time — we are blockaded in — the Michicott mail started out this morning, but could not get through and returned here — we can't get out and our mails can't get in, so we are without any late news to give our readers...

Frequent complaints and an occasional compliment appear in the pages of the *Advocate* over the years. A typical one published April 17, 1873 noted that

The Green Bay mail due here last Wednesday night did not reach here until the next morning, and the Friday night mail did not come at all. These delays are proving a serious annoyance to our business men and should be stopped. Although

the roads are in a bad condition, we believe, with proper management, the mail could come through on time, especially when private teams go through in a day.

A more recent recognition of a postal problem, captioned "Unusual Rural Routes," appeared in the *U.S. Postal Guide* of December, 1923:

Among the most dangerous and difficult to perform service on are the routes from Newport to Otter Rock, Oreg.; Ellison Bay to Detroit Harbor, Wis.; Rocky Bar to Atlanta, Idaho; and from Sandusky to Kelly's Island, Middle Bass, and Put in Bay, Ohio...The routes from Ellison Bay to Detroit Harbor and from Sandusky to near-by islands must be operated over the ice in winter and in fall when the lake is freezing. In the spring, thawing it is extremely difficult and hazardous to perform the service, and a considerable number of carriers have lost their lives in endeavoring to transport the mails.

Post offices continued to come and go in the 1880s and '90s under the influence of economics and local politics, since postmasterships were strictly political appointments and were subject to change whenever the political party holding the presidency in Washington was changed. The postmaster usually was expected to serve as the local head of the political party that appointed him.

By 1880, postal services had expanded greatly. There were twenty-four offices in the county that year. Charles Martin, writing in 1881, reported that

*From Sturgeon Bay, the county seat, mails and express make daily connections with railroad routes at Green Bay. All over the county but a few miles apart, are established post offices, conveniently located for settlements and settlers. Mail matters are carried to the post offices by stage lines, and parties desiring to reach any part of the county can secure passage in the mail coaches at reasonably low prices. (*History of Door County Wisconsin, *p. 12, 1881)*

As a matter of record, the "coaches" were more often than not a horse and wagon or buggy.

The peak period for post office numbers was 1898 to 1902, when thirty-six offices were operating in the county. This was at the end of several decades of rapid rural settlement when it was Post Office Department policy to have offices located so that no one had to go more than just a few miles to get their mail. By 1908, the number had declined to thirteen, primarily due to the establishment of Rural Free Delivery, which closed many of the smaller village and rural offices all over Wisconsin.

Since then, Maplewood was reestablished in 1913 (having been closed in 1904), Washington Harbor closed in 1916, Sawyer closed in 1938 to become a still-existing station of the Sturgeon Bay office, Jacksonport became a rural station of Sturgeon Bay in 1958 and closed for good in 1970, and the remaining eleven are still handling all the county's mail: Washington Island, Ellison Bay, Sister Bay, Ephraim, Fish Creek, Egg Harbor, Baileys Harbor, Sturgeon Bay, Brussels, Maplewood, and Forestville. In total over the years, Door

County has had forty-eight different post offices, with fifty-six names due to eight name changes.

In the early years, it seemed to be a status symbol to obtain a post office for your community, become its postmaster, and have it named after yourself. At least seven of the county's offices bore the name of the first postmaster. For example, Marcus McCormick was the first postmaster at Marcus, the village that later was renamed Forestville. Voseville is another example. Thomas Vose was the first postmaster of this office, which was located first at Valmy and later at Whitefish Bay. Other offices in this category include Duchateau, Horn's Pier, Stevenson's Pier, Stokes, and Williamsonville.

The rewards of a nineteenth century postmaster almost certainly had to be mainly local status, because they were not money. Stipends were often less than ten dollars per year. Francois Pierre, who was Brussels' postmaster from 1870 to 1902, earned salaries ranging from $12 to $120 per year. In the first three months of the Nasewaupee post office in 1858, Postmaster Nelson Fuller earned 37¢.

Postmasters' compensation at fourth-class offices, which most were during this period, was computed as a fraction of the dollar business done at their offices rather than paid as a fixed salary. Every three months the postmaster was paid all of the first $50 of office revenue, fifty percent of the next $200, and forty percent of everything over $350, but at a total to the postmaster not to exceed $250. This put a cap of $1,000 per year on salaries but did not guarantee a minimum wage. Assuming post office revenues reflected the number of people using the mails, these salary levels are good indices of human population growth in each community.

Women were not slighted as postmasters. In 1878, Mrs. Matilda Hunt at Ellison Bay became the county's first female postmaster. Other women were postmasters before 1900 at Baileys Harbor, Evergreen, Forestville, Hainesville, Institute, Namur, Sevastopol, Sister Bay, Stokes, Tornado and Valmy. Incidentally, "postmaster" is a word that has no gender; you are a postmaster regardless of your sex.

Baileys Harbor

Established December 4, 1860, and is still in service. Zip Code - 54202.

Location: In the present village of the same name in the southwest quarter of section 20, Town 30 North, Range 28 East, Town of Baileys Harbor.

The early history of Baileys Harbor is unusual. Its name originated in the mid-1840s, when a ship captain named Bailey took emergency refuge from a northeast gale in the previously unknown harbor. Captain Bailey took a glowing report of the area back to his employer, Alanson Sweet of Milwaukee, who owned a large shipping business on the lakes. In the summer of 1849, Mr. Sweet bought 125 acres of land at Baileys Harbor and drew up plans for a village to be called Gibraltar. He sent Solomon Beery, later a Baileys Harbor postmaster, to be in charge of opening a stone quarry and building a pier. In 1851, Sweet built the first lighthouse at the harbor entrance under a government contract.

An 1869 cover postmarked in blue ink.

When Door County was established by the state legislature in 1851, Mr. Sweet persuaded the lawmakers to designate his planned village at Baileys Harbor as the county seat even though no village existed there. A short time later, for obscure reasons, Mr. Sweet closed his business and left Baileys Harbor without ever building his village. Other settlers came, however, and the village eventually prospered.

The matter of the county seat was not easily resolved. H.R. Holand described the event this way:

> *Bailey's Harbor...continued as the county seat until 1857 when the energetic hustlers of Sturgeon Bay took the necessary steps to have the county seat removed to the latter village. Notices were posted in Baileys Harbor and elsewhere, chiefly inspected by chipmunks, stating that an election would be held to learn the wish of the people as to the location of the county seat. A cigar box was then carried around*

1886 registered letter with a fancy oval postmark.

> *to the scattered fishermen and a few dozen farmers inviting them to vote for the rising metropolis, Sturgeon Bay, which they obligingly did.* (History of Door County, *Vol. I:385-386, 1917)*

✉

Mail service was not the greatest in the 1860s. The *Door County Advocate* of July 12, 1866, noted that

> *the mail route between this place [Sturgeon Bay] and Baileys' Harbor has been discontinued for the present, for the reason that no bids were sent in to the Post Office Department for carrying the mail. For the present, the mail for that place will go in the Egg Harbor mail every Thursday.*

✉

H.R. Holand provided a glowing description of the first postmaster at Baileys Harbor:

> *Moses Kilgore was among the earliest permanent settlers of the town and it is commonly asserted that he did more for the improvement of the town than any other man. He was a remarkably energetic Yankee from the State of Maine with*

a picturesque flow of profanity and unadorned speech which was exceedingly entertaining or dreadfully horrifying according to the temper of his audience. He was the first great booster for good roads in the county. When he represented the county in the State Legislature in 1867, he succeeded in putting through an appropriation for building the state road that runs through the county on the Lake Michigan side. He was also a prominent business man, stage driver and member of the county board for a number of years. His epitaph might be: 'He was an indomitable hustler from his cradle to his grave.' (History of Door County, Wisconsin, *Vol. I:389, 1917)*

Mr. Kilgore apparently was good at his job, judging by comments in the *Door County Advocate*:

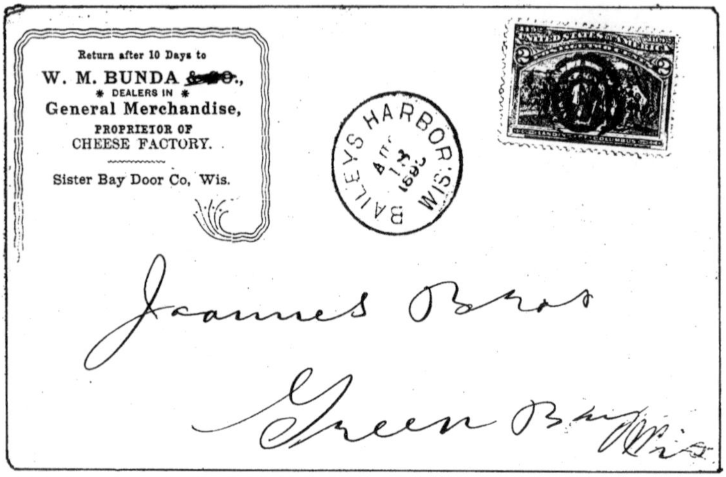

1893; the apostrophe in "Bailey's" was officially deleted in 1892.

Mr. Moses Kilgore has obtained the contract for carrying the mail twice a week between this place (Sturgeon Bay) and Bailey's Harbor, for $400 per year. The service will probably be increased to three times a week and the compensation to $600. (March 19, 1874)

We are indebted to Mr. M. Kilgore, our enthusiastic mail carrier, for his promptness with mails during stormy and rough roads, as well as when it is pleasant, for the extra mail we receive through his enterprise and for the many favors he confers upon us from day to day. (December 17, 1874)

On the other hand, mail service continued to be erratic, as indicated in a letter to the editor of the *Advocate* from "IRA" at Baileys Harbor:

...Again we are compelled to make mention of the fact that no letters were received at this post office last Saturday, when we are confident that there must have been some at any rate.—This result of negligence on the part of some of the postmasters along the line is far from being a convenience to business men, as well as not being in accordance with the requirements of the Postal Laws. This is the

third time to our certain knowledge that this community has been served in this way. (September 19, 1875)

✉

When the first post office opened in 1860, the name was spelled "Bailey's Harbor." This spelling was retained until December 15, 1892, when the apostrophe was officially removed by the U.S. Post Office Department.

A spelling problem of a different sort come to light in 1988. At least as early as September of that year, the post office began using a hand canceler with the "E" missing in Baileys. When I inquired at the Baileys Harbor post office on June 5, 1989, about the use of this misspelled device, the window clerk had not noticed the error, even after nine-plus months of use, nor had the postmaster. The clerk also stated that the Green Bay Sectional Center, which supervised their office, also was not aware of the mistake. This postmark was used until the mid-summer of 1990.

✉

Post office notes from the *Door County Advocate*:

April 2, 1868 - The Post Master General has appointed Spencer B. Ward postmaster at Bailey's Harbor, in the place of Solmon Beery, resigned. Mr. Ward has been a very efficient deputy in that office for several years, the office being kept in his store. He is well drilled in the service and will fill the whole bill.

October 6, 1870 - Mr. J.P. Phillips has been appointed Postmaster at Bailey's Harbor in place of S. B. Ward, deceased. Messrs. Severn, Phillips & Co. have completed their new store and made it one of the finest in the county.

February 23, 1871 - The time for the arrival and departure of the Bailey's Harbor mail has been changed to connect with the Green Bay mail. It arrives Mondays and Fridays at 6 P.M. and departs Tuesdays and Saturdays at 6 A.M.

✉

The story of the Jacob Appel family of Baileys Harbor, written by Fritzie Jackson (a grandchild), appeared in the *Door County Advocate*, December 9, 1994, and told of some early-1900s mail arrangements:

...My mother, Augusta [Appel] worked at Panter's hotel in Bailey' Harbor for $1 a week washing, cleaning, baking and scrubbing...

While working at Panter's, my mother met my dad, August Jackson, who drove the mail stage from Sturgeon Bay to Ellison Bay. He and my uncle (his brother, William Jackson), who rode shotgun, carried the mail in a stage drawn by two horses he kept at Panter's barn. He had six teams of horses, and proceeded to Ellison Bay to unload the mail, pick up a fresh team to go back the same route to Sturgeon Bay.

Dad lived at the Carmen Hotel in Sturgeon Bay with his family then. On their trip, the two men each wore big black bearskin long coats with felts on their feet to keep them warm. Each night my mother would place a huge flat stone in the oven all night so it would be hot on their trip. Each man carried a pistol to ward off the wild animals and intruders from attacking the horses to get at the mail. When my dad retired, he still kept one team of horses, Dick and Dan. His brother then went into the cigar-making business (Cherryland Cigars) with his wife, Hulda...

✉

An extract from a Toft family history in the *Door County Advocate*, December 1, 1992:

...In 1920, Henry Heinrichs no longer wished to be postmaster of Bailey's Harbor, and Will Toft became postmaster. The north front room of the Will Toft house in the center of the village became the post office and continued into the late 1940s. Anna [Mrs. Will Toft] was assistant postmaster. The mail was brought from Sturgeon Bay daily, by truck in summer and by a leftover WWI sleigh or a stagecoach in winter

Early drivers were Charley Panter, Henry Schultz and Dave Jacobsen. The roads were bad, sometimes under water, sometimes impassable. About half way between Baileys Harbor and Sturgeon Bay the driver would change horses. When the snow on the road was too deep, the fence lines, with permission, would be cut and the sleigh would run across the farmer's fields. A small pot-bellied stove heated the stagecoach...

For many years the rural mail carrier was Jens Jensen. He was a kindly man who was wooing a daughter, and was maneuvered into marrying the mother. Jens didn't work on Saturdays, so Will would sort the mail and on Sundays give it to the church-going Polish people.

Will would have the post office open from 8 A.M. to 8 P.M. every day. He would accommodate the village by cashing checks and supplying change for the small businesses. In the 1980s, when the home was being readied for sale, we found the Post Office wall above the business shelf to be covered with graffiti. Names of teenagers like Bernice Hartwig, Helen Herbst, etc. brought on a wave of nostalgia for the late 20s and 30s...

✉

Another family-history feature, this one by Mary Ann Johnson on the descendants of Martin and Reinhard Hickey of Baileys Harbor, appeared in the *Door County Advocate* of October 21, 1994. It included the story of Jim Hickey, a Baileys Harbor rural mail carrier:

...In 1962, Herb Pleck told Jim that Reuben Larson had retired from the post office and there was an opening for a new rural mail carrier. Jim took the test and

qualified for the position, getting the number one rating. He received the appointment, crediting his success with having served with the U.S. Army during the war. For years Jim worked closely with Tony Paul, postmaster, and Florence Paul, who was postal clerk at this time...

Jim served for twenty-three years as rural mail carrier for Baileys Harbor, beginning in 1962 and retiring in 1985. His route included a total of eighty-five driving miles daily, with 440 mail boxes to oversee. His route went as far as the Jacksonport swamp, then out west to Peninsula Center, part way to Egg Harbor, all of the Kangaroo Lake route, north past Koepsel's market on Highway 57 up to Highway Q and then right to Q to North Bay, returning to Baileys Harbor via Highway 57, and then out to Harbor Point (known in earlier days as Swede Point). He spent two hours each morning in the post office sorting out the rural route mail and then six hours completing the entire route. He returned to the post office at 4 p.m., having started out at 8 a.m. Jim furnished his own car during these years, and was reimbursed for mileage. He put on a whopping 40,000 miles per year...

...[An] incident he recalls involved a nudist family on Ridges Road. Jim had a package to deliver to the home one day, and when he went to the door he saw they were all nude, but had come to the door to sign for the package. Also on Ridges Road, there was a group of children living in the Law cottage who put frogs into their mailbox. When Jim opened the mailbox, the frogs jumped out and into his car...

Jim retired from the postal service in 1985 at the age of 65...

Baileys Harbor Postmasters and Dates of Their Appointments

Moses Kilgore - December 4, 1860
Solomon Beery - September 10, 1861
Spencer B. Ward - March 23, 1868
Joseph J. Phillips - September 16, 1870
William Jeneese - September 12, 1871
Frederick Wohltman - July 31, 1873
Christian Pfeifer - April 19, 1881
Frederick Wohltman - May 3, 1881
Mrs. Augusta Wohltman - July 29, 1892
Hugh G. Spring - December 16, 1892
Roger Eatough - February 2, 1895
John Anclam - May 25, 1898
Henry H. Hinrichs - February 10, 1915

William T. Toft - December 10, 1918
Eben R. Hanson - August 16, 1939
Otto R. Voeks - February 5, 1947
Anton R. Paul - October 11, 1949
Thomas A. Abrahamson - July 11, 1981
Michael Liska - June 16, 1990

Postmaster's Salaries

1860-61	Moses Kilgore (6 months only)	$ 5.33
1864-65	Solomon Beery	$ 22.87
1871	William Jeneese	$ 72.00
1873	Frederick Wohltman	$ 64.00
1877	Frederick Wohltman	$102.29
1879	Frederick Wohltman	$108.01
1883	Frederick Wohltman	$182.48
1885	Frederick Wohltman	$237.72
1887	Frederick Wohltman	$250.97
1889	Frederick Wohltman	$222.93
1891	Frederick Wohltman	$249.27

BAILEYS HARBOR

SEC. 19, 20
T30N - R28E
TOWN OF BAILEYS HARBOR

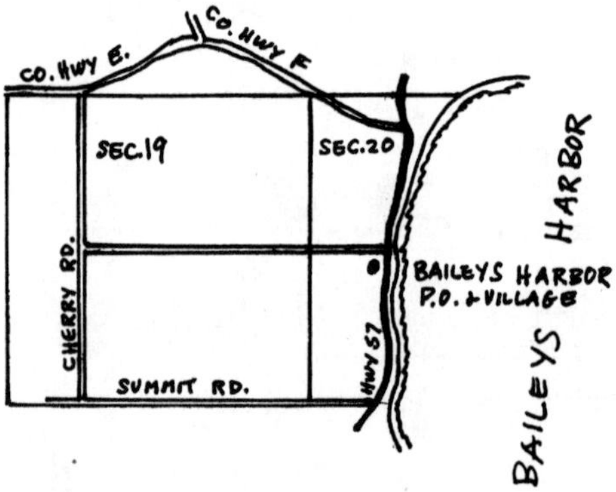

Brussels

Established November 14, 1862. Discontinued January 15, 1867.

Reestablished January 27, 1870, and is still in service. Zip Code - 54204.

Location: In the present village of the same name in Town 26 North, Range 24 East, Town of Brussels. In the 1860s, the location was in the SW 1/4 of section 9; in 1918, 1943 and at present, it was in the SW 1/4 of section 8.

The post office was named for the township and village, which had been named after the capitol city of Belgium by the first European settlers, who were mainly Belgian immigrants.

A variation in the spelling of the name occurred in the canceling device used by the Brussels post office in 1908. Here the name was spelled as "Brussells." The length of time in which

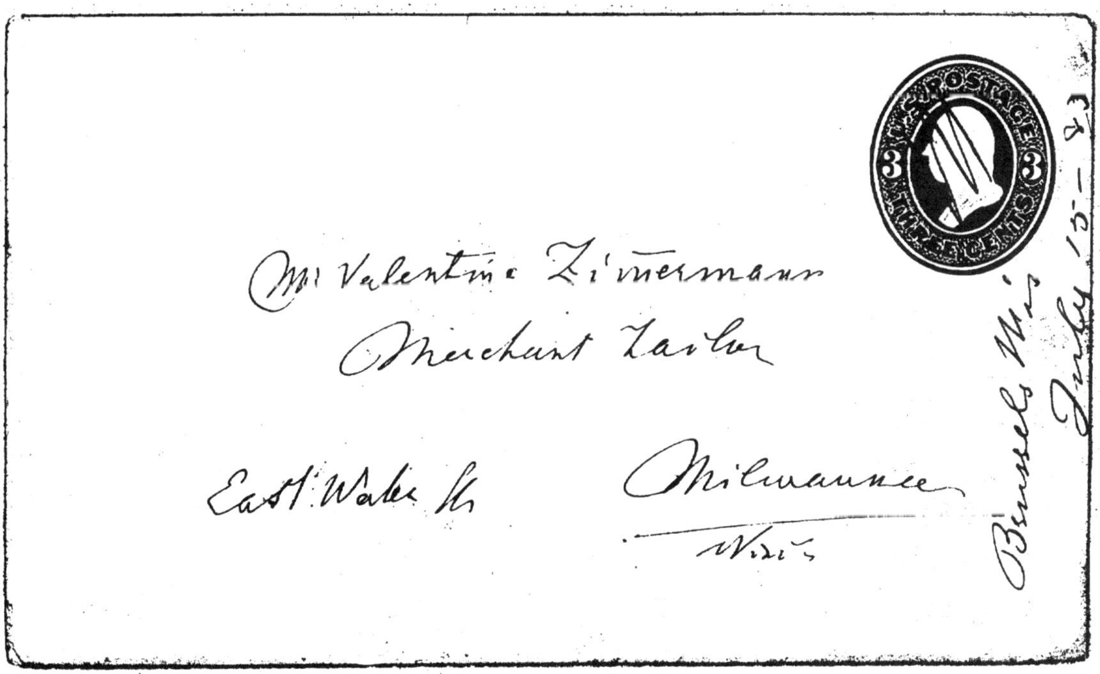

1883 manuscript postmark. Postmasters had to provide their own canceling devices in the early years, but many stayed with pen and ink.

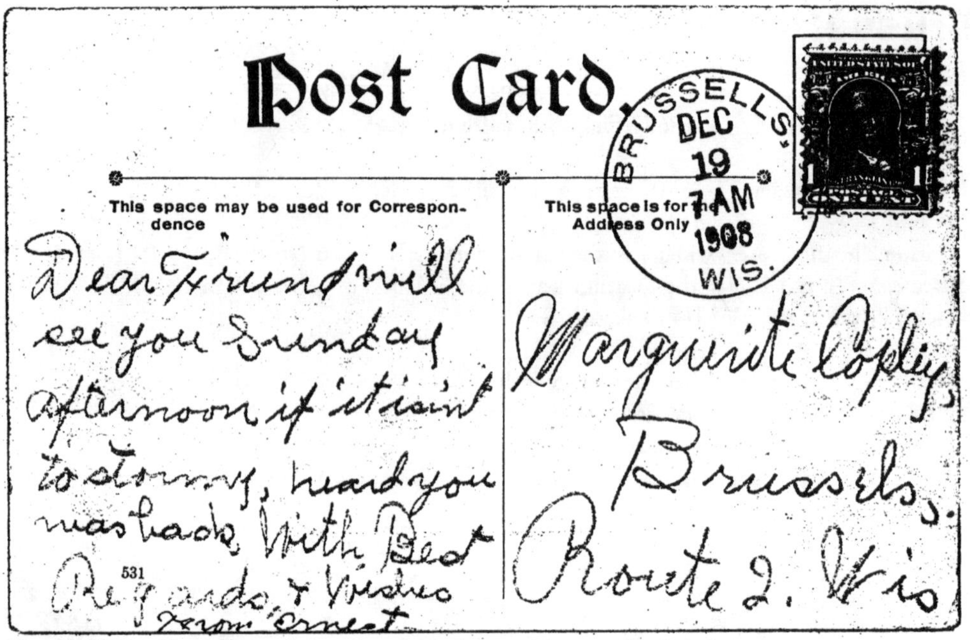
Post Card.

This space may be used for Correspondence

This space is for the Address Only

BRUSSELLS DEC 19 7AM 1908 WIS.

Dear Friend will see you Sunday afternoon if it isn't to stormy, heard you was back. With Best Regards & Wishes from Ernest

531

Marguerite Copley, Brussels, Route 2. Wis

Note the "LL" spelling of Brussels; how long it was in use at the post office is unknown.

this postmark was used is unknown.

✉

In 1918, Post Office documents listed an estimate by Brussels postmaster, Jules Pierre, that his office supplied 1,853 people with mail.

Brussels Postmasters and the Dates of Their Appointments

Jean F. Gilson - November 14, 1862
Marc Naniot - March 24, 1865
Francois Pierre - January 27, 1870
Frank G. Quartemont - April 5, 1902
Moses Gilson - November 3, 1904
Jules G. Pierre - January 12, 1906
Alvin E. Simon - September 1, 1947
Roger L. Miller - November 16, 1948
Margaret Miller - March 4, 1972
Evelyn Kerscher - May 21, 1977
Debbie L. Lemmens - May 6, 1993 (Officer-in-Charge)
Judy Karas - October , 1993

Postmasters' Annual Salaries

1864-65	Jean Gilson	$ 3.84
1871	Francois Pierre	$ 12.00
1873	Francois Pierre	$ 12.00
1877	Francois Pierre	$ 28.00
1879	Francois Pierre	$ 27.63
1883	Francois Pierre	$ 59.61
1885	Francois Pierre	$146.63
1887	Francois Pierre	$106.24
1889	Francois Pierre	$137.50
1891	Francois Pierre	$120.17

BRUSSELS

SEC. 7, 8, 17, 18
T26N - R24E
TOWN OF BRUSSELS

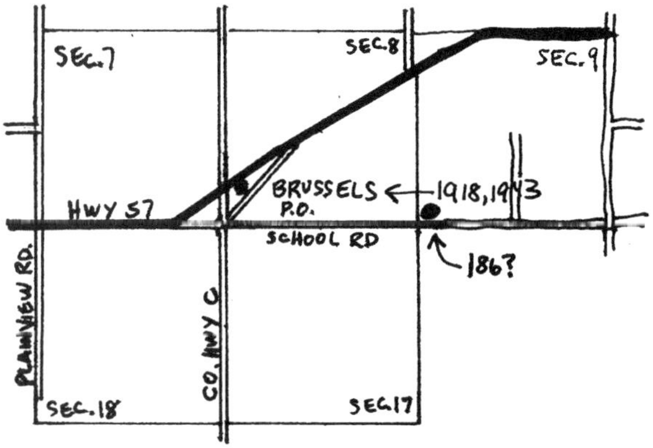

Carnot

Established June 23, 1891.

Discontinued May 15, 1907, with mail service at Forestville.

Location: In the present rural community of the same name on the northeast side of the crossroads between sections 23, 24, 25 and 26, Town 26 North, Range 25 East, Town of Forestville.

"Forest" was proposed originally to be the name of this office, but it was turned down by the U.S. Post Office Department, probably because it was too close to the Forestville post office both in name and in distance (four and a half miles). The application for the Carnot office stated that it would serve a population of "about 600" people.

The *Door County Advocate* reported on September 19, 1891, that "A new post office for Clay Banks has been established under the name of Carnot with John Burnham as postmaster." This statement is not especially accurate, since the Carnot post office was in the Town of Forestville, and the name of the first postmaster was Borrmann, not Burnham, according to the original application for the office.

The origin of the name Carnot has had at least three interpretations. The *Door County Advocate* of October 17, 1891, reported that "the name Carnot given to the post office in Clay Banks was selected by the department in Washington and may refer to a prominent French political leader who opposed Napoleon I. Carnot, born in 1801, at last reports was still among the living though a very old man."

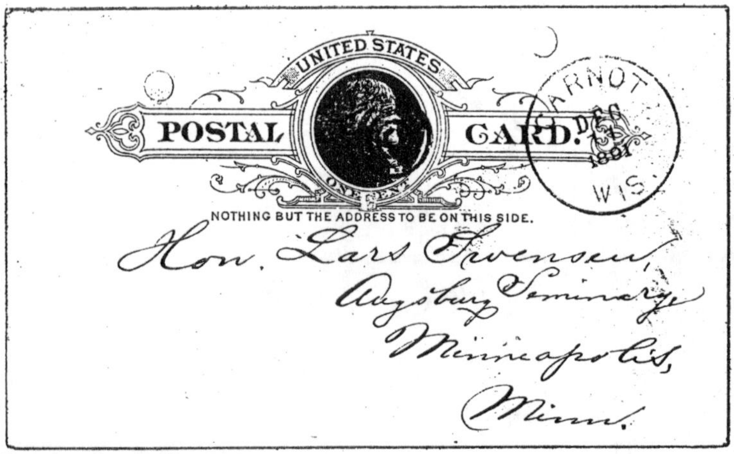

Postal card mailed in 1891.

In 1975, as the result of an inquiry from a reader, Mrs. John Peters, author of the Clay Banks-South Sturgeon Bay column in the *Door County Advocate*, contacted several local people about the naming of Carnot. The reader had suggested that Carnot might have been named for Francois Carnot, the President of France in 1891 when the Carnot post office was established. Mrs. Peters reported on the matter as follows in the *Advocate* of October 16, 1975:

> *I received a letter from a person who wishes to remain anonymous, in regard to the naming of Carnot. It seems said person thinks the previous account a bit on the fishy side, in fact he thinks there is definitely something rotten under the barn. (Everybody's a critic.)*
>
> *It seems this fellow's grandfather was one of the earliest settlers and here's how he tells it. Now I guess there really was a disagreement between the Norwegians and the Germans about the choice of a name.*
>
> *The Norwegians wanted it named after one of their kings, while the Germans wanted it named after their emperor. Neither side would give in, so as a compromise they named it after a famous French military leader, Lazare Carnot (Kar-No, 1753-1823), who by the way, had a very able general under him by the name of Napoleon Bonaparte.*
>
> *Well, anyway everyone finally agreed on that name but they pronounced it Kar-Not. Now that's the way it was folks, and remember, you were there.*

✉

Carnot had only two postmasters during its sixteen-year life. John Borrmann was appointed June 23, 1891, and Herman J. Teske was appointed January 10, 1896.

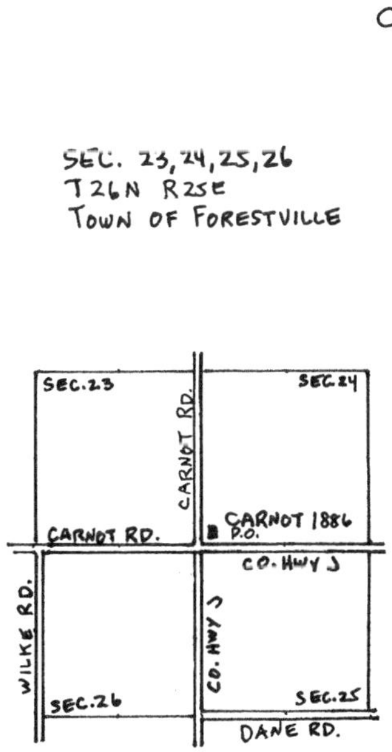

Chambers Island

Established April 26, 1866.

Discontinued August 13, 1868.

Location: On the north side of the island of the same name in Green Bay, in the northwest quarter of section 4, Town 31 North, Range 26 East, Town of Gibraltar. The application for this post office filed with the U.S. Post Office Department in 1866 gives the proposed location as the northeast quarter of section 4. However, this quarter section lies in Mackaysee Lake, so it seems likely that the northwest quarter was the intended location. The sawmill and other buildings of the island's residents were mostly in the northwest quarter.

The application for the proposed post office in 1866 stated that the office would serve fifty-one island residents.

> *New Post Office.—We learn from Washington that a new post office has been established at Chamber's Island, and J.S. Ferson, Esq., appointed postmaster. This will be a great convenience to the people of the island, who have heretofore had to go to Fish Creek for their mail. (*Door County Advocate, *May 10, 1866)*

✉

The post office was named for the island, which Martin (*History of Door County, Wisconsin*, 1881, p. 56) said "...was so named in honor of Capt. Chambers, who lost his life there during the Black Hawk War." This was obviously not possible, since the Black Hawk War was fought in southern Wisconsin entirely in 1832, while Chambers Island appears on maps and in travelers accounts predating 1830.

It is generally accepted that the island was named in 1816 after Colonel Talbot Chambers, second in military command of an expedition sent from Mackinac Island to Green Bay to establish a military post at Fort Howard. It was on this same expedition that Washington Island was named. C.B. Eaton wrote that

> *Talbot Chambers commanded at Fort Howard after [Colonel] Miller's departure and a year later took command of Fort Crawford at Prairie du Chien. A contemporary said of him: 'Col. Chambers was a brave soldier in the field...not qualified for commandant...overbearing...when intoxicated was desperate and dangerous...Once he chased a young female into the house of Jacque Menard, with no good motive for doing so...' Chambers, 'for cutting off both ears of one soldier, and one of another, was tried and cashiered...and was in the Mexican Army at the surrender of the City of Mexico...' Talbot Chamber's name, as any Wisconsin map*

will show, remains anchored to a Door County island after nearly a century and three-quarters. (Washington Island Insights *1987, pp. 5, 6)*

Settlement of the island began about 1850. In 1858, the Door County Board established Chambers Island as a separate township. For the next ten years a full set of town officers was elected and met annually. As a result of internal jealousies among the island residents, no town officers were elected in the late 1860s, so in 1869 the County Board dissolved the township and attached the island to the Town of Gibraltar. (See Holand, *History of Door County, Wisconsin* I:330, 1917)

✉

James S. Ferson, who operated a sawmill and store on the island, was the only postmaster in the life of the office.

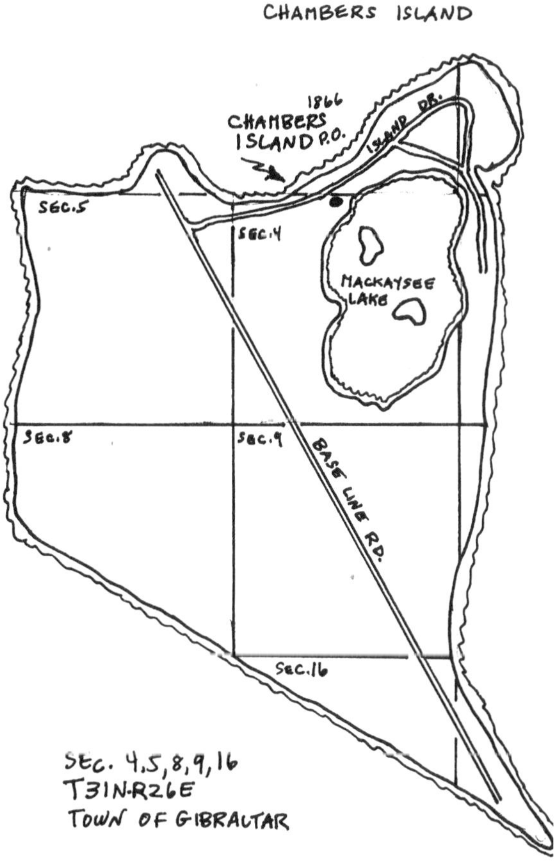

Cheeseville

see Warren's Corners

Chickatock/Gardner

Established as Chickatock October 27, 1858.

The name was changed to Gardner on March 21, 1866, and was so noted in the *Door County Advocate* on April 5, 1866.

Discontinued April 24, 1867.

Reestablished as Gardner November 9, 1888.

Discontinued January 14, 1905, with mail service at Brussels.

Location: The office in the 1860s was located in the southwest quarter of section 25, Town 27 North, Range 23 East; in 1888 and thereafter it was in the southwest quarter of section 29, Town 27 North, Range 24 East. Both locations were in the Town of Gardner.

The application for the reestablishment of Gardner in 1888 stated that the population to be served by the proposed office was "about 300."

The name Chickatock is of Indian origin, possibly a chief associated with the Little Sturgeon Bay area. It is said to have been supplied by the Green Bay postmaster, who was also alleged to have named the Nasewaupee post office (another Indian name) when it was established a month before Chickatock.

The Gardner name was for the township, which, at its establishment in 1862, was named for F.B. Gardner, the most prominent businessman in southern Door County.

Mr. Gardner came to Little Sturgeon in the early 1850s and turned out to be one of the more remarkable men who have come to Door County. He built an industrial complex that at its height employed 400 men. It included a sawmill, lath mill, shingle mill, shipyard, ice-house, and a large retail store for hardware and farm machinery. He also built a hotel in Chicago, Illinois and a large sawmill and hotel in Pensaukee (Marinette County), Wisconsin across Green Bay from Little Sturgeon.

> *Mr. Gardner was a quick, dapper little man of instant decisions. He was careful in little things but bold and adventurous in big enterprises. He was very popular with his employees as he was sympathetic, generous and always ready to help an unfortunate whether he was an employee of his or some poor struggling Belgian farmer back in the brush. Many of these had bought their farm lands from Mr. Gardner, paying for them in work...He was very popular with his Belgian associates. (H.R. Holand,* History of Door County, *Vol. I:431-432, 1917)*

Mr. Gardner died in 1878.

Postmasters and Dates of Their Appointments

Chickatock:

- Michael Schmitz - October 27, 1858
- Charles Enoch - March 28, 1867

Gardner:

- Jean Henquinet - November 9, 1888
- Jule Gerndale - January 22, 1904

Postmasters' Annual Salaries

1860-61	Michael Schmitz	$ 9.28
1864-65	Michael Schmitz	$12.53
1889	Jean Henquinet	$ 8.28
1891	Jean Henquinet	$26.15

CHICKATOCK
GARDNER

SEC. 25 - T27N R23E
SEC. 29,30- T27N R24E
TOWN OF GARDNER

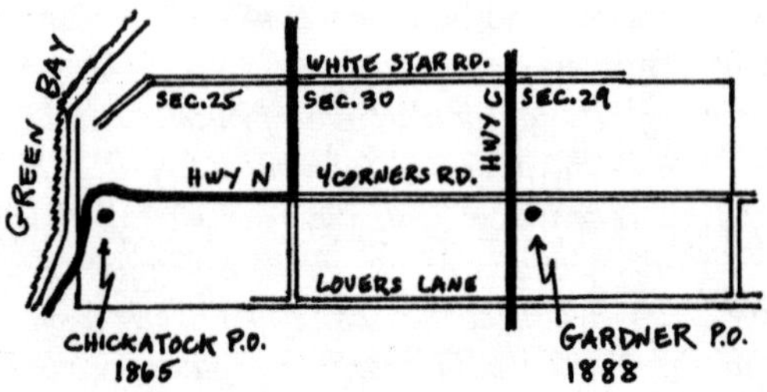

Clay Banks

Established December 16, 1862. Discontinued September 7, 1893, with mail service at Vignes.

Reestablished October 6, 1893. Finally discontinued February 28, 1903, with mail service at Algoma, Kewaunee County.

This post office had at least three different locations in its lifetime. There may have been more; the U.S. Post Office Department records are incomplete in this respect. All three were in Town 26 North, Range 26 East, Town of Clay Banks. In 1865 the location was in the southeast quarter of the northeast quarter, section 20; in 1878 it was in the northwest quarter of section 28; in 1893 it was in lot four, section 21.

✉

The name 'Clay Banks' is one of long standing, and originated among the sailors on the Lake. The high clay banks loomed up wonderfully, and sailors could readily recognize them many miles distant. In passing up and down the Lake, 'clay banks' was sort of a point to reckon distance from. When this section began to settle up, names for that portion of the county were numerous, but to make known the location, the words 'Clay Banks' always had to be attached, and to save time and get immediate recognition, all other names were dropped, and Clay Banks adopted as the name. (C.I. Martin, History of Door County, *Wisconsin, p. 65, 1881)*

In the early 1870s, Clay Banks had more shipping than any other port in Door County. It also had the county's longest pier (1,600 feet), which was destroyed by a storm in March, 1886. (H.R. Holand, History of Door County, Wisconsin, *Vol. I:442, 1917)*

✉

Under the heading "Clay Banks Correspondence," the *Door County Advocate* of August 7, 1873, published this unsigned letter from a disgruntled postal patron:

Mr. Editor:—Having leisure we once more condescend to favor you with a communication from this locality, tho' if we do not have an opportunity to forward it by private conveyance, it will probably be a week ere it reaches you as we presume there is not another county of our growth and population in this broad land that has not greater or more convenient mail facilities than the southern part of ours, and we earnestly hope that before the letting of another mail contract upon this route the matter will be laid before the proper authorities and an effort made to form a new route and change the present inconvenient schedule; for at present it

An 1886 usage.

takes eight days time for mail from this place to reach Sturgeon Bay, which is but nine miles distant, and in the town of Forestville, that is supplied by the same route, it requires a like amount of time to receive communications from Sturgeon Bay. The mail matter in both cases lying over a week's time at the Ahnapee post office. Whilst if the present route could be so changed as to go and return via Clay Banks and a branch route established to and from via Forestville from Ahnapee to Sturgeon Bay, mail facilities would be greatly increased and the cost of the new route would be a mere trifle compared with the many advantages and benefits arising therefrom and it would not then as at present require the same length of time to receive intelligence from nine miles distant as it does from across the Atlantic Ocean. But perhaps the day of the chemin de fer *is not far distant when pedestrian or equestrian modes of transporting mails will be unknown and those green hills and forests will ring with the reverberations of the iron steed's whistle and the rushing crowds swaying to and from will be a grand memorial to the pioneers who hewed civilization from a wilderness of woe.*

Clay Banks must have had more than its share of post office problems, judging by the turnover rate of its postmasters. In the last eighteen years of its existence, there were thirteen postmasters appointed - four in 1893 alone - and only one of the eighteen served longer than two years.

✉

Harry Schuyler, writing in *Fish Creek Voices - An Oral History of a Door County Village*, recounted that

I was born in the town of Clay Banks on April 17, 1897. My father was born in the county in 1868...My grandfather, Albert A. Schuyler, came from New York to Door County to install the first circular saw in the county. The mill was on the shore in Clay Banks, right near the Tufts pier. Clay Banks at that time consisted of a post office, saloon and boarding house for the men that worked in the saw mill.

Clay Banks is just north of what is now known as Bronsdorf Beach...There is a little creek that runs into the lake just north of Bronsdorf Beach, and it was just this side of the creek. I remember it very well—I got mail in the post office in Clay Banks. That is, my folks did, I was probably too young; but I remember going there. Of course I couldn't go into the saloon. That was bad! (p. 42)

✉

Clay Banks Postmasters and Dates of Their Appointment

George A. Prescott - December 16, 1862
Franklin Tyrrel - August 4, 1863
Albert J. Schuyler - August 18, 1865
Benjamin Minsker - January 26, 1875
Halver Halverson - December 26, 1877
Theodore Pieplow - May 13, 1878
Fritz Paarman - October 31, 1879
Benjamin Minsker - August 8, 1882
Fritz Paarman - June 22, 1883
Benjamin Minsker - August 13, 1883
Joseph A. Fellner - June 15, 1885
James Tufts - October 4, 1889
Charles I. Hitt - April 17, 1893
Thomas O'Neill - June 2, 1893
Abraham Ranhalt - August 2, 1893
Charles I. Hitt - October 6, 1893

Postmasters' Annual Salaries

1864-65	Franklin Tyrrel	$ 7.17
1871	Albert Schuyler	$ 16.00
1873	Albert Schuyler	$ 30.00
1877	Benjamin Minsker	$ 75.17
1879	Theodore Pieplow	$ 51.16
1883	Fritz Paarman	$ 78.03
1885	Benjamin Minsker	$ 72.57
1887	Joseph Fellner	$121.34
1889	Joseph Fellner	$127.28
1891	James Tufts	$ 56.00

CLAY BANKS

SEC. 20,21,28
T26N R26E
TOWN OF CLAY BANKS

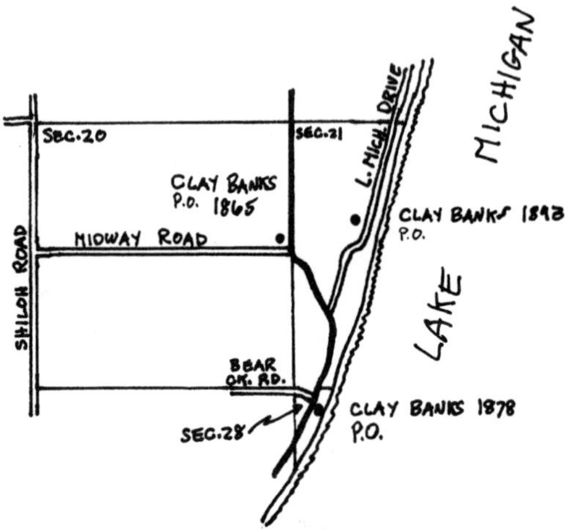

Detroit Harbor/Washington Island

Established as Detroit Harbor May 3, 1892.

The name was changed to Washington Island on September 15, 1926, although the post office remained in the Detroit Harbor community. The office has had three locations in the northwest quarter of section 12, Town 33 North, Range 29 East, Town of Washington.

While the history of Washington Island's four post offices is presented alphabetically, their chronological order is the reverse. Washington Harbor was the earliest office, followed by Fagerwick and Detroit Harbor/Washington Island.

The Detroit Harbor post office was named for the community where it was located, which bears the name of the shallow bay lying between Washington Island and Detroit Island. The harbor, in turn, was named for the "petite detroit" (little strait), the waterway known as the East Channel between Lake Michigan and Green Bay which runs through Detroit Harbor. Early French explorers gave the name.

Conan Bryan Eaton has written extensively on the island's postal history. He had this to say about Detroit Harbor:

> *The new post office will be called Detroit Harbor, and will soon be in operation. This was the lead on a May, 1892 Advocate column headed 'Washington Island' and signed by one Myrtle Hope. Government records list May 3 as the establishment date and Bo Leopold Anderson postmaster. An oddity which history has ignored: On his application to the Post Office Department, Mr. Anderson clearly proposed calling the new office Fagerwick (thus reviving the name of the office discontinued*

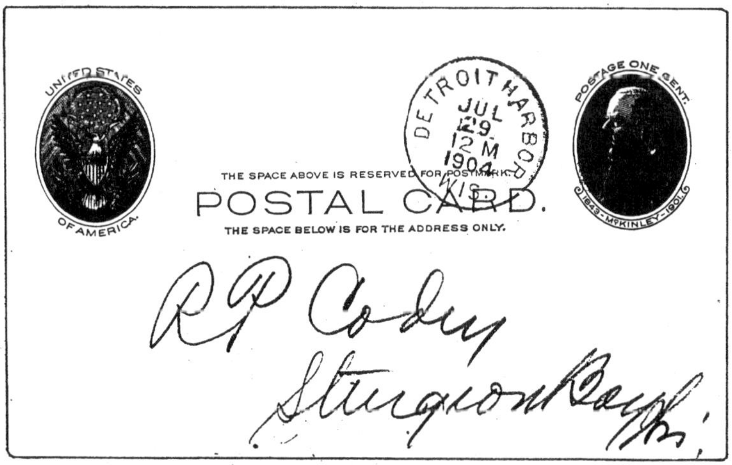

1904 postal card with a cork "killer" cancellation.

nearly ten years earlier, which had been headed by his sister's father-inlaw, K.O. Shellswick. It may have been a minor Department employee who found Fagerwick already listed, drew a line through that name on the application and wrote above it 'Detroit Harbor.'

Unlike the pattern of rapid change at Washington Harbor, the post office at Detroit Harbor, Wisconsin displayed a solid and settled character. Bo Anderson kept the office until 1907 and was followed by William Jess, who held on until 1922. John A. Gudmundsen's tenure of some twenty months broke that pattern, but established another: His clear Icelandic ancestry was matched by his successor, Magnus Magnusson, who served thirty-four years up to 1958, and by the next incumbent, Theresa Rainsford, who retired in 1987 after twenty-nine years...

*One change, probably inevitable, came a decade later. Complying with an order from the Post Office Department dated September 15, 1926, Postmaster Mac Magnusson stamped his outgoing mail on October 19 as usual: DETROIT HARBOR, WIS. The next morning he used his new stamp: WASHINGTON ISLAND, WIS." (*Washington Island Insights *1988, pp. 1-2)*

✉

"B.L. Anderson has been appointed postmaster of the new office established at Detroit Harbor on Washington Island." (*Door County Advocate*, July 30, 1892)

✉

In a 1910 Washington Island business directory, Captain Pete Anderson advertised "U.S. MAIL BOAT, Detroit Harbor to Ellison Bay daily except Sunday, with passenger service." The same directory announced that "Detroit Harbor and Washington Harbor are the only post office points on the island, but mail is delivered to all parts. All mail matter for Jackson Harbor or West Harbor should be directed to Detroit Harbor, the distributing point, unless otherwise specified."

✉

Getting the mail from the Door County mainland to Washington Island has always been a difficult proposition, even in recent years. S.S. Telfer, Sr. wrote about one mail contractor in the *Door County Advocate* of August 10, 1978:

In the early 1920s and for some time before Pete Anderson, a Dane, living on Washington Island with his wife and five sons, carried the mail across the Door in good and inclement weather.

Pete was a sociable man, having the mild characteristics of the Scandinavian Islanders. He was resourceful and daring, ever ready to take chances, risking his life many times in crossing.

He carried the mail for seventeen years from 1906 to 1923, having a contract with the government which was renewed every two years and awarded to the lowest bidder.

Pete was not a large man. He had a quizzical, impish smile and with one noticeable feature, a single white eyebrow. A friend facetiously suggested it came from over-enthusiasm in looking in the top of a bottle to see if there was another drink in it.

Pete was somewhat careless in the more essential requirements of a good mail carrier. His equipment was never too sturdy, often held together with rope and bailing wire. Stories were often told of some of his more hazardous experiences ending with the statement, 'He will never die in bed; he will die with his boots on.'

Pete once told of an experience he had in crossing with a horse and sleigh. It was necessary to cross on safer ice on Green Bay; he took a long circuitous route away from Lake Michigan.

He was carrying the mail but no passengers when he ran into ice which was unsafe for him with the added weight of the horse and rig. He got out of the sleigh and ran from the horse, but not wanting to be left alone, it followed tight on his heels until they reached firmer ice. A race, man and horse, on unsafe ice, which Pete won.

On one trip with his horse, a large floe of ice was set adrift with them on it. Pete and the horse were towed and pushed to a firm area by the Coast Guard boat best known as 'The Bull' which was a very solid and heavily constructed ice-breaking craft...

After Pete's death, his widow told a friend of the time Pete was driving a team of broncos that broke through the ice and drowned, losing all the mail and his sleigh, leaving him alone far from shore.

When large cakes of ice, which would carry a load, were floating in the Door, Pete used a skiff with runners attached. Passengers who wished to cross helped haul the boat with the mail across the ice and man the oars through the open water to the next ice floe and again pull the boat. Trips were timed to reach the Coast Guard Station at meal times if possible. Pete and his passengers were always welcomed and fed in the Bum Shack, the Coast Guard dining room. No charge was ever made for the meal. The crew was always glad to have company to hear the latest island and mainland gossip.

When shore was reached, Pete charged the passengers for the trip, they having done most of the work, and also for the meal at the station.

One forenoon in the fall of the year, when the weather can be quite changeable, the lookout at the station reported the mail boat was adrift and moving out into Lake Michigan where the waves were white capped. Pete was apparently in trouble although no distress signals were given.

The crew launched the life boat and went to investigate. Coming within hail-

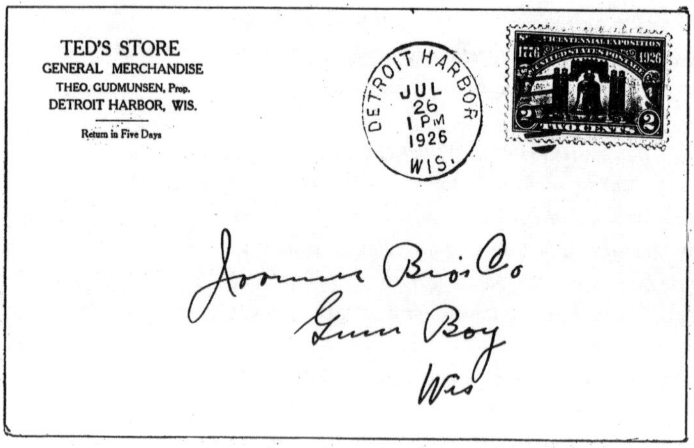

1926 cover with a business corner-card.

ing distance of the mail boat in the heavy seas, they shouted to Pete. There was no response after several calls. Pete must be in serious trouble, so with great care the life boat was maneuvered as close as possible to the distressed mail boat and a guard, with careful timing, boarded it. Pete lay on one of the seats in the cabin.

The guard was afraid he had suffered a heart attack in the rolling boat and shook and called him. Pete opened his eyes and asked what he wanted. When told of his position and danger, Pete calmly said, 'I ran out of gas and there was nothing to do, so I took a nap.'

In the cemetery on Washington Island, down near the lower edge, there is a small marker inscribed: Pete Anderson, November 3, 1880–March 3, 1923.

Pete Anderson, age 42, died of pneumonia at home on Washington Island. He was still under contract to the U.S. Government to deliver the mail across the treacherous Death's Door...

He risked his life many more times than anyone knows of and he is almost forgotten. If a commemorative stamp for Pete Anderson were ever issued, it would be for a man who well deserved it.

Carl Christiansen with his 'Sea Queen' and later the 'Charlotte C' carried mail and freight in 1923, finishing Pete Anderson's mail-carrying contract. (Washington Island Insights *1988, p. 31)*

Similar events occur to this day. On March 27, 1936, the *Door County Advocate* reported that

Another narrow escape from an ice tragedy occurred at Washington Island Tuesday when William P. Jepson, hauling the mail from the mainland, just reached safety before the ice of Death's Door broke up and started out.

A near tragedy occurred in 1943:

Just to show that it is still as treacherous as ever, the 'Door' played this grim trick February 24, 1943. Carl and Arni Richter and Lucien Boshka made their trip for the mail across the ice, leaving from West Harbor with a sedan and a truck. Crossing was as usual.

On the return trip, a twelve-foot crack appeared where none had been before. Lucien says it's the first time he ever had the opportunity to see an ice crack open. It was just like it was unzippered faster than a car could follow. They followed the crack until they were off John Larsen's trying to find a safe place to cross.

Then Arni, who was driving the sedan, decided to jump the crack. He held the door open for safety which caused it to be 'sprung' when the ice cracked off under him. The speed of the car carried it on to safe ice.

Planks were laid for the truck and when Lucien, who was driving, heard the words 'Step on it' - he did, with the result that one plank was thrown from under the car and the truck went down on one side. 'Step on it' in this case meant 'Step on the plank, Arni.' Right then, Arni says he would have taken two and a half cents for the whole outfit.

*The truck was finally raised and it was a thankful crew who returned home that night. After two days in the garage for repairs, the cars were ready for service again. Needless to say, we've been getting our mail via boat since then. (*Washington Island Insights *1988, p. 75)*

*A blizzard all day Saturday, March 12, kept the ferry from leaving the Island until afternoon. That day's mail could not be delivered. Also there was no delivery of Monday's mail because of ice conditions. (*Door County Advocate, *March 18, 1988)*

✉

For months in the fall and spring no man is sure of his footing crossing the Door. Where the ice may be perfectly safe in the morning, the waves may wash in the evening. The shifting winds that rush through the Door play all sorts of havoc with the ice.

The following is an account of the various modes of crossing the Door on a single day in March, 1914, copied from a Door County paper:

St. Patrick's Day will long be remembered as a remarkable day on account of the various modes of crossing and the abundant travel across the Door. The mail went and returned in a motor boat; Pete Anderson drove across the Door after passengers with a sleigh; Bo L. Anderson returned from the county seat with a horse and cutter; Charles Jensen arrived home from Chicago with a horse and buggy; and Harry Dana came across with an auto. Each one of these parties report that the going was good for this particular rig. (H.R. Holand, History of Door County, *Vol. I:297-298, 1917)*

✉

Magnus "Mac" Magnusson was the postmaster at Detroit Harbor and Washington Island for thirty-four years. His story was told by Gladys Jepsen in a feature printed by the *Door County Advocate* August 14, 1969:

...Mac became postmaster on Washington Island in 1924 when Calvin Coolidge was president. The post office was then in the basement of the Boese home. In 1926 it was moved to the Magnusson home across from Cornell's Clover Farm store where it remained until the new post office was built in 1962...

Mac said, 'It was a great day for the Island when Rural Free Delivery first came in 1902. John Malloch was our first mail carrier. The one-cent postcards and two-cent stamps for letters were in use then.'

Mac received a citation for selling more savings bonds than any other third class post office in Wisconsin. This was during the first year that savings bonds came out.

Cecelia (his wife) said, 'One Easter a jug of syrup that was in one of the mail sacks was broken. It must have been very poorly packaged. Twenty-five packages were completely covered with syrup. Goodness? What a sticky mess to clean up!

Another amusing incident happened one Christmas. A man came in for his mail and became very excited because he had received so many packages. He grabbed them up in his arms and ran home, completely forgetting that he had driven his car to the post office...

How peaceful it must have seemed to the Magnussons to have their home all to themselves after having part of it used by the public after so many years.

✉

In the late 1890s, Nels Jepson was one of the men who carried the mail across the Door. He walked across the ice in winter and used to sail in a sailboat in the summer. The name of the sailboat was the 'Razorback.' After he finished carrying the mail, I believe the Kincaide brothers carried it a few years. These brothers were David and Armour. They had a gas engine in their boat, named the '45/90.' It was said that it was named after a 45-90 rifle that Davey owned. One day the Revenue Cutter 'Tuscarora' caught up with them and told them it was illegal—that is, the name was. They were told to change it, so they named their boat the 'E.A. Clayton,' after their children.

Pete Anderson took over the mail route after the Kincaides in about 1907. Pete was quite a character. He was a jolly man and well-liked. He had a small boat named the 'Razorback,' no doubt the same one his father-in-law had before him, except this boat was not powered by a gasoline motor and did not depend on sails. After using this boat for a number of years, he acquired the gas boat 'Volunteer,' which was larger, faster and not so old. After using this boat for a few years, he bought the 'Navarre,' a larger boat. He used this one a year or two before his death...in the winter of 1923...

Carl Christianson took over the mail route after Pete's death and continued carrying the mail until the contract expired. He had the gas boat 'Charlotte.'

Bill Jepson received the next contract for carrying the mail, until in 1931, Carl Richter was awarded the contract. This contract was held by Carl Richter until 1940, when the Richters purchased the ferry line from Bill Jepson. The mail has been carried by Carl Richter and the ferry since 1931 to the present day. (R. McDonald, Four Islands: A History of Detroit, Rock, St. Martin's and Washington Islands, *pp. 145-146, 1984)*

✉

Mail hauling seems like a lost art today when hearing of the exploits of yesterday's carriers. Winter posed the greatest challenge, and for the Island, it was either go without mail until the first ship arrived, or find someone who would make the trip over the ice, on foot if necessary. Bill Jepson recalled his father, Nels, doing just that in the 1890s, an effort made twice a month in winter.

Mail boats for summer duty also carried freight and passengers, which is true today. Nels Jepson had the sloop 'Razorback,' and in 1899, the 'Minnie S.,' which he built. In the early 1900s, David Kincaide's 'E.A. Clayton' carried mail. Kincaide was well known in later years for his many seasons as light keeper on Povery and St. Martin Islands. Although names of carriers, subs, mail boats and contracted mail carriers are difficult to pin down, records being incomplete. Pete Anderson was the next contract carrier from 1906 to 1923.

Anderson used the 'Volunteer' and the 'Navarre' for summer duty. When Pete died in 1923, Carl Christiansen and Bill Jepson finished the contract. Carl had the 'Charlotte C.,' and may have carried for Pete in his later years. (Bill and Carl were partners for a time with the hooker, 'Wisconsin;' later to become a ferry.)

Bill Jepson applied for and got the contract in 1924, and continued with his ferries and snowmobiles until 1931, when Carl and Arni Richter won a four year contract. Bill got the contract back again from 1936 through 1940.

Pete Anderson was known as a character. Esther Waal writes about when the Island was 'dry':

'...The revenuers never found any violations on Washington Island. That was because when Pete suspected that he had revenuers on the mail boat, he found it necessary to stop at Plum Island, where he phoned ahead to his friends, and by the time they reached the Island there was not a still in sight.' Esther also recalled...an excursion that Pete conducted from the Island to Plum Island. Lots of women and children on board...on the way back they were struck by a violent storm. Grandma didn't know which was worse...the terror, or the seasickness, or the water coming in. Everyone was soaked. But Pete got them back safely, in spite of the problem that his dog got its tail caught in the wheel of the engine.

Boats were not the only mail transportation. I have a snapshot of my father (Carl Christiansen) and four others. One is probably Hannes Hannesson, and the others might be 'passengers.' The horse is Spark Plug. I remember one day in Chicago picking up a copy of the Tribune and finding an article on the front page of Captain Christiansen and his horse and sleigh drifting out into Lake Michigan. You can imagine the phone lines were buzzing until I reached my mother and found out that they had been rescued by the Coast Gaurd. (Esther Christiansen Waal)

Harry Newman brought the mail from Ellison Bay to Door Bluff in winters to meet Island mail carriers, Carl Christiansen, and later Bill Jepson and the Richters. Hannes Hannesson recalled, 'One time Harry came over to the Island with his horse because there was too much mail for just one horse. There was a dance that night and he meets this girl, Rebecca Garrett, and that was it! The next thing you know, they were married!

My first job was working for the mail carrier, Carl Christiansen, for three winters. One dollar a day plus board, and I always had money in my pocket! You had to take care of the horse, besides going across on the ice with the mail and freight and whatever was carried. Passengers we'd charge one dollar a head. I used to skate across behind the horse and sleigh. The horse just followed the track. We'd set out cedar bushes to mark the route. (Hannes Hannesson)

My father, Carl Christensen, was the first person to carry the mail by automobile. In the dead of winter, when the mail sometimes did not arrive until after dark, suddenly one day he took his old Model T and was back with the mail by noon. The switchboard lit up like a Christmas tree, with people calling friends: 'Have you heard that Carl is back already with the mail?' Now this is important! By the time my father got the contract, they had to at least try every day. (Esther C. Waal) (D. Purinton, Over and Back, *pp. 34-35, 1990)*

✉

Detroit Harbor, Wis., April 2, 1920.—The mail carrier from Ellison Bay to Washington Island crossed over on the ice for the last time this winter on the 22nd (of March); from that day until the 26th we received no mail. On the 23rd, Peter (Anderson) started out with the mail as usual, and had two lady passengers, Mrs. Hedwig Anderson and Miss Tillie Petersen, going to Chicago. When about half way across the Door he noticed some poor spots in the ice and later it seemed that the weight of the horses and rig would settle the ice. He turned back for shore and the water oozed up into the track in spots as they went.

On the 24th he hired the motorboat 'Bub,' Capt. J.W. Cornell, owner, Leon Cornell, pilot, and Claude Cornell, engineer. Starting from the east channel of

Detroit Harbor, they set out into the teeth of a southerly gale to go to the mainland and get the mail and passengers. They had telephoned to Gills Rock to send mail and passengers to Northport (so called being the most N.E. part of the mainland in Door County). The mail, a sleigh load, left Ellison Bay in the morning and did not reach Gills Rock until noon and the rest of the way was almost impassable, so he turned back. The passengers, Mrs. Thelma Fons and baby, Dell Klingenberg and Bernt Gunnlaugsson managed to get to the beach at Northport so the 'Bub' got them on board.

As the wind and sea increased, they started back for the east channel of Detroit Harbor. When nearly ready to turn into the channel and running under check, a big wave of solid blue water crashed down on the boat and almost swamped it. As it was, it passed the forward deck several inches, pushed the cabin back, and broke three plate glass windows, broken pieces of which hit Claude and Leslie Cornell, cutting them badly in the face. One man was knocked into the engine and the fly wheel threw him to the side of the boat. It looked blue for a few minutes, but they got into the Harbor all right. Leslie went to the doctor to get the pieces of glass out of his face.

*—-This article was submitted by Thelma Pons who made this trip with her baby, three weeks old, who was tied into a fish box and never woke up during the trip. (*Washington Island Insights *1987, p. 18)*

✉

*...From the Island Observer comes news of the October 2 retirement of Island Postmaster Wayne Rupiper who has worked for the U.S. Postal Service for twenty-three and one-half years. He was a rural route carrier for sixteen years. When he started there were about 250 stops; now there are about 380... (*Door County Advocate, *September 29, 1992)*

✉

Detroit/Washington Island Postmasters and Dates of Their Appointment

Bo Leopold Anderson - May 3, 1892
William Jess - September 28, 1907
John A. Gudmondson - January 21, 1922
Magnus Magnusson - September 29, 1924
Teresa Rainsford - June 30, 1958
Wayne J. Rupiper - August 1, 1987
Bernice Reilly - October 4, 1992 (Officer-in-Charge)
Don Riewe - December 29, 1992 (Officer-in-Charge)
Richard Jepsen - October 16, 1993

March 1927 - an early use of a Washington Island postmark.

DETROIT HARBOR
WASHINGTON ISLAND

SEC. 12
T33N R29E
TOWN OF WASHINGTON

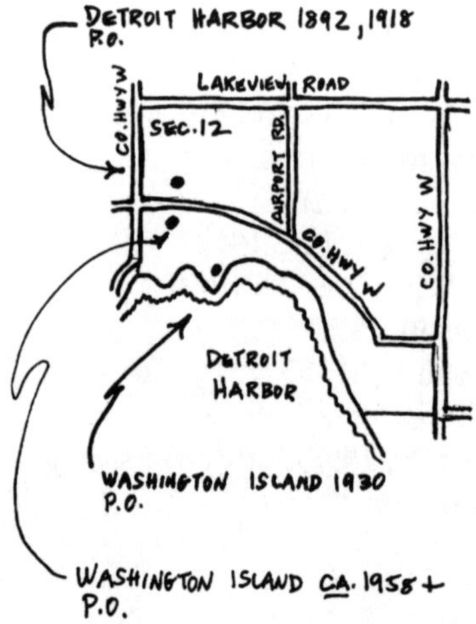

Duchateau

Established December 12, 1862.

The name was changed to Red River on November 13, 1873. At the same time, the office was moved into Kewaunee County. Charles Scofield retained the postmastership after the move.

Discontinued December 3, 1887, with mail service at Dyckesville, Kewaunee County.

Another Red River post office in Kewaunee County was established June 7, 1870, and discontinued November 13, 1873. Constant Martin was the postmaster of this office.

Duchateau was located in the northeast quarter of the southeast quarter, section 10, Town 26 North, Range 23 East, Town of Union. After the name change and move into Kewaunee County in 1873, the office was located in the settlement at the mouth of the Red River just south of the Door County line on the Green Bay shore. This location is today a Kewaunee County Park. Duchateau was named by, and probably for, its first postmaster. Red River was named for its location.

✉

Duchateau/Red River Postmasters and Dates of Their Appointments

Duchateau:

- Abeillard Duchateau - December 12, 1862
- Xavier Brans - February 17, 1865
- William van der Gete - April 9, 1867
- Dennis Befay - September 23,1869
- Charles Scofield - March 8, 1872

Red River:

- Charles Scofield - November 13, 1873
- Thomas H. Smith - December 15, 1874
- Charles Scofield - February 13, 1879
- David A. Gibson - December 14, 1881

Postmasters' Annual Salaries

1871	Dennis Befay	$9.00
1873	Charles Scofield	$9.00

DUCHATEAU

SEC. 10
T26N R23E
TOWN OF UNION

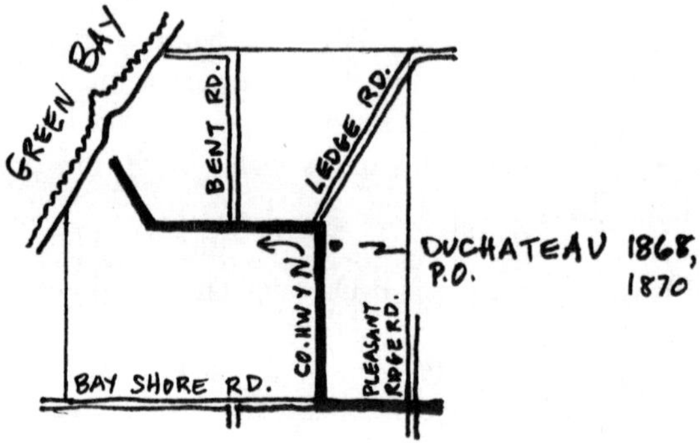

Egg Harbor

Established August 3, 1861. The office is still in service. Zip Code - 54209.

Location: In the present village of the same name on Green Bay in the northeast quarter of Section 25, Town 30 North, Range 26 East, Town of Egg Harbor.

There is quite a selection of stories about the naming of Egg Harbor. The least credible (source unknown) is that the harbor was so-called because it was shaped like an egg, an image that is difficult to discern. Charles I. Martin wrote that

> *As to the origin of the name 'Egg Harbor,' there is some variation in the statements of the 'old settlers.' One statement is, that Mr. Claflin (the first white settler in Door County) so named it, because while coasting along the shore, he got good shelter there, and on the beach he found a nest full of eggs – those of some wild fowl. Another report is, that Col. Robinson, and other gentlemen from Green Bay, many years ago, took a cruise in a small sail yacht, going as far north as 'Death's Door.' They visited most of the Harbors along the way, and had a good time – in the old fashion meaning of the word. On one occasion they got to throwing eggs at each other and did not 'let up' until every egg they had was thrown, and the contestants completely smeared over with the shellcovered hen-fruit. Afterward, to distinguish the 'battleground' from other places and little harbors along the coast, the Green Bay gentlemen referred to it as 'egg harbor.'* (History of Door County, Wisconsin, *1881, p. 77)*

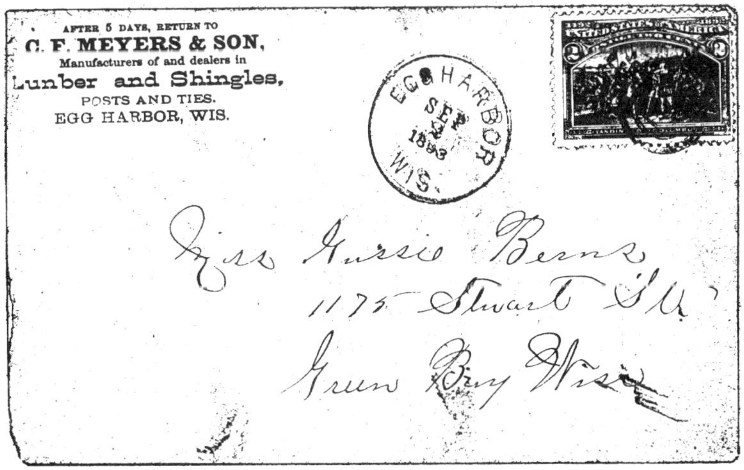

1893, with a misspelling in the corner-card.

Martin's story of increase Claflin's duck eggs is based on a letter from Jacob E. Thorp, Claflin's son-in-law, written in 1880 and published in Martin's history (p. 95).

The remaining version, and the oldest if not the most credible, describes another egg fight, this one by members of six American fur company boats traveling along the Green Bay shore on their way from Prairie du Chien, Wisconsin to Mackinac Island, Michigan in 1821. The incident was recorded by Mrs. Henry Baird in an article from the *Wisconsin Historical Collections* (14:55-62), "Early Days on Mackinac Island," cited by Holand (*History of Door County, Wisconsin*, p. 74, 1917):

At one of the party's campsites...we all noticed that strange appearance which Edward Ploudre presented. He had on white duck pantaloons and a frock coat, and had both pockets filled with eggs which he...fancied his coat would conceal. But the keen eyes of both Mr. Kinzie and Mr. Baird were too much for him, as was their fleetness, for they immediately set in pursuit of him and when they caught him slapped his pockets until the eggs were broken and the contents ran in a stream down his pantaloons and white stockings and into his low shoes. The men laughed until exhausted. Then there was another call for more eggs, and another fight ensued, which only ceased for want of ammunition. Never did anyone enter with greater zest into any sport than did the gentlemen on this occasion. However, at last quiet was restored and we found ourselves with good appetites for supper, and soon retired to refreshing sleep. The next morning the field of battle presented a strange appearance, strewn as it was with egg shells, and many were the regrets expressed that the ammunition was exhausted.

Backstamped 1895, this cover was mailed at the 1¢ rate for printed matter.

Before leaving the shore, speeches befitting the occasion were made by most of the gentlemen, and the place was formally christened 'Egg Harbor,' the name it has ever since borne.

✉

Jacob Thorp's letter to Martin mentioned above also include this information:

...In 1862 I built a large hotel at Egg Harbor and carried on Hotel keeping until 1867, when my house burned and I moved to Fish Creek. While at Egg Harbor I was intrusted with a number of public offices. In 1862 I was appoint-

ed Postmaster, which office I held until I moved away. (p. 96)

His son, Roy, was the first white child born in Egg Harbor, on October 29, 1855. Roy served as Fish Creek postmaster from 1893 to 1907.

✉

*Post Office Change.—We learned that Sheriff J.F. Thorp has been appointed Postmaster at Egg Harbor, Vice Judge Lyman resigned. (*Door County Advocate, *July 16, 1863)*

✉

*Gustav Tanck was the first rural mail carrier who served a twenty-seven mile route out of Egg Harbor, from 1924 to 1929. He was a farmer and dairyman, with 160 acres at one time. He also was assessor of Egg Harbor Township, Town Clerk and Justice of the Peace. (*The Peninsula *7:25, 1963)*

✉

In an article published in the *Door County Advocate* of December 29, 1977, John Enigl reminisced about winters in rural Door County during his younger years, including the hardships of moving the mails:

...Before dawn on a December morning in 1923, Gus' Tanck harnessed his gelding, Prince, and hitched it to the sleigh with one little cab on top. He had milked the cows already and was about to set out for the post office in Egg Harbor to start his mail route. Gus couldn't forget to wear his sheepskin coat and sheepskin mittens—the bite in the air would remind him. Mrs. Tanck would have Dexter or Queen harnessed, ready for the second half of the route.

Since the Hastings post office five miles to the south had closed, Tanck's route now extended as far south of Egg Harbor as Albert Carmody's—a great distance to cover, indeed, 27.8 miles. Gus preferred the winter to the springtime, for in spring the foot of Plum Bottom Hill would be flooded. Sometimes the only way to get across from Egg Harbor was by boat, or by taking the long route around the hill to west, near Hans Hanson's farm.

The scene changes. Joseph Paul 'Bub' LeMere is now mail carrier for the Egg Harbor route. We see him at Birnschein's garage readying his Model 'A' Ford snowmobile for the 1935-36 winter season. The vehicle was built from the chassis of a 1928 Ford Roadster that Gerald Carmody had owned...Bub thought of the old post office pledge and how it applied to him: 'Neither snow nor rain nor gloom of night shall stay these faithful couriers from the swift completion of their appointed rounds...'

✉

Completion of a new post office building in the Village of Egg Harbor is nearing. Begun about a month ago, the building was built almost before anyone had *heard about it. It has been constructed on the Marvin Trodahl lawn. People couldn't figure out what was happening when a bulldozer moved in and masons began laying a foundation. The neat little building with a picture window is almost ready for occupancy. Postmaster Lester Olson says, 'When you see the flag waving over the front door, you'll know we've moved in.' (*Door County Advocate, *October 5, 1954)*

✉

Egg Harbor Postmasters and Dates of Their Appointment

Milton E. Lyman - August 3, 1861
Jacob E. Thorp - June 25, 1863
Levi D. Thorp - September 25, 1868
Lyman D. Mowry - April 29, 1874
Jacob J. Barringer - February 21, 1882
Lyman D. Mowry - April 29, 1883
Truman A. Thorp - October 30, 1889
Fred L. Hanson - March 24, 1900
Truman A. Thorp - February 23, 1904
Charles A. Speaker - December 22, 1906
John M. Phillips - September 6, 1907
Claud W. Gard - October 14, 1909
Anna K. Colomb - November 15, 1917
Lester H. Olsen - January 1, 1938
Herbert J. Anschutz - August 28, 1964
Gladys M. Giesseman - August 25, 1982

Postmaster's Annual Salaries

1864-65	Jacob Thorp	$ 16.81
1871	Levi Thorp	$ 17.00
1873	Levi Thorp	$ 21.00
1877	Lyman Mowry	$ 50.19
1879	Lyman Mowry	$ 64.83
1883	Jacob Barringer	$161.80
1885	Lyman Mowry	$148.86
1887	Lyman Mowry	$183.56
1889	Lyman Mowry	$176.48
1891	Truman Throp	$192.50

EGG HARBOR

SEC. 25 T30N R26E
SEC. 30 T30N R27E
TOWN OF EGG HARBOR

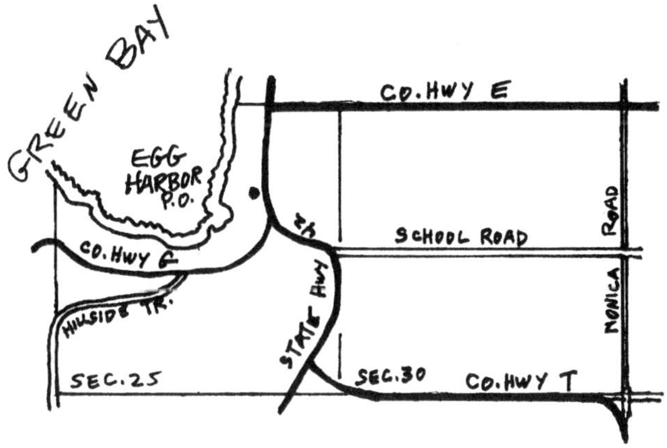

Ellison Bay

Established March 17, 1873 and is still in service. Zip Code - 54210. The *Door County Advocate* of April 3, 1873 noted this event: "Post offices have recently been established at Sister Bay and Eliason's Bay in the northern part of the county. Mr. Henderson is Postmaster at the former place and Mr. John Eliason at the latter."

This office always has been located in the village of the same name on the Green Bay shore in the northeast quarter of Section 15, Town 32 North, Range 28 East, Town of Liberty Grove.

The chief factor in the promotion of the settlement of the northern part of Liberty Grove was a Dane by the name of John Ellison (Eliasen). After him is named Ellison Bay. He came to Ephraim in 1854 and was for many years a member of the Ephraim community. At Ephraim he owned an exceedingly stony forty of land and made but little progress. By 1870, however, he must have accumulated some means as we then find him at Ellison Bay preparing to build a large pier and systematically advertising in the newspapers for settlers. The pier was built in 1872 and also a store. One or both of these must have been profitable as Ellison in 1878 was the owner of 8,000 acres of land. (H.R. Holand, History of Door County *1:372-373, 1917)*

The name of the proposed postmaster of Ellison Bay on the application for establishment of a post office is given as "John Eliason" and is signed with that spelling. His name in various writings over the years has had several versions:

Johan Berndt 'Eliasen' was the European way of spelling the immigrants name. Evidently, Eliasen got through the port of entry with less damage to his euphonious name than befell many newcomers. Time, however, had its influence on the name, which came to have many variations, with plain 'John Ellison' finally being the one most used. But inconsistency about it never ceased to the end of his life. In the Ellison obituary in the Door county Advocate of October 1, 1908, the name is a hybrid 'John Eliason.'

John Ellison was born in Europe on September 12, 1823...Records as to the place of his birth do not agree...(Most of them) indicate that he was born in Denmark. Testimony exists, however, to show that he was born in Sweden...; that (he) used to sail between Sweden and Denmark; that he left Sweden to live in Denmark after he and the Swedish government differed over observance of a certain law by him; and that after that episode he lived in Denmark, from which country he came to the United States...

Finally, Ellison left Ephraim to live in Liberty Grove, presumably before 1865, for in that year government surveyors named Ellison Bay after him. In his history, Martin (History of Door County, Wisconsin, 1881) states that Ellison did not know this until two years later, when he learned of it by looking at a government map. A printed business card reads as follows:

JOHN ELIASON
DEALER IN
CORDWOOD, CEDAR POSTS
AND TELEGRAPH POLES
ELLISON BAY, DOOR CO., WIS.
P.O. EPHRAIM, WIS.

On the card in question, Ephraim is crossed out and Ellison Bay written in as the 'P.O.' in excellent handwriting. His preliminary work was completed, and Ellison became identified with Liberty Grove...

Ellison's work in Liberty Grove was of a directive nature...First came the essentials, such as building the pier and the large house, with wings, that was to be home, post office and store...Aside from the wood business there was the store to keep, the selling of lost and larger tracts of land, and serving as postmaster after he was appointed by T.W. Marshall, acting postmaster of the United States in 1873...

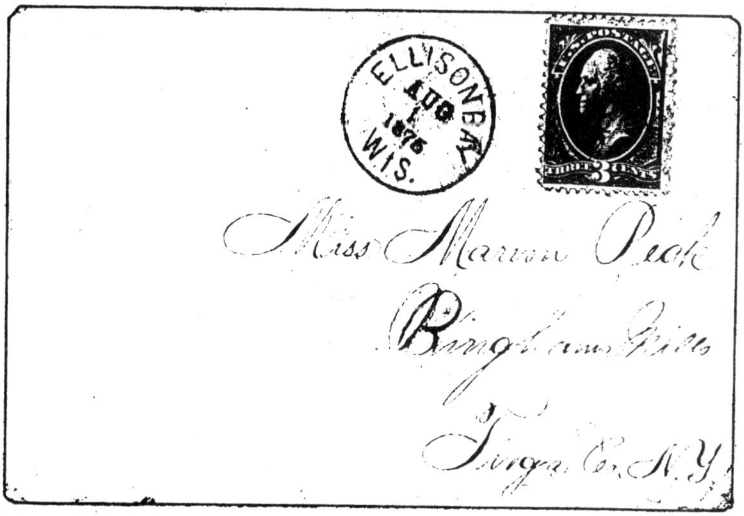

Postmarked 1875.

In his latest years, Ellison expressed hopes of going back to visit in Sweden and Denmark...That hope was never realized. The next report about him appeared two months later in the Advocate of September 26, 1908. It was a report of his death after a day's illness, and of the funeral service...He was buried in the church yard of the Lutheran church, and on the tombstone marking his grave are these lines:

JOHN ELLISON
Born September 12, 1823
Died September 26, 1908
age 85 years 11 days
He was the founder of Ellison Bay
coming here in 1866 and was
the first postmaster
So ended the life of a pioneer. (M.G. Powers, The Peninsula *4:6-13, 1959)*

✉

Locations of Ellison Bay post offices up to 1966 were described by Grace Grasse and Lorraine Varnell in their book *A Century in God's Country 1866-1966.* John Ellison's office was in his home, now (1966) the Moore property. In 1903, Mrs. Matilda Hunt Tostenson kept her office in what is now the Lutheran parsonage. She also had a hat shop on these premises.

From 1903 to 1915, the post office was in Charles Ruckert's store. From 1915 to 1935, three locations were used, first in the Disgarden Hotel (now Kramer's), then in the former Ed Evanson store, and finally in the Disgarden home (now the home of Harvey H. Olson).

From 1935 to 1947, the post office was in the former schoolhouse, now the Rogers' home. In 1947, the office was moved to the new home and post office built by the postmaster and was still in service there in 1966.

✉

Walter Severson, postmaster from 1942 to 1972, compiled a history of his years in office. Some abstracts from it follows:

...The mail arrived about 9:45 a.m. via Star Route, six days a week, originating from Green Bay (later from Sturgeon Bay), and it left at 3:45 p.m. to make outgoing train and truck connections for next-day delivery in Milwaukee and Chicago. The Star Route drivers were hired by contract and were not civil service employees. Quite a bit of our parcel post in the later 1940s was cartons of smoked fish addressed to Chicago and other large

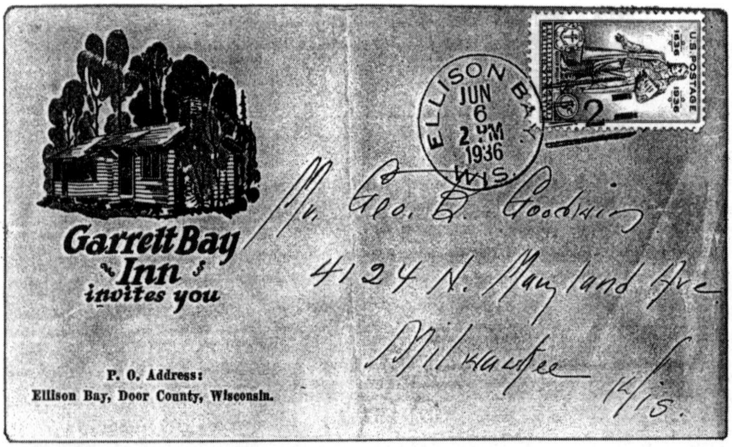

1936, a late usage for this "Doane" style of postmark.

cities as far away as California.

...Early in my tenure, one Star Route driver started delivering unaddressed smoked fish parcels along his route for private charges, and , because our rural carrier was usually able to complete his deliveries by 3 p.m. the contractor somehow arranged a 3:15 p.m. departure time from Ellison Bay in order to give himself more time for personal stops. However, on days when we had snow-covered roads or when we had an especially heavy volume of mail..., the rural carrier was not through with his deliveries in time to make the 3:15 dispatch, and I complained to the railway mail service office in Milwaukee...They arranged that a 3:15 departure was permissible, but, if the carrier was late, a 3:45 departure time would apply. Once, during World War II gas rationing, the Star Route driver stopped at a garage and had the valves on this truck engine ground, which caused an 11 a.m. Star Route arrival in Ellison Bay...

A later contractor had a younger driver who appeared inebriated at departure time one day, so I refused to give him the mail and got a local driver and truck to take the mail to Sturgeon Bay...A few weeks later, when that driver had been replaced by his brother, the new driver was backing towards the back door when he collided with a car. He then got away and backed into my office..., damaging the eaves troughs. He also was inebriated. I told him he wouldn't get the mail and locked the door. He got a tire iron and started for the front door. I locked that one too and once more called for the substitute driver with his truck. The contractors after that were satisfactory.

Mail for Washington Island also had a Star Route, starting at Ellison Bay. A local driver with a pickup truck took the mail and met the ferry at Gills Rock (or at Northport on blustery days) and brought back the outgoing mail from the island each morning...A few times mail for Washington Island remained at Ellison Bay for two or three days before a delivery connection could be made due to severe ice or weather conditions...

Because Jay Rogers, the owner of the post office quarters wanted to retire, we had to secure other living and post office quarters in Ellison Bay. He agreed to sell me a quarter-acre of the old school grounds, and I designed and built my present home, with postal quarters included, at 12044 Highway 42. The Ellison Bay post office was located there from March 1947 until 1974, when the post office moved to its present location in the Liberty Grove-Ellison Bay Fire Department building on Garrett Bay Road...

The Door Reminder, a 3rd-class-mail advertising weekly, began publishing in 1947...After several years of expansion of Reminder mailings, the receipts therefrom promoted Ellison Bay from being a third-class to being a second-class post office...

✉

The Pioneer Store (in Ellison Bay) was built in 1900 by Mr. and Mrs. Charles Ruckert. From 1903 to 1915 it also was the village post office, with Mr. Ruckert the postmaster. (J. Kahlert, Early Door County Buildings, *p. 90, 1976)*

✉

Walter Cornelius Olson, the owner of the United States mail and stageline between Sturgeon Bay and Ellison Bay, was born December 15, 1880... When [he] was twenty years of age he enlisted in the U.S. Life Saving Service and for ten years was connected with the station on Plum Island...In 1910, Mr. Olson left the Life Saving Service and obtained the contract for carrying the mail between Sturgeon Bay and Ellison Bay. Up to this time the stage line had been worked with horses and the long journey in slowly moving wagons was one of great hardship both to the passengers and beasts of burden. Mr. Olson at once began to install up-to-date automobile trucks, adding to the efficiency of the service until he at present is operating two heavy freight and mail trucks and three large automobile passenger busses. The service is now as prompt, rapid and pleasant as on the average railroad line in the state (H.R. Holand, History of Door County, Wisconsin, *II:476, 1917)*

✉

On November 16, 1988, fire damaged an Ellison Bay landmark. The *Door County Advocate* of November 18 reported that

"Fire, the enemy of at least three historic Door County hotels in the past six years, was vanquished Wednesday when Sister Bay-Liberty Grove fire fighters saved the Norrland Hotel in Ellison Bay from being destroyed..."

The 86-year-old Norrland Hotel, built by Mr. and Mrs. Ed Disgarden, also escaped a serious damage October 3, 1903 (the night the Hackley went down) when it was struck by lightning. During its long history, the three-story wooden structure served as an office for visiting doctor, G.R. Egeland, a dental office for Dr. Uno Nyman and as a post office.

Records show that the high cost of living at the Norrland during those early years was $1 a day for room and board and if one could just afford the price of a meal, it cost 25¢...

✉

Ellison Bay Postmasters and Dates of their Appointment

John Eliason - March 17, 1873
Mrs. Matilda E. Hunt - May 29, 1878
Albert Icke - August 4, 1893
Matilda E. Hunt-Tostenson - May 25, 1897

Charles Ruckert - April 7, 1904
Elmer A. Disgarden - February 10, 1915
Clyde A. Olson - May 27, 1935
Winfield Rogers - November 26, 1935
Walter H. Severson - October 10, 1942
Patricia Peterson - September 30, 1972
Karen Sunstrom - September 30, 1992 (Officer-in-Charge)
Gloria A. Johnson - June 3, 1993 (Officer-in-Charge)
Karen Sunstrom - October 6, 1993

Postmasters' Annual Salaries

1873	John Eliason	$ 12.00
1877	John Eliason	$ 38.88
1879	Matilda Hunt	$ 38.86
1883	Matilda Hunt	$141.92
1885	Matilda Hunt	$164.66
1887	Matilda Hunt	$200.51
1889	Matilda Hunt	$171.87
1891	Matilda Hunt	$132.22

ELLISON BAY

SEC. 15
T32N R28E
TOWN OF LIBERTY GROVE

Ephraim

Established November 13, 1861, and is still in service. Zip Code - 54211.

Location: In the present village of the same name at several sites in Town 31 North, Range 27 East, Town of Gibraltar. The first Ephraim post office was in Lot 4 of section 13; later offices have all been in the northwest quarter of section 24.

The village of Ephraim was founded in 1853 by the Rev. Andrew M. Iverson and his small Moravian congregation of Norwegian settlers, who came to Door County from Green Bay. These settlers gave the village its name. In Biblical terms, Ephraim means "doubly fruitful." In the Old Testament, the name was applied to the Tribe of Israel which occupied Mount Ephraim. In the New Testament, Ephraim was a city on the edge of the wilderness where Jesus went after raising Lazarous.

✉

The early days of postal service at Ephraim have been describe by H.R. Holand:

> *The nearest post office was at Green Bay, and between this town and Ephraim...lay a dense forest of seventy-five miles without either road or path...By boat in summer or over the ice in winter, it was possible to reach civilization. When all conditions were perfect, it was possible to make the round trip in a week. But usually there were long delays due to storms and head winds or rough ice...During the first five years the pioneers of Ephraim therefore seldom got their mail oftener than two or three times a year. But in the fall of 1857...a road was opened up to Egg Harbor (from Sturgeon Bay) and prompted the people of Sturgeon Bay to do likewise to the south toward Green Bay. Before spring came, sleigh bells jingled between Green Bay and Sturgeon Bay...*

Overlook of Ephraim, 1910.

This prompted a demand for postal connections. This was, strangely enough, speedily granted, not only to Sturgeon Bay, but also to Egg Harbor, Fish Creek and Ephraim.

To be sure, there was no road whatever beyond Egg Harbor, but the monthly mail deliveries to various post offices on the peninsula were not so large in volume as to require a horse and wagon. Gullik Goodletson, a young fellow of about eighteen years of age who lived in Ephraim, undertook to carry the mail between this place and Green Bay...

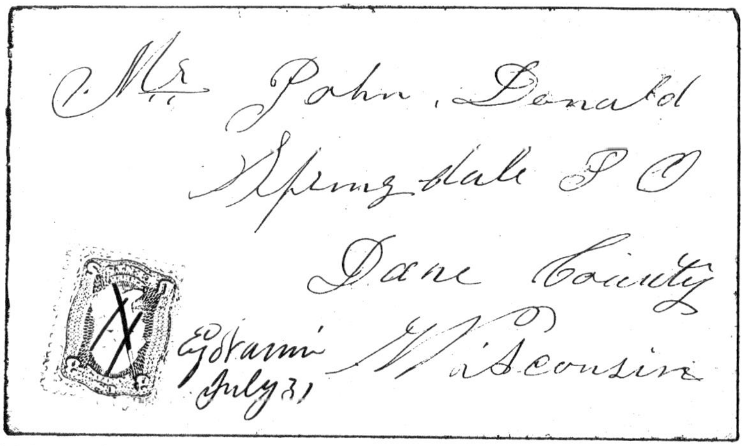

This cover is undated but probably is from around 1865.

The post offices of those days were as unpretentious as the mail carrier. They were much the same, so a description of the Ephraim post office will suffice for all. Like the mail carrier, there was noting impressive about this post office. It was confined to a small shelf in a corner of Hans Jacob's sitting room-kitchen-dining room-bedroom. On this shelf stood a tin box about a foot square and six inches deep. This was the office itself and was treated with profound respect by all as being dedicated to the service of the U.S. Government. It was always kept carefully locked, and Mr. Jacobs would never permit anyone but himself to touch the sacred treasure chest.

The contents of this box were rather disappointing. It had two compartments, in the smaller of which was about a dollar's worth of stamps and a pamphlet of post office regulations. The large compartment was intended for outgoing and incoming mail, but was usually empty, for the pioneers of Ephraim very seldom wrote or received letters.

*The monthly arrivals of the sturdy little mail carrier were festivals toward which everyone looked with great expectancy. On the evening he was expected, almost every man in the village was usually at the door of the post office to bid him welcome. (*Peninsula Historical Review *5(1):19, 1931)*

✉

The *Door County Advocate* printed several comments about mail service in the Ephraim area:

July 26, 1862: Mail Route to Eagle Harbor.— We understand that Congress has provided for an extension of the Green Bay and Sturgeon Bay Mail Route to the Post Office at Ephraim, via Egg Harbor and Fish Creek. It will be recollected that, in an early number of our paper, we called attention to the necessity of an extension of this route through the Northern part of the county, and we congratulate the people of the Northern towns on the early communication of their wishes. The necessary estimates are being collected for letting the route at an early day.

Ephraim post office about 1940.

October 20, 1864: Ole Larson, Esq., of Ephraim, the man who carries the mail between that place and Sturgeon Bay, is running a meat market at Ephraim, and supplies the People there and on the route with fresh meat each week.

February 24, 1870: Bidders for the Ephraim mail route should put in bids for carrying the mail to North Bay as a post office will be established there and the route extended.

October 5, 1871: Ephraim Mail Arrangements - Southern Mail via Fish Creek and Egg Harbor to Sturgeon Bay departs every Monday and Friday at 6 a.m., arrives every Tuesday and Saturday by 6 p.m.

Eastern Mail to North Bay departs every Wednesday at 6 a.m., arrives same day by 6 p.m.

Northern Mail to Washington Harbor arrives every second and fourth Wednesday of each month by 6 p.m., departs next day at 6 a.m., from December to May each year. (H.P. Jacobs, P.M.)

January 23, 1873: The people in the northern part of the county want three more post offices north of the present one at Ephraim.

✉

Hans Peter Jacobson was one of the original Ephraim settlers and became the first postmaster. He built a log home where the Anderson Hotel now stands. During the early years of the village it served as his home, the council room where village business was settled and as the post office. After he settled in Ephraim he dropped the "on" from his name and added a "Doctor." As Dr. Jacobs, he served the sick who came to him for help as best he could.

On September 22, 1880, he wrote a letter to C.I. Martin about his beginnings at Ephraim, which Martin printed in his *History of Door County, Wisconsin*:

> *I first landed in Door County at Sturgeon Bay, October 1852, and settled on what is now known as E.C. Daniel's place, where I resided for eight months. The government sold the land, and I tore down my house, loaded it into a boat, and came to Ephraim. This was then such a dense forest that, with axe in hand, I had to step ashore and clear a placed to unload the boat...Rev. A.M. Iverson, now of Fort Howard, was one of the first settlers in this place, and the first town Superintendent of Schools. He was also pastor of the United Brethren Church of the Moravians, and it was at that time our church here (Ephraim) was built. It was the first in the county—I do not remember the date...I have often said: 'I was the first in this place,' but I shall never again be the first to make a new settlement. It sometimes make me shudder, even now, when I think of those first days, and it makes me wonder how we got through. (p. 52)*

Also undated but probably about 1875.

It's interesting to note that Ephraim had only five postmasters in the first 125 years of its post office. In contrast, Sister Bay had eighteen postmasters in a similar period. The reasons for such a difference are not clear.

✉

Ephraim Postmasters and Dates of Their Appointment

- Hans P. Jacobs - November 13, 1861
- Andrew O. Hanson - March 14, 1894
- Samuel M. Hogenson - July 23, 1915
- Bert E. Thorp - October 31, 1951

J. Hansons Store and Post Office, 1906.

Irene E. Meyer - April 16, 1983
Lenn Seppi - February 27, 1988
Gerald Roberts - July 13, 1991

Annual Salaries of Hans Jacobs as Postmaster

1864-65	$ 33.81	1883	$192.55
1871	$ 90.00	1885	$ 91.86
1873	$130.00	1887	$204.51
1877	$ 92.35	1889	$190.02
1879	$ 92.36	1891	$171.91

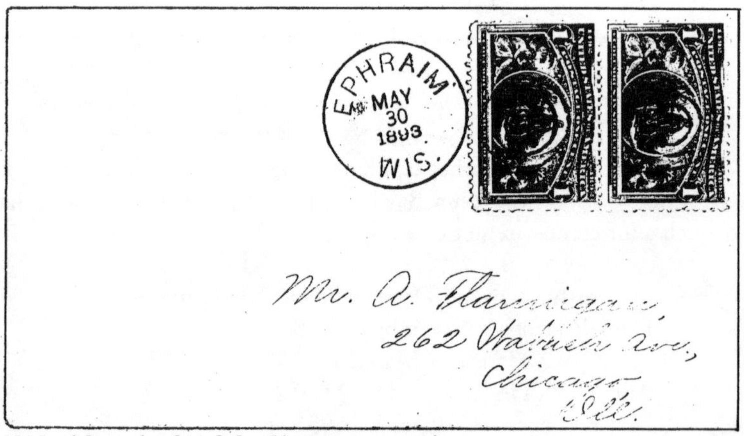

1893 with a pair of 1¢ Columbian commemoratives.

EPHRAIM

SEC. 13, 24
T31N R27E
TOWN OF GIBRALTAR

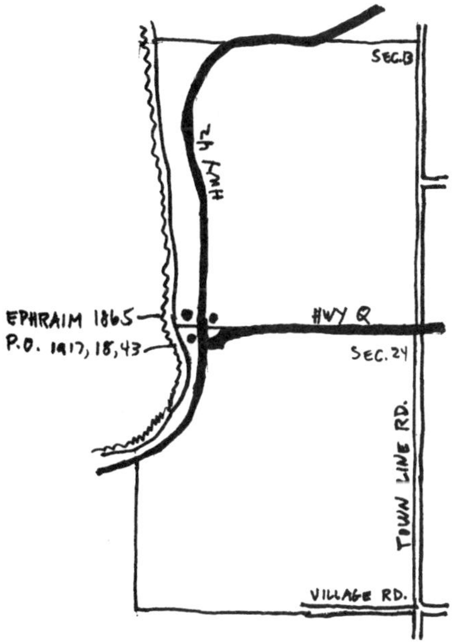

Evergreen

Established November 16, 1885.

Discontinued September 23, 1898, with mail service at Sturgeon Bay.

Location: At the Evergreen Nursery Company, Inc. on County Highway TT, three miles east of Sturgeon Bay, in the northwest quarter of the northeast quarter, section 11, Town 27 North, Range 26 East, Town of Sturgeon Bay.

The post office was named for the nursery. It was originally proposed to be "Pinney," but the Post Office Department objected. A second proposal, "Evergreens," was also rejected. Finally, "Evergreen," without an "s," was approved. The reasons for disapproving the first two names were not stated by the Department, although they probably were related to the instructions on the application form for a new post office, which stated that "The name of the candidate for postmaster should not be applied as the name of a post office. It is preferable to have some LOCAL or PERMANENT name, which must not be the name of any other office in the State; and you should aim to select a name not appropriated to any office in the United States."

On the Evergreen application, it was entered that the post office was estimated to serve "twenty-five families or 125 persons."

The Evergreen post office was conceived as a convenience and died thirteen years later as a victim of local politics. During its life, however, it did a remarkable business.

The story began in 1864, when George Pinney went into the tree nursery business at Sturgeon Bay, selling evergreen planting stock to all comers. His first nursery is said to have been located on the site of the present Sturgeon Bay post office. He was a firm believer in publicity and put a good deal of effort into newspaper advertising and instructing his customers how to handle their trees, something none of his competitors did. He also published a magazine for the nursery trade which was widely circulated and helped to spread his reputation. His firm was and is called the Evergreen Nursery Company.

As the business grew, headquarters were established three miles east of Sturgeon Bay. A small community known as Evergreen grew up there, but the record is not clear as to which came first, the nursery or the settlement. At any rate, by the time the 1880s arrived, Evergreen had a blacksmith shop, store and several houses, as well as the nursery. By 1885, Evergreen Nursery was reputed to be the largest mail-order tree nursery in the world.

In that year, Mr. Pinney was able to demonstrate that his business alone sent and received more dollars in postal money orders than all the other patrons of the Sturgeon Bay post office put together. He also had substantial mailings in nursery correspondence, price lists and catalogs. So, being a staunch Democrat in the Democratic administration of President Grover Cleveland, he petitioned for and was awarded his own post office, to be located at the Evergreen Nursery headquarters. His appointment as postmaster was dated November 16, 1885.

The *Door County Advocate* for November 11, 1886 announced that the contract for carrying the mail daily between Sturgeon Bay and Evergreen had been awarded to Alonzo S. Putnam for his low bid of $156 a year.

The local community apparently was proud of the Evergreen Nursery operation because of its size and the publicity it brought to Door County. The *Door County Advocate* for May 9, 1886, offered considerable editorial comment about it:

> *There are probably not many of our readers who are aware of the extent and importance of the evergreen business in this county...The business was begun in 1864 by George Pinney...In the spring of 1883, he began advertising largely, and since that time has established an immense trade. Up to the present date he has received more than eleven hundred orders for the spring business, and before the season closes will doubtless book from fourteen to fifteen hundred, supplying about two thousand customers, many orders being for clubs of from five to ten persons. Since March 1st, his average daily mail has been from sixty to seventy-five letters and postal cards, and he has received as many as fifty-seven orders in one mail. Large quantities of small plants are sent by mail, the postage on these for the month of April being $157.75. The office work occupies the entire time of two persons, and on some days additional help is required. In packing, sorting and box-making ten persons are kept busy.*
>
> *During the present season, Mr. Pinney will ship from two to three million of plants and trees...The business is more than three times that of last year, when 467 orders were booked. This increase is in a great measure due to liberal advertising, Mr. Pinney having expended about $500 for that purpose this year, being nearly*

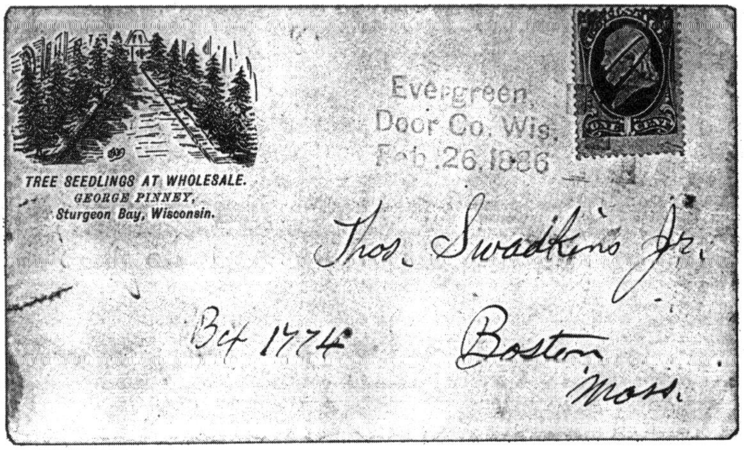

An 1886 straight-line postmark applied in light blue ink.

twice as much as he paid in 1885.

Much of Mr. Pinney's trade was at first with nurserymen, while farmers are at present his principal customers, these having generally been successful in evergreen culture. This success is undoubtedly due to the instruction they have received from Mr. Pinney, whose various treatises on this subject have been circulated throughout the whole of the North American continent. He was the pioneer of the evergreen business, and there is probably no better authority than he in the land.

George Pinney died of cancer on November 2, 1894. His daughter, Flora C. Pinney, was appointed to succeed him as the second and last Evergreen postmaster on December 13, 1894.

Postal matters apparently went smoothly until 1898, when trouble arose. In the county was another local Democrat who had his eye on the Evergreen postmastership. He was alleged to have arranged things so that he was in line for the appointment. The nursery managers heard about this, of course, but would have none of it, for they wanted to retain control of the post office.

Since the Pinney family could not change things politically, they ended the matter by moving the business office of the nursery to Sturgeon Bay. Thus, nursery mail came and went at the Sturgeon Bay post office. Business declined rapidly at the Evergreen post office, since the community was not large enough to support it, so on September 23, 1898, the office was closed for good. Evergreen most likely would have continued in operation for several more years had it not been for the political squabble, since the nursery business was doing well. But it didn't, and the nursery has had a Sturgeon Bay address ever since.

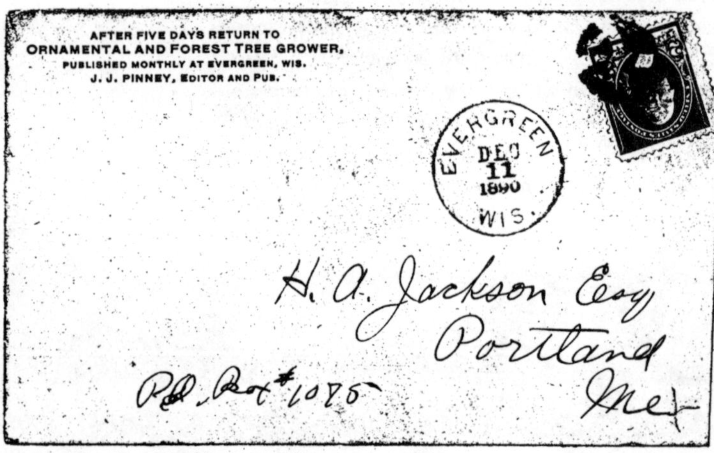

1890 cover from the Evergreen Nursery.

The Evergreen post office building was destroyed by fire in 1915, and as of 1972 the foundation was still visible on the nursery grounds. The Evergreen settlement, however, has long since disappeared and is now marked only by the nursery buildings and a farmstead across the highway.

Annual Salaries of George Pinney as Postmaster

1887	$687.09
1889	$649.56
1891	$655.39

EVERGREEN

SEC. 11
T27N R26E
TOWN OF STURGEON BAY

Fagerwick

Established January 25, 1881.

Discontinued October 23, 1882, with mail service at Washington Harbor.

Location: At the south end of Washington Island on Detroit Harbor in the southeast quarter of section 12, Town 33 North, Range 29 East, Town of Washington, where the postmaster was involved with an unsuccessful real estate development.

At the time Fagerwick was established, Robert Severs, the long-time Washington Harbor postmaster, was also serving as town clerk and correspondent for the *Door County Advocate.* C.B. Eaton noted that

> *In late February of 1881, Severs wrote for the Advocate: 'Report says we are to have a second post office on this island...The government gives this bit of a place about $140 a year for mail service...I think we all ought to be satisfied and grateful.' The Washington Harbor postmaster must have been reacting to the establishment on January 25 of Fagerwick Post Office on the Detroit Harbor shore, with Knud O. Shellswick postmaster. (The Scandinavian Fagerwick is usually translated 'Beautiful Bay.') One can only speculate concerning Severs' possible reaction if he had read the Fagerwick application filed with the Post Office Department by Mr. Shellswick. To the question, What post office will be left out by this change? Mr. Shellswick wrote in: 'None, except Washington Harbor might be starved out in course of time.' Possibly Washington Harbor's well established status and its location at the shipping and commercial hub of the Island, together with slower-than-expected development in Detroit Harbor, was responsible; in any case, it was Fagerwick Post Office which seems to have 'starved out' until its discontinuance on October 23, 1892. (*Washington Island Insights, *p. 2, 1988)*

Mr. Shellswick was postmaster for the life of the Fagerwick office. On his application for the post office, in addition to his appraisal of Washington Harbor, he added the overly optimistic estimate that the office would serve "two-thirds or three-quarters of the inhabitants of the Island."

✉

The Fagerwick name was still current at Detroit Harbor in 1892 when Bo L. Anderson applied for a post office there. His application requested that Fagerwick be the name of the new office; however, the Post Office Department turned him down and designated Detroit Harbor as the office's name. C.B. Eaton pointed out (in personal correspondence) that Bo

Anderson's sister married a son of Knud Shellswick, so there was some connection.

Mr. Shellswick was born in Norway in 1810, came to America in 1861, and was a sea captain, farmer and land developer. His descendants say that his name was Knud Olson in the Old Country, but he changed it to Skjelsvig when he came to America, and later to Shellswick (*fide* C.B. Eaton).

FAGERWICK

SECTION 12
T33N R29E
TOWN OF WASHINGTON

Fetzer

Established January 11, 1887.

Discontinued July 18, 1888, with mail service at Egg Harbor.

Location: On the Green Bay shore south of Egg Harbor in lot 1, section 4, Town 29 North, Range 26 East, Town of Egg Harbor.

Fetzer was one of the shorter-lived post offices of Door County, being in service for only eighteen months. The *Door County Advocate* reported on December 9, 1886 that "Fetzer is the name of the post office to be established at Horseshoe Bay upon the petition of Youngs and Fetzer and others interested in the matter." The application for the office, dated November 26, 1886, noted an estimate that the office would serve a population of "300 to 400." Considering the short life of the office, this was substantially more than an optimistic prediction.

From 1870 to about 1890 there was a thriving sawmill, pier and small village at Horseshoe Bay. During this period, John Fetzer and Walter Youngs, who had business interest in the Town of Forestville south of Sturgeon Bay, bought the property and employed many men. The post office was named after the senior partner.

✉

The village of Horseshoe Bay had its history described by H.R. Holand:

> *Andrew Anderson...built the first pier about 1870. He bought and shipped cordwood and kept a store. In a few years he sold out to Albee & Taylor and they pushed the business energetically. They had a mill and vessels daily came and went from Horseshoe Bay. A cooper shop, a blacksmith shop, a general store, a school and a dozen dwelling houses were soon erected there. All roads led to Horseshoe Bay and business was booming. Later Fetzer & Youngs bought the property and employed many men. In 1890 an ice company made up of Sturgeon Bay people started cutting ice there, employing about sixty men. The ice harvest farther south was poor and the Horseshoe Bay company were confident that the price would go high up and all would make much money. They therefore held the ice, that is, that which did not trickle away. Little by little, the ice melted. When the ice speculators were ready to sell the ice had turned to water and their dreams of gold turned to dross.*
>
> *That was the last exploit in the Village of Horseshoe Bay. The mill was closed, the schoolhouse was moved away, the buildings fell into decay and the grass and*

brush grew up in the roads. Soon, almost everyone forgot that there ever had been such a place as Horseshoe Bay where the schooners in olden times dropped anchor. (History of Door County, Wisconsin, *I:399, 1917)*

Today, the former village of Horseshoe Bay and the Fetzer post office is the site of Frank E. Murphy County Park.

✉

George Walter Youngs, a relative of the junior partner in Fetzer & Youngs, was the postmaster for the life of Fetzer post office.

There is some confusion about the spelling of the names of the partners in the Horseshoe Bay enterprise. Their firm has been variously listed as Fetzer and Young, Young and Fetzer, Youngs and Fetzer, and Fetzer and Youngs. Mr. Fetzer probably was the senior partner; hence he gained the post office name. The application for the Fetzer office was signed by the first postmaster as George Walter Youngs. Presumably Mr. Youngs knew how to spell his own name.

John Fetzer, the Forestville and Horseshoe Bay entrepreneur, was born in Germany, came to America in 1850 and to Door County in 1867. He gained prominence as a merchant, mill owner and politician. In the latter capacity he represented the Town of Forestville on the Door County Board of Supervisors for twenty years and also served terms as an assemblyman and senator in the state legislature.

✉

Increase Claflin moved from Little Sturgeon to Fish Creek in 1844 to become the first white settler there. He named several places from Little Sturgeon to Death's Door, including Fish Creek. Horseshoe Bay he called by that name because he found his horses there when they were on their way back to Little Sturgeon after his move to Fish Creek. One of the horses lost a shoe at the place. Mr. Claflin thereupon named Horseshoe Bay and the place has gone by that name ever since. Mr. Claflin lived at Fish Creek until his death in 1867 at age 83 years. (C.I. Martin, *History of Door County, Wisconsin*, p. 96, 1881)

FETZER

SEC. 3,4,9,10
T29N R26E
TOWN OF EGG HARBOR

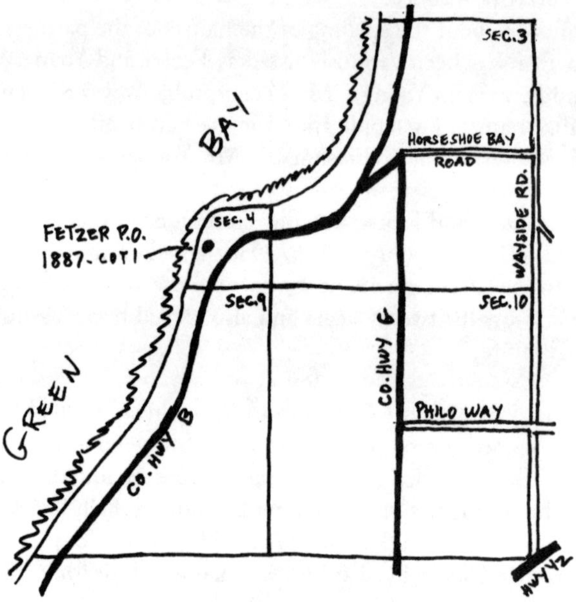

Fish Creek

Established August 26, 1858. The office is still in service. Zip Code - 54212.

Location: In the present village of the same name on the Green Bay shore in the southeast quarter of the southwest quarter, section 29, Town 31 North, Range 27 East, Town of Gibraltar.

The name is locally descriptive of a small creek in the village which was important to the early settlers, and was given by Increase Claflin, who settled there in 1842.

Fish Creek and its post office were isolated by land from the rest of the county to its south for several years. "As late as 1869, according to Henry C. Graham, who carried the mail between Sturgeon Bay and Fish Creek for $125 per year, there was no road between these two villages but only a rough trail through the forest." (H.R. Holand, *History of Door County, Wisconsin* I:180, 1917)

Ruby Hill Wons, born in Fish Creek in 1892, described her childhood memories of the post office in an article she wrote at age 99 for the Gibraltar Historical Association:

> *It is always fun to go for the mail. I wait outside the post office on the wooden platform of the scale there until I see the stage with team coming down the hill. It is a pretty sight. They reach the turn, make a wide flourish around the curve, and draw up in front of the post office. May Thorp is tending the post office. I may get the Youth's Companion, The* Door County Advocate, *and even possibly a volume of the Chatterbox series, a book for children.* (Door County Advocate, *April 13, 1991)*

Fish Creek Post Office, 1910.

On October 3, 1990, the *Door County Advocate* published a short history of the Fish Creek post office written by Ann Thorp:

> *Fish Creek's attractive and spacious new post office*

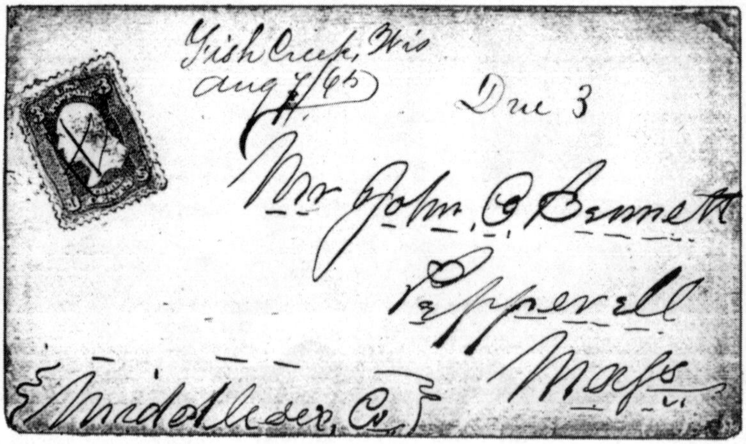

1865 manuscript cancel.

opened September 10, 1990, a little more than 142 years after the first village postmaster was appointed.

...Around the turn of the century when the resort business was thriving, automobiles had begun to make their appearance and the mail-order catalog became a household fixture, the post office was focal point of activity in the village.

In 1898, it was located in a house on Main Street where the present home of Roy and Virginia Kinsey stands, and that house was destroyed by fire. Roy Thorp was postmaster there until 1907, when Mabel Vorous became postmistress for seven years and the facility was in the present Christmas shop on Main Street just west of the Cookery Restaurant. The building had been a butcher shop, restaurant, electric shop and village library in its long and colorful history.

May Thorp Kinsey, daughter of Roy Thorp, was appointed postmaster by President Woodrow Wilson in 1914 and held the post for twenty years. The office was in the present Kinsey home on Main Street. Rural Free Delivery had begun. Mail came to Sturgeon Bay by rail and to Fish Creek by truck. Parcel Post shipments brought baby chicks early each spring and their cheeping could be heard for blocks. Other birds and animals came in crates—geese, mink, bees and once a bear cub for the game farm in Peninsula Park. May Kinsey was a good-natured woman, staying open long hours to accommodate everyone. If people came in from Chambers Island at night, May let them pick up their mail.

Carl Seiler took over in 1935 and the facility was set up in the front of his garage on Main and Pine Streets, now Hide Side Casuals clothing shop. In 1941 Anita Schulz was hired as a clerk and in her thirty-two years with the post office, she was acting postmaster for a time, then officer-in-charge, after Elliott Hodgins left. She was advanced to postmaster [in 1971], the first in Door County to be appointed under the newly created U.S. Postal Service (formerly the U.S. Post Office Department). In 1960 a new facility was dedicated in a new building across the street...

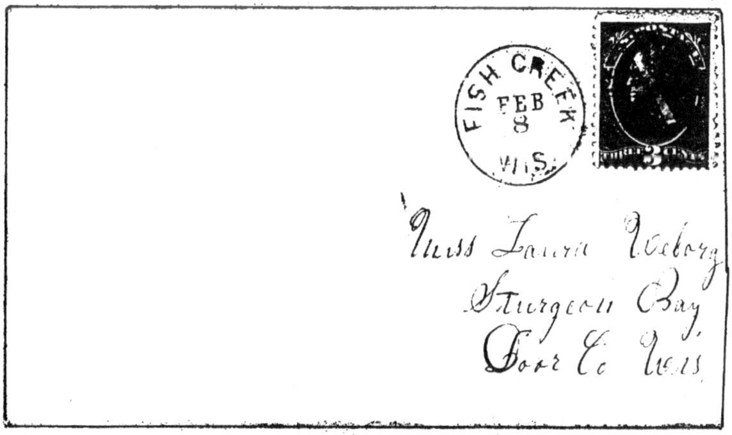

This cover is not dated, but the letter it contained was headed 1877.

James Gogats and David Davis each served for eight years and Jill Goking began in December, 1989. She was officially installed at the opening of the new post office September 10. Bunny Spearo works with her and Carla Stenzel and Roger Ohnesorge are rural carriers.

Roger's career started in 1959, when he drove a forty-mile delivery run Monday through Saturday. Now his territory is a ninety-mile trip, and includes parts of Baileys Harbor, Ephraim and Egg Harbor. At Baileys Harbor he sorts mail for one hundred boxes and he and Carla deliver to about 400 boxes in summer and 325 in winter.

By now Roger is accustomed to steering the car from the passenger seat and the route is so much a part of his life that when he's driving off duty he sometimes stops if he sees a red flag up. He still delivers baby chicks, geese and bees, which he says always means a few are on the outside of the box to keep him company. Occasionally he has delivered cremated remains to the Blossomberg Cemetery custodian. Of this, he says he gets no complaints on the ride. Since he began, the amount of mail has increased greatly. Everyone has some mail daily, he said, and if people leave for a week, they may have a bushel of mail waiting on their return.

Carla Stenzel has been a rural carrier for sixteen years and is also responsible for sorting that mail. She and Roger enjoy their work and have had no complaints about their service. There have been few times in their tenures when mail was not delivered because of severe winter storms, and then it was because it didn't get to Fish Creek.

Among the thousands of pieces of mail to and from the village over the years, our postal workers have handled good news and bad; the untold numbers of 'Having a Good Time' postcards sent from Door County, wedding invitations, birth announcements and sympathy cards, tax notices and Social Security checks, Christmas cards and gifts, and more recently, more and more 'junk' mail...

Gibraltar Township people are proud of their new post office and its staff, who, like their earlier counterparts, play a vital part in all their lives.

✉

More about life at the Fish Creek post office was written by Duncan Throp:

The daily arrival of the U.S. mail by truck at Aunt May Kinsey's post office during the 1920s was an occasion for many visitors, including us kids. One day a crate arrived containing a tiny black bear cub. I poked at him and listened to his squeals. Suddenly the cub broke one of the slats and escaped from his cage. He scooted across Main Street and finding a tall box elder tree raced to a top-most branch. Somebody phoned the game farm at Peninsula Park and the sent Oscar Nelson, a DNR handyman, to capture the cub. Oscar was known to 'have a way' with animals.

Joe Duclon, Fish Creek Mail Carrier, 1912.

He located the treed animal and forthwith climbed the tree, speaking soothingly to the bearlet above him. The cub answered with snarls and growls that promised war to the death. Oscar persevered until he was able to get the cub inside a gunny sack he had tucked in his belt.

The two began the descent. Halfway down the cub managed to bite through the sack, Oscar's pants and into his leg. It was a good bite and Oscar completed his descent with a few howls of pain and blood running down his leg. On the ground, he took the cub to his car and hauled him back to the game farm in triumph, ignoring his scars of battle.

*Any place that could provide such an eventful afternoon was a great place and it paid to check the post office and the coming and going of the U.S. mail. (*Door County Advocate, *October 3, 1990)*

✉

Edward Schreiber offered further reminiscences about the Fish Creek mails:

In the early days (of the 1900s) it sometimes required great effort for the postal service to deliver the mail daily. Rail service brought the mail as far as Sturgeon Bay, but it had to be delivered to the villages north of there using horses. In sum-

mer, the mail came from Sturgeon Bay by wagon, but in winter it arrived in a large bob-sleigh fitted with a cab enclosure large enough to accommodate the driver and a small stove. The bags of mail were stacked in a box at the rear of the sleigh and were covered with a heavy tarp to protect them from the snow and ice. When the roads hadn't been cleared and the frothy, snow-covered horses pulled the sleigh into town, they were a sight worthy of a Christmas card...

There were several...businesses in the village, including three stores. The store owned by the Vorouses was in a building that later housed the post office and also had a garage located at the rear of the building operated by two local men, Carl Seiler and Henry Stenzel...Previously the post office was in the Al (now Roy) Kinsey home across the street, with Mrs. Al (May) Kinsey as postmistress. (E. & L. Schreiber, Fish Creek Voices: An Oral History of A Door County Village. *278 pp., 1990. See pp. 16 18, 28)*

✉

H.R. Holand chronicled how the first Fish Creek postmaster came to the village in the fall of 1857:

*...A man with a small trading vessel had put into the harbor so late that when he woke up next morning he found the bay frozen over. His name was Jacob St. Ores. Being obliged to winter there he found the few pioneers who settled there such good company that he decided to make Fish Creek his home. Moreover he made a trip back to Ozaukee County, his former home, to tell his relatives about the delightful place he had discovered. As a result, his brother in law, Martin Minor, with his family, including his sons, Edward S. and Augustine A. Minor, moved up in 1858... (*History of Door County, Wisconsin *I:354, 1917)*

Fish Creek Post Office, 1920.

✉

Anita Schults, a former Fish Creek postmaster, wrote of her years with the Fish Creek post office in a reminiscence made available to me by Ann Thorp:

Just a year after we moved to Fish Creek, in 1940, I started working in the Fish Creek post office as a clerk. Little did I know that someday I would retire as postmaster from that same office.

In those early years, the wages were low and the rewards seemed nil. I often asked myself 'Is this to be my lifelong career?' Now, in my retirement years, I think about those years often, and if someone would ask 'Would you do it again?', I would truthfully answer 'Yes, I would!' I never got rich money-wise, but the memories I took with me mean far more than material wealth.

I started working in the old post office, which later was an ice-cream parlor and is now a clothing shop, across the street from the present post office, which is about to move to the Community Center. It was a building owned by Carl Seiler (the postmaster then) and Henry Stenzel, who owned the Fish Creek Garage. The post office proper was one room in front of the building, with the garage occupying the larger part in the rear. Divided by a partition, half was the lobby which housed a small antique table, two chairs, and a writing desk that was originally a Clark's Spool Case, sitting on a stand. The other half was the work area, with only one small window for ventilation. I worked in this building for twenty-two years and it holds the most poignant memories.

Fish Creek Post Office, 1930.

I remember well my first 'bad' experience (bad then, humorous now). I had worked there only a few days when Mr. Seiler asked me if I would mind staying alone while he walked across the street to the Schreiber Grocery Store. I was very confident, and told him I could handle any situation. He had been gone only a short time when I looked out the window and saw a truck stop. A man stepped out and walked toward the post office. He was dressed in bib overalls and had a beard that almost covered his face. Being a young girl from the city, all I could think of was that here was a man coming to rob the post office. I quickly locked the door and hid behind the lock boxes. When he came to the door and found it locked, he mumbled something and walked away. Soon I saw him returning with Mr. Seiler, who introduced me to Claude Kihl, a well-known resident of Juddville.

His gruff demeanor and appearance certainly was enough to ignite a young girl's vivid imagination and cause fear and trembling!

Although many people come to mind as I think back over the years, I will never forget Lilia Dyer and Ella Weborg.

Miss Dyer, a very well-educated lady from Missouri, spent her summers in a log cabin near the entrance to Peninsula State Park. She always carried an umbrella (which she definitely told me was a 'parasol') to shade her face from the sun as she walked the mile and a half to town. She came into the post office every day during the summer and asked me if I would please show her how to open her box. I knew that she knew how to open it, but this was her way of getting personalized attention—attention that she wanted NOW! If I was busy with other customers and told her she would have to wait her turn, she would stand and pout. After finally helping her, she would say 'You weren't very nice to me today.' After more than twenty summers, this characteristic behavior became an established custom. I became very fond of her.

Miss Weborg was a woman of limited financial means but with a wealth of knowledge. She always had many interesting stories to tell when she came into the post office. Whatever the weather, either hot or cold, you could recognize her dressed in an old cloth coat. When you saw her, you would think she had stepped out of an old photograph album. Elliott Hodgins, the postmaster at this time and also a good photographer, once asked her to sit in one of the lobby chairs to be photographed. I have often wondered what happened to this photo.

Miss Weborg also loved making flowers from toadstools and fungus that grew on the trees. She was constantly giving me these gifts she had made, not knowing I was allergic to mold. I was grateful for her thoughtfulness and took them home, placing them, because of my allergy, on the window ledge in my father's tool room.

Camp Meenahga, a girl's camp, was located in the State Park. It seemed never to fail that on the hottest day of the beginning of the summer season, we were deluged with duffel bags belonging to the girls going to camp. Then, on the hottest day at the end of the summer, we were again greeted by those same bags being sent home again.

There was also a boy's camp on Adventure Island run by Charles Kinney, also known as 'The Skipper.' The boys would come to town in an old boat that looked like a Viking vessel. Weather permitting, they would pick up their mail daily. It usually consisted of packages of various shapes and sizes containing goodies sent from home. They were never allowed to open them until they were back at camp, where each boy was made to share what he received.

In 1947, when Mr. Seiler transferred from postmaster to rural carrier, I

Fish Creek street scene about 1905.

became acting postmaster until Elliot Hodgins was appointed postmaster. It was during this time that it was decided a new post office was needed. A new building was erected across the street in 1960. There were protests from some who felt that the old building was in keeping with the quaintness of the town and should remain as it was, but the new post office was certainly a pleasure for those of us who worked in it. It was large and airy with windows on three walls. We now had a washroom, a utility room with a furnace, and all new furnishings, including two new lobby desks.

When Mr. Hodgins moved to California in 1949, I became the officer-in-charge and then advanced to postmaster. I was the first postmaster in Door County to be appointed under the newly created U.S. Postal Service. Previously, it had always been the U.S. Post Office Department. When I retired in 1973, William Wedepohl of Ephraim became acting postmaster until James Gogats became postmaster.

As I said, those years were rich in memories, many happy ones, but some sad ones, too. The saddest was the day an officer from Green Bay transferred all of my records to Mr. Wedepohl, and I lowered the flag for the last time at 4:30 p.m.

⊠

Events other than those that created nostalgic memories have happened at the Fish Creek post office:

Due to problems with vandalism, "Fish Creek Postmaster Jill Goking has announced that the Post Office lobby will no longer be open twenty-four hours.

*The facility will be open Monday-Friday, 7:30 a.m.-4:40 p.m., Saturdays, 7:30 a.m.-4:00 p.m., and will be closed on Sundays. 'I'm very disappointed,' said Goking in announcing the decision. 'It's another example of a few vandals ruining it for the whole community. But I felt I had no choice.' (*Door County Advocate, *April 13, 1991)*

✉

Fish Creek Postmasters and Dates of Their Appointments

Jacob St. Ores - August 26, 1858
Alexander Noble - August 6, 1859
Michael F. Kalmbach - April 7, 1865
John Brown - January 10, 1873
Frank G. Blakefield - December 19, 1884
Alexander Noble - June 15, 1885
Samuel Churches - June 14, 1889
Roy F. Thorp - October 26, 1893
Mabel A. Vorous - August 23, 1907
May T. Kinsey - January 25, 1915
Carl E. Seiler - July 25, 1935
Anita H. Schulz - March 6, 1947
Elliott M. Hodgins - October 10, 1949
Anita H. Schulz - March 6, 1971
James Gogats - March 17, 1973
David D. Davis - July 11, 1981
Jill Goking - December 2, 1989
Debra Kinner - March 7, 1992

Postmasters' Annual Salaries

1860-61	Alexander Noble	$29.65
1864-65	A. Noble to May 15, 1865	$35.08
	Michael Kalmbach to June 30, 1865	$4.29
1871	Michael Kalmbach	$56.00
1873	John Brown	$54.00
1877	John Brown	$70.62
1879	John Brown	$77.57
1883	John Brown	$161.26
1885	Frank Blakefield	$168.01
1887	Alexander Noble	$144.42
1889	Alexander Noble	$156.95
1891	Samuel Churches	$158.40

FISH CREEK

SEC. 28, 29
T31N R27E
TOWN OF GIBRALTAR

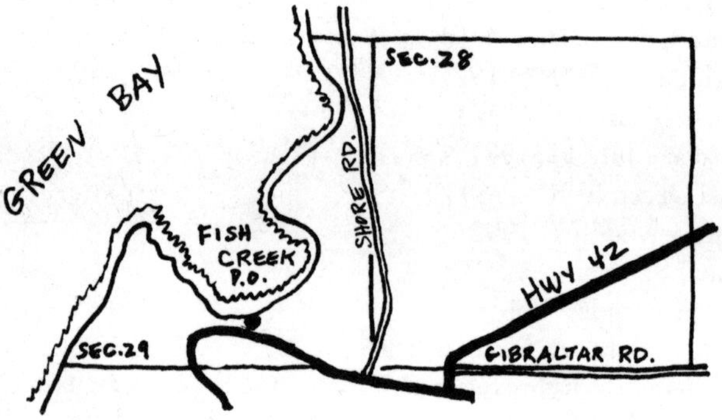

Forestville
see Marcus

Forestville post office about 1930.

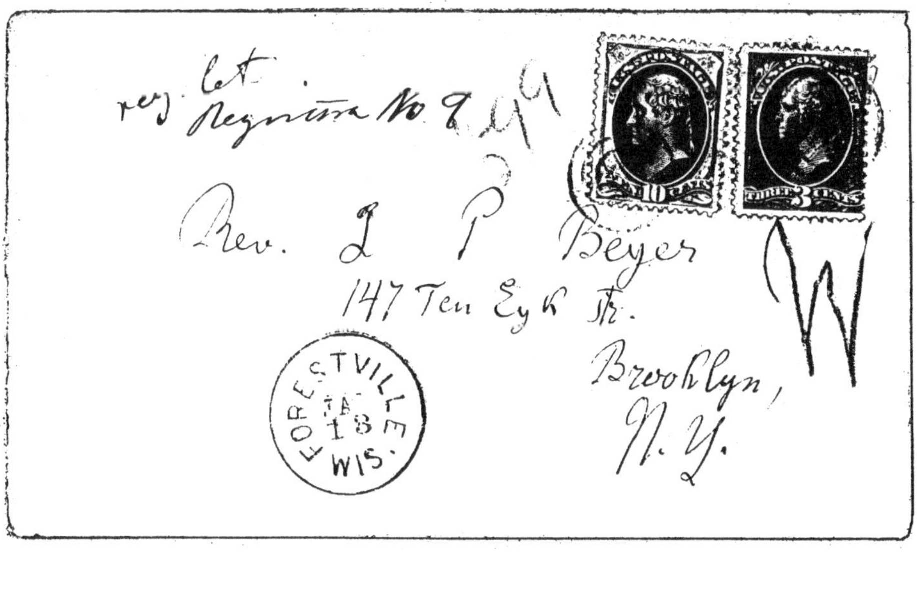

A registered cover backstamped 1882.

1906 usage of a "Doane" style of postmark.

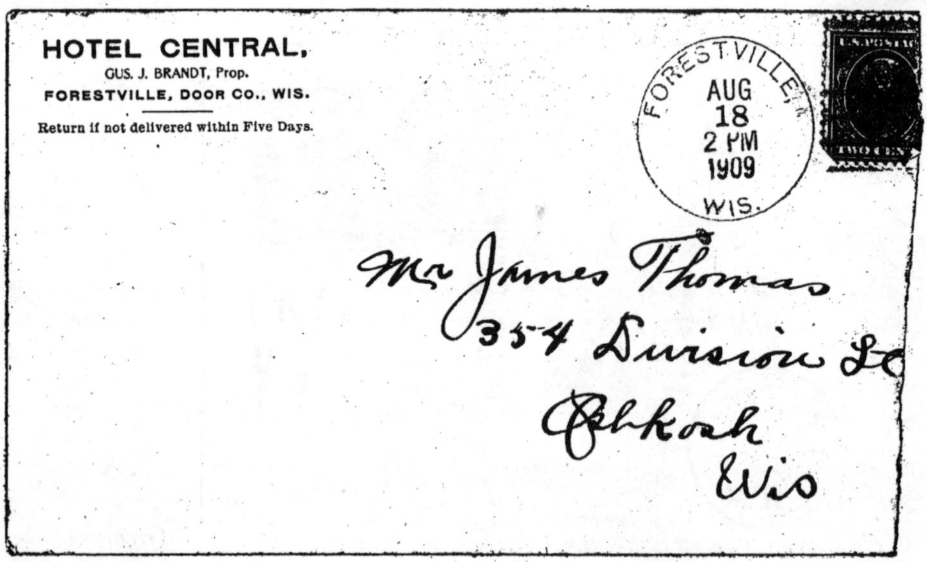

1909 hotel cover.

Foscoro

Established August 14, 1871, but discontinued February 2, 1876.

Reestablished February 28, 1878, and finally discontinued November 15, 1902, with mail service at Algoma, Kewaunee County.

Location: When the office was established in 1871, it was just south of the extreme south east corner of Door County in Kewaunee County. On April 10, 1894, the office was moved into Door County near the Lake Michigan shore in the south part of lot 3, section 32, Town 26 North, Range 26 East, Town of Clay Banks.

> *Along Clay Banks' half-dozen miles of water frontage there were at one time three hopeful villages—Foscoro, Clay Banks and Horns Pier. All of these villages were once upon a time post offices and telegraph stations. Now their very existence is forgotten except by the oldest inhabitants.*
>
> *Foscoro was in the extreme southeastern corner of the town where Stony Creek rambles down among its rocks to the lake. Some time in the '60s three enterprising men came along and decided that here was a most favorable spot for the construction of a mill and pier for shipping forest products. Their names were Foster, Coe and Rowe. They planned a village which they fondly hoped would grow and become a mighty city. In order that their village might have the benefit of a real distinctive name they combined the first syllables of their surnames into the name Fos-Co-Ro. Being thus happily named after three mighty men, they hoped it would have a threefold happy growth.*
>
> *Foscoro was so near the Kewaunee County line that it sometimes was not sure which county it belonged to. In all events, it was so far removed from the currents of life in Door County that it was little known and less visited...Now all remains of the village, the pier, the mill and the mill race have disappeared. (H.R. Holand,* History of Door County, Wisconsin *I:441-442, 1917)*

✉

In 1894, Charles Fellows, the Foscoro postmaster, submitted information to the Post Office Department in Washington which stated in part that while his office was named "Foscoro," the local name of the village where it was located was "Stony Creek."

✉

An article about Foscoro appeared in the *Door County Advocate* of April 13, 1871:

> *Foscoro. The Kewaunee Enterprise says: Stony Creek, where Messrs. Foster, Rowe & Co's saw mill is situated, is invested with a halo of romance by "Jeanie,"*

who writes to the Milwaukee News an enthusiastic descriptive letter, the concluding portion of which we copy below. The letter is dated "Foscoro."

...To the north of the village plat, about a quarter of a mile, the high bluff at the Lake recedes some forty or fifty rods and diminishes to a gentle hill...Within this amphitheater is in the future the sweetest village that the waves of Lake Michigan shall kiss...I thought when I first saw the spot that imagination might call it the home of the fairies...

In this amphitheater comes a stream,...bounding along as if glad to get there, and then stops in a quiet estuary at the Lake and smiles upon the scene. The Indian name of this stream I understand to be Sensippi, which I am informed means 'stream of rocks,' a name very appropriate, as its bed is filled with the freight of some former glacier.

Such was the place when the canny hand of God left it. But then came a Mr. Rowe, from Chicago, and a Mr. Foster from Port Washington—and must is be!—dug a large race for the water of this Sensippi to run in, built a large saw mill, where they are destroying those beautiful cedars and other trees, those suggestive monuments of by-gone ages, and converting them into lumber, to be sent to Chicago, perhaps, that place devoid of all beauty or sense of poetry.

Nor is this all; only a short distance from the mill and connected with it by a wooden railroad, is a pier run out into the lake a thousand feet. How it mars the beauty of this fair nook! It is as if some beautiful girl, with a mouth to excite an irresistible desire for a kiss, should all at once run out a tongue like an anteater...

✉

Foscoro Postmaster and Dates of Their Appointments

George A. Rowe - August 14, 1871

Charles L. Fellows - October 1, 1872

FOSCORO

SEC. 31, 32
T26N R26E
TOWN OF CLAY BANKS

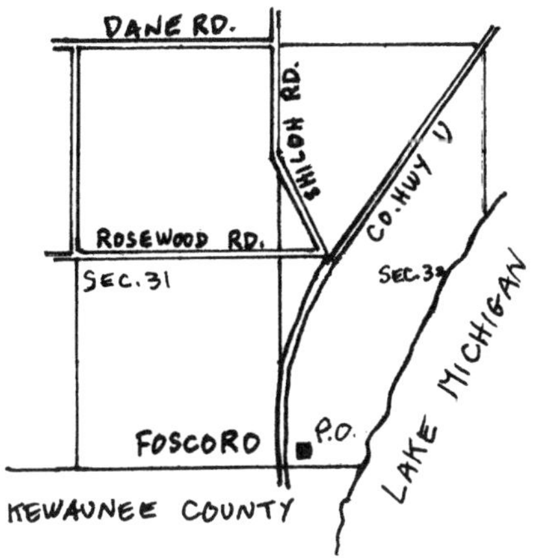

Gardner
see Chickatock

CHICKATOCK
GARDNER

SEC. 25 - T27N R23E
SEC. 29,30- T27N R24E
TOWN OF GARDNER

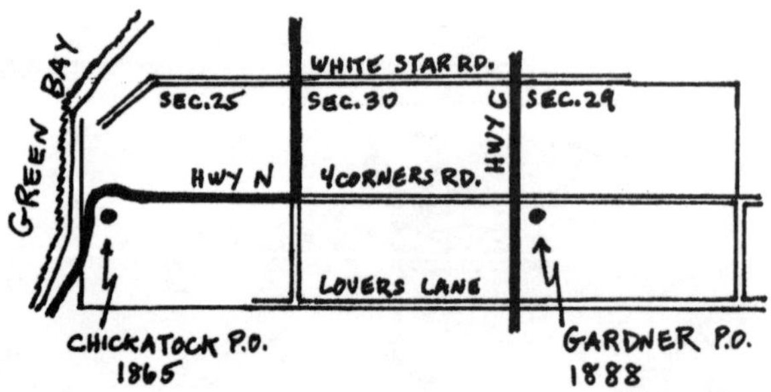

Gills Rock
see Hedge Hog

HEDGE HOG
GILLS ROCK

SEC. 6, T32N R29E
SEC. 31, T33N R29E
TOWN OF LIBERTY GROVE

Graceport

Established January 4, 1898.

Discontinued April 30, 1904, with mail service at Sturgeon Bay.

The exact location of this post office has been a somewhat confused situation. Some authors have placed it in the northwest corner of the Town of Sevastopol, while site documents filed by Graceport postmasters with the U.S. Post Office Department list two locations. Both were in the extreme southwest corner of Town 29 North, Range 26 East, Town of Egg Harbor. The original post office application filed by Henry Meisner on November 30, 1897, stated the location to be in the southeast quarter of section 31. This was on the shore of Green Bay. Then, on April 2, 1902, Henry Paschke, in a site document requested by the Department, stated that the information submitted was "for new site as moved 3/4 miles east" and listed the location as the Southwest Quarter of the Southeast Quarter, section 32.

All this seems to establish Graceport post office at two sites in the southwest corner of Egg Harbor township, but never in Sevastopol township.

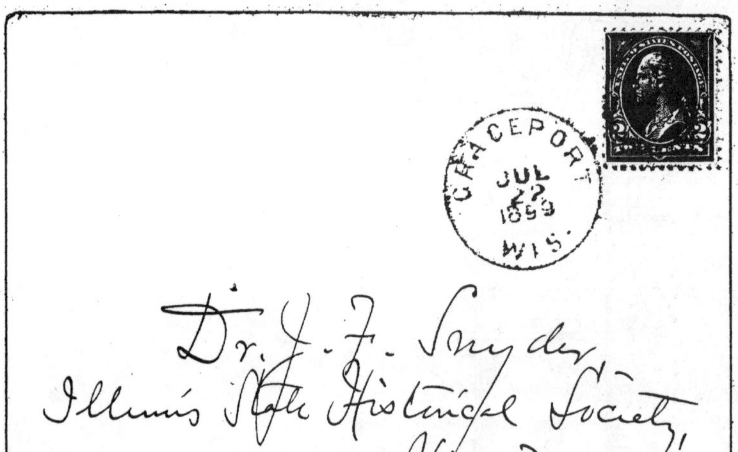

1899.

In the 1897 post office application, the population to be supplied by the proposed office was estimated at 150.

The former fishing and lumbering village of Graceport was located just south of the former Chateau Hutter buildings on County Highway B between Sturgeon Bay and Egg Harbor. The village was originally called Podunk and was named by its founder, George A. Marsh, in 1867. Much timber was shipped from the pier he built there. In the 1870s, Chauncey R. Thayer succeeded Marsh as the owner of Podunk and renamed it Thayersport. In 1883, W.B. Cheeseman took over the village from Thayer and gave it still another name, Graceport, which the area retains today. Later owners of the site were R.H. Parkinson and John Hutter.

Indications are that Cheeseman named the village after either his daughter Grace, or his wife Grace, but there is no conclusive proof as to which was the case.

Graceport Postmasters and Dates of Their Appointments

Albert C. Meisner - January 4, 1898

Henry A. Paschke - March 3, 1902

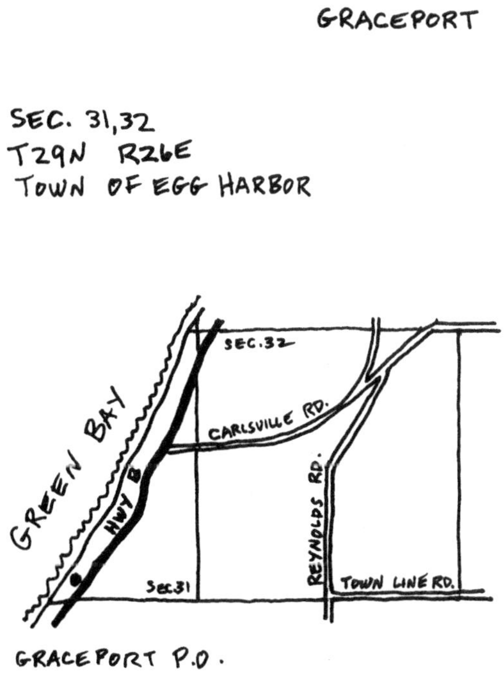

Hainesville

Established September 22, 1896.

Discontinued November 15, 1902, with mail service at Sawyer.

Location: In the southeast quarter of the southeast quarter, section 28, Township 28 North, Range 25 East, Town of Nasewaupee.

Hainesville was a rural community apparently named for the Talleck Haines family, who came to Nasewaupee Township in 1855.

Mrs. Stina Torgerson was the postmaster for the life of the office. In the application for her post office, she estimated that it would serve 190 persons.

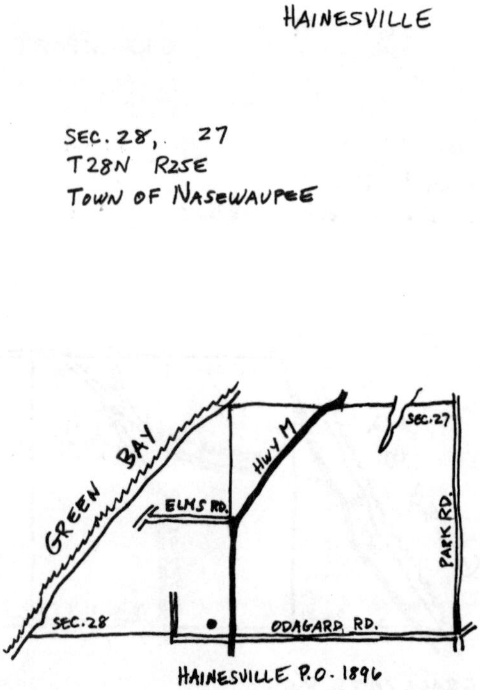

Hastings

Established January 4, 1902.

Discontinued April 30, 1904, with mail service at Egg Harbor.

Hastings was located in the home of the postmaster in the northwest quarter of Section 22, Town 29 North, Range 26 East, Town of Egg Harbor. This location is about 1 3/4 miles north of the present community of Carlsville on State Highway 42.

The postmaster for the life of the office was Anton Burlo, Jr. His application to the U.S. Post Office Department for his office proposed that it be named Plum Bottom, but this was denied in favor of Hastings. The denial apparently was in line with an 1894 Order of the Postmaster General, which stated that "To remove a cause of annoyance to the Department and injury to the Postal Service in the selection of names for newly established post offices, it is hereby ordered that only short names or names of one word will be accepted."

Mr. Burlo's application gave the population to supplied by the proposed post office as "125 or 150."

The *Door County News* of January 11, 1902, reported that

"A new post office is to be established in this town at a point near Plum Bottom. It is to be named Hastings in honor of the judge of this circuit, and Antoine Burlow, Jr. will be named postmaster."

Judge Samuel D. Hastings was Circuit Judge of the District comprising Brown, Oconto, Marinette and Door Counties. He was a resident of Green Bay.

John Enigl of Egg Harbor told me that his Grandfather Bavry had sued postmaster-to-be Burlo in Judge Hasting's court, but lost the suit, so Burlo called his post

Burning of the Hastings post office, 1992.

office Hastings to honor the judge that saved him.

The old residence that once housed the Hastings post office was burned down as a fire-fighting training exercise in April, 1992, by fire departments from Egg Harbor, Ephraim and Washington Island.

Burning of the Hastings post ofice, 1992.

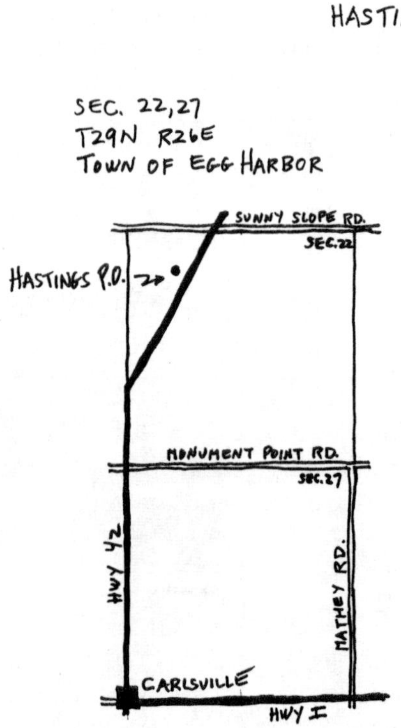

Hedge Hog/Gills Rock

Established as Hedge Hog on April 16, 1883.

The name was changed to "Gillsrock" on February 11, 1902. Spelling the name as one word was required by a U.S. Post Office Department policy on new post office names in effect at the time. The office was discontinued on July 30, 1904, with mail service at Ellison Bay.

Location: In the present village of Gills Rock on the Green Bay shore in the Town of Liberty Grove. The Hedge Hog office was in Lot 2, section 6, Town 32 North, Range 29 East, while the Gillsrock office was in the southwest quarter of the southeast quarter, section 31, Town 33 North, Range 29 East. These two locations were about a quarter-mile apart.

The Hedge Hog post office seems to have been named for Hedgehog Harbor, which includes both the Garret Bay and Gills Rock areas on U.S. Government maps. Oliver P. Graham, who came to Door County in 1841 described the origin of Hedgehog Harbor in an 1880 letter published in C.I. Martin's *History of Door County, Wisconsin*, p. 78, 1881:

> *A comical genius, by the name of Lovejoy, was an old bachelor that lived in the county for some time. He had been away from the society of women so long that the sight of one would make him jump as if struck by electricity, and he would run off into the woods. However, some time afterward he became more reconciled and finally got so close to a woman as to marry her. He was the first shipbuilder in these parts. He built a small vessel at Big Sturgeon—sloop-rig, good model, and fine sailer. The craft was used for fishing and freighting about the Islands. The first winter after she was launched, he laid her up in a little inlet about a mile or so from the Door bluffs. The water fell so much that he could not get the boat afloat the next spring. During the summer the porcupines gnawed several holes in her, which gave rise to the place being called 'Hedgehog Harbor.'*

In H.R. Holand's version of this episode, the beaching of George Lovejoy's boat was said to be "near the present [1917] Gills Rock pier" in 1856. (*History of Door County, Wisconsin* I:375)

Holand also states (op.cit., p. 373) that Gills Rock was named for Elias Gill who owned the warehouse, fishing boats and pier there, as well as 1,300 acres of land in the vicinity.

✉

When the post office was being established in 1883, the name Point Harbor was proposed but turned down by the Post Office Department, as was a second proposal for Hedgehog Harbor. Finally, Hedge Hog was approved. It was estimated that the new office would supply a population of "about one hundred" people.

Hans Tostensen, the Hedge Hog postmaster, was known as "The King of Gills Rock." He had been a successful business man at Ellison Bay. When he came to Hedge Hog he acquired several hundred acres of land, built a pier and went into the wood business. "Mr. Torstenson is one of the best known men in his section, and for fourteen consecutive years was the faithful and efficient postmaster at Hedge Hog, having but recently removed from the office, for political reasons only, he being a staunch member of the Republican party." (*Commemorative Biographical Record of Brown, Kewaunee and Door Counties*, p. 604, 1895)

The statement of Tostensen's fourteen years of service does not agree with U.S. Post Office Department Records which indicate a ten-year tenure at Hedge Hog.

The spelling of Tostensen is believed to be the proper one, since it is the way Hans Tostensen signed his name on his application for a post office. Other and later sources used the spelling Tostenson and Torstenson.

> *Junius Garrett has found it anything but pleasant to fulfill his contact for carrying mail to and from Washington Island. He alternately uses a small boat, a horse and cutter and snow skates to cross the Door and effect a landing at Hedgehog Harbor on the mainland. (*Door County Advocate, *February 21, 1891)*

Postmasters and Dates of Their Appointments

Hedge Hog: Hans Tostensen - April 16, 1883

Gills Rock: Gottlieb Voight - July 20, 1893

Andrew Nelson was appointed postmaster on May 23, 1894, but the appointment was rescinded May 29, 1894. Political reasons probably were involved.

Annual Salaries of Hans Tostensen as Postmaster

1883	$ 1.34
1885	$10.05
1887	$16.41
1889	$22.24
1891	$45.57

HEDGE HOG
GILLS ROCK

SEC. 6, T32N R29E
SEC. 31, T33N R29E
TOWN OF LIBERTY GROVE

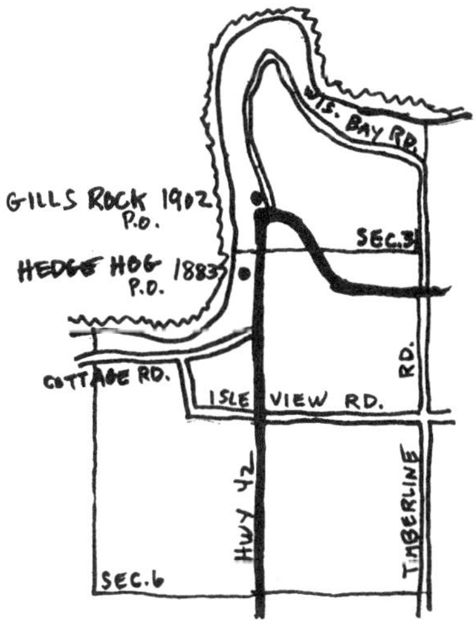

Horn's Pier

see Warren's Corners

Unusual 1885 octagonal postmark in purple ink.

The message on this postal card is dated 1878.

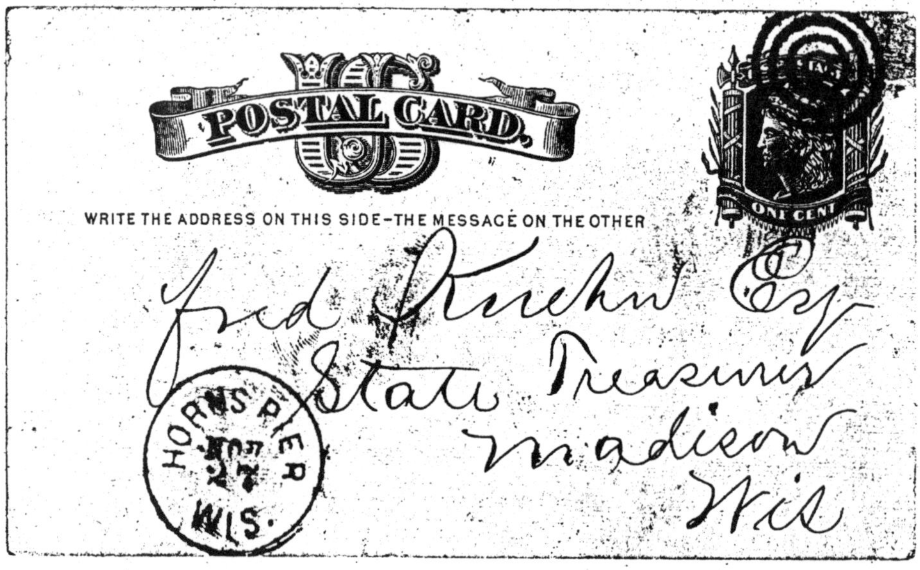

Horn & Joseph,
DEALERS IN
Lumber, Shingles, Wood,
Ties, Bark, Telegraph Poles, Posts, &c.
AT HORN'S PIER, WIS., and
General Commission Merchants
234 SOUTH WATER STREET,
CHICAGO, ILL.
(OVER.)

A Horn's Pier business card.

SALONA
WARREN'S CORNERS
HORN'S PIER
CHEESEVILLE

SEC. 3, 4, 5
T26N R26E
TOWN OF CLAY BANKS

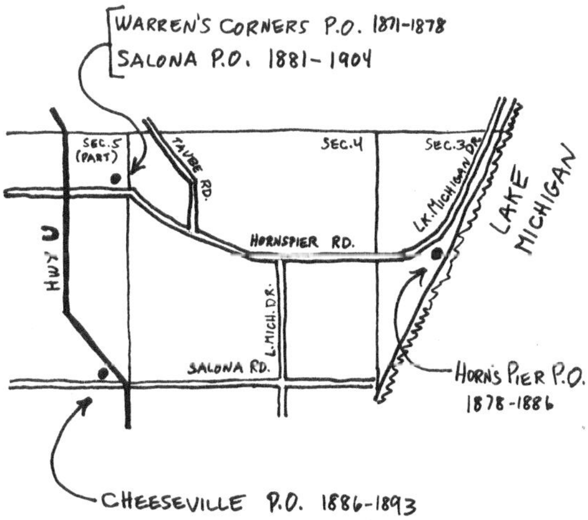

Institute

Established December 24, 1892. Discontinued April 22, 1895, with mail service at Voseville.

Reestablished January 14, 1897. Discontinued April 30, 1906, with mail service at Sturgeon Bay.

This office had two locations in the present village of the same name on State Highway 57 in the Town of Sevastopol. Both were in the northeast quarter of the northwest quarter, section 24, Town 28 North, Range 26 East.

From 1892 to 1895, the office was in St. Aloysius Institute, a Catholic boarding school offering education to all the children in the Door County Catholic community. Children also came from Milwaukee, Chicago and Michigan. Many were orphans or from families of single parents. Benedictine Sisters from New Jersey provided the faculty and taught both religion and traditional school subjects. Room and board was four dollars per month. One of the Sisters, Clementine Braunroth, was Institute's first postmaster. In 1896, Sisters of the Franciscan Order from Bay Settlement took charge of the school and still provide faculty for the school today, which was renamed St. Peter and Paul after the local parish in 1920. At that time the boarding school was discontinued. The original Institute building was replaced in 1953 by the present school building.

Even though St. Aloysius did not have the post office after 1895, people kept calling the community Institute, and so it remains today. When the post office was reestablished in 1897, the name Wester (after the new postmaster) was proposed for it, but the Post Office Department decided to retain the Institute name. The move of the post office from a Catholic school to Wester's saloon is an interesting juxtaposition. The saloon and post office building still stands on Highway 57.

Site of Institute post office, 1897-1906 (1991 photo).

When Sister Clementine submitted the application for a post office in 1892, she answered the question

"If the office be in a village, state the number of inhabitants," by stating that "it will be a little village in the future." She also stated that the population to be supplied by the office would be "150 pupils, four teachers, and about fifty families nearby."

Site of Institute post office, 1895-1906 (1924 photo).

The new post office at Institute, John Wester, P.M. is not yet ready for business, but will be soon. Those of our subscribers in the Town of Sevastopol who desire to receive their paper through the Institute office will please notify us to that effect. (Door County Democrat, *February 6, 1897)*

Institute Postmasters and Dates of Their Appointments

Clementine Braunroth - December 24, 1892
John Wester - January 14, 1897
James Hanrahan - May 26, 1900
John Moore - October 29, 1900

1898.

INSTITUTE

SEC. 13,24
T28N R26E
TOWN OF SEVASTOPOL

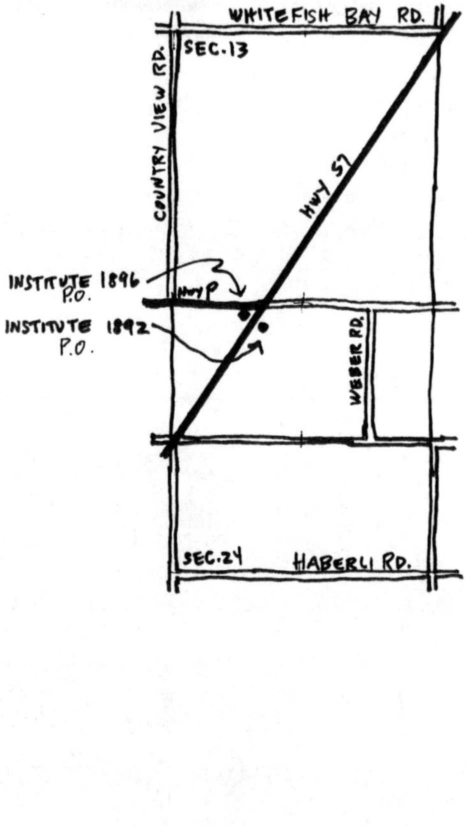

Jacksonport

Established May 29, 1867.

On February 1, 1958, Jacksonport post office became a Rural Station of the Sturgeon Bay post office. Also on that date, Fred Erskine retired as Jacksonport postmaster after forty-three years of service, and Mrs. Joan LeClair became Clerk-in-Charge. The office in her tenure was first located at the back of her residence and then relocated in 1967 to the newly constructed laundry fronting on State Highway 57. She campaigned after 1958 for more salary (which she was granted) on the basis of mail volume handled, and her own canceler (to replace the Sturgeon Bay Rural Station canceler) because she was proud of Jacksonport and wanted the ninety-year-old name retained on outgoing mail. When Jacksonport obtained its Zip Code number (54236) in 1964, a regular Jacksonport canceler was put in use and the old Rural Station canceler was relegated to use as a Money Order stamp. The office was finally discontinued on May 15, 1970.

In an interview on June 1, 1970, Mrs. LeClair said that "thirty or forty" pieces of mail were canceled on the last day of operation, only one of which was a last-day cover request from a collector. The office was closed out by Fred Erskine and the Sturgeon Bay postmaster, Francis Tachovsky; the latter told me he canceled three stamped envelopes with May 15 postmarks, of which he gave me two. He also added that Jacksonport patrons now get rural delivery service from Sturgeon Bay or Baileys Harbor, depending on their location.

The Jacksonport post office was located in the present village of the same name in the northeast quarter of the northeast quarter of section 23, Town 29 North, Range 27 East, Town of Jacksonport.

H.R. Holand recorded how the village of Jacksonport was named:

Jacksonport post office about 1920.

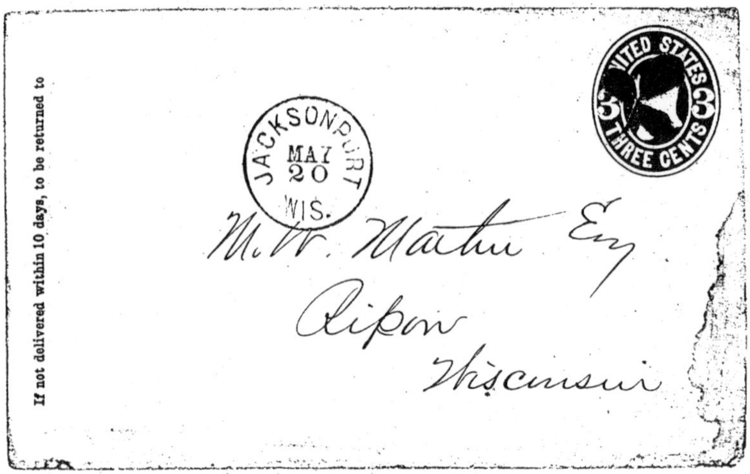

Internally dated 1869; note the unusual cloverleaf cancel.

> *...In 1867, three men in Madison were busy planning the future of Jacksonport. It was a nameless lakeside forest then, but it formed a very definite picture in their minds and they had high hopes that it would become their Eldorado. These three men were Col. C.L. Harris, John Reynolds and Andrew Jackson. Harris and Reynolds had about seven thousand dollars each and were now casting about to see how they might increase these seven thousand to seventy times seven. Andrew Jackson was in charge of the Government Land Office in Menasha and learned of the great abundance of cedar and cordwood near the later village of Jacksonport and of the facilities for water transportation. He suggested that as land and labor were cheap...there ought to be a mint of money in the cedar and cordwood business...*
>
> *[After buying land] the next step was to give a name to their embryo city. One suggested Harrisport, another Reynoldsport and a third, Jacksonport. Finally, the last name was adopted in honor of Mr. Jackson who was really the father of the plan. (*History of Door County, Wisconsin *I:404-405, 1917)*

Jacksonport township, unlike the other Door County towns, was not organized by the Door County Board. Instead, Col. Harris and others got the state legislature to set off Jacksonport from parts of Baileys Harbor and Egg Harbor as a separate township in 1869. This event occurred before most of the people in the town knew of the matter.

Thus it seems that the post office and the township were both named for the village of Jacksonport. Other authors have stated that the village was named for U.S. President Andrew Jackson, but there is nothing to confirm such a conclusion.

On July 6, 1867, the first Jacksonport postmaster, George F. Rowell, filled out a site-description form for the U.S. Post Office Department. He submitted his form with a letter which said that "I have the honor to return herewith a very rough filling out of the diagram of this place, but presume it will be sufficient explanation when I inform you that we are in the lumber woods and have not the convenience for completing such a work."

*Mr. M. Kilgore has been treating the people of Bailey's Harbor and Jacksonport to a tri-weekly mail for some time past. He will keep it up as long the roads remain good. (*Door County Advocate, *February 27, 1874).*

Families living in Jacksonport in the 1870s had limited communication with the outside world. Roads were very poor. There were long stretches where there was only a single track. It took six or more hours with a good team to make the trip from Jacksonport to Sturgeon Bay. At first, mail was received and sent only once a week. Not until February, 1877 was it increased to three times a week. (L.W. Reynolds, "The Jacksonport Story." The Peninsula *5:1-17, 1960)*

From *The Milwaukee Journal*, September 7, 1947:

FAMILY HABIT HANDLING MAIL

Post Office job stays in hands of Erskines for fifty years Jacksonport, Wis.—This summer marks the fiftieth year that Uncle Sam's mail has been handled here at the same site and by the same family, starting with Lincoln Erskine in 1897. His son, Fred, the present postmaster took over in 1915.

During the period that 'Linc' was the official dispenser of the village mail, children soon learned to pay proper respect to the dignity of this service. Many of the older generation of Door County today recalled how 'Linc' would not tolerate any rowdyism or 'smarty' manners in children calling for mail. The penalty for such conduct was not only a flat refusal to give them their mail, but also as prompt shooing from the premises.

But children who found favor with him often were invited to view his interesting collection of curios which he kept in a glass case.

Many of these curios were later given to the next generation of Erskine children. Some were sold to collectors and the remainder was given to the Milwaukee Museum.

Royal Erskine, brother of Lincoln, built the present post office building, parts of which are well over eighty years old since the north and south sections had served for other purposes. One portion had been a boarding house for the boat crews and lumbermen at the beach.

The enlarged building became a combined hotel, saloon and dance hall. When Lincoln Erskine was commissioned postmaster, he bought out his brother Royal and discontinued the saloon.

In the horse and buggy days, a trip from Sturgeon Bay to Jacksonport represented a half day journey, so that travelers often spent the night in Jacksonport.

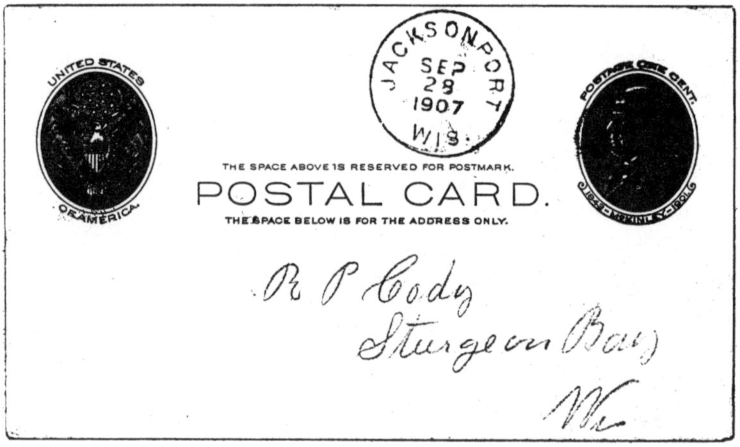

1907.

Fred Erskine well remembers how he and his brothers were kept busy taking care of the horses of travelers and looking after the stables.

Another need for a hotel in the early days arose from the successive industries which were born, flourished and died in Jacksonport with changing conditions, each employing large crews of workers.

(Note: The old hotel-post office (Eureka House) referred to above stood at the corner of Highways 57 and A in what is now the Erskine Rest Area. It was torn down shortly after Fred Erskine retired as postmaster.)

✉

Jacksonport Postmasters and Dates of Their Appointments

George F. Rowell - May 29, 1867
Michael Reynolds - December 3, 1869
George F. Rowell - August 28, 1871
Michael Reynolds - April 22, 1873
Charles Reynolds - June 4, 1877
Joseph LeMere - September 9, 1893
Lincoln H. Erskine - September 18, 1897
Fred Erskine - February 1, 1915
Joan LeClair - February 1, 1958 (Clerk-in-Charge)

Postmasters' Annual Salaries

1871	George Rowell	$ 22.00
1873	Michael Reynolds	$ 22.00
1877	Charles Reynolds	$ 49.61
1879	Charles Reynolds	$ 78.75
1883	Charles Reynolds	$181.37
1885	Charles Reynolds	$204.11
1887	Charles Reynolds	$215.89
1889	Charles Reynolds	$223.36
1891	Charles Reynolds	$216.11

JACKSONPORT

SEC. 22,23
T29N R27E
TOWN OF JACKSONPORT

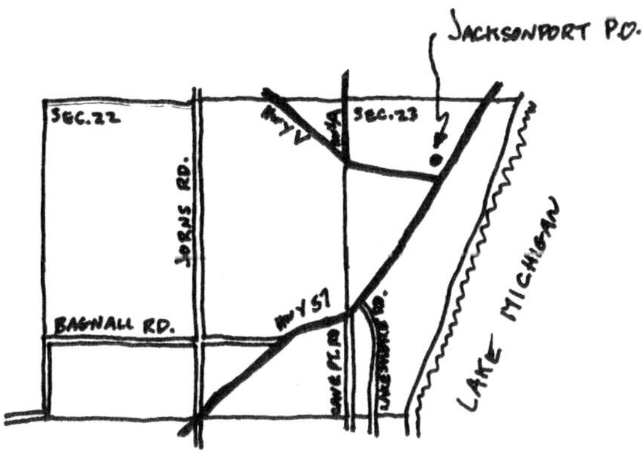

Kolberg

Established January 12, 1895.

Discontinued February 15, 1907, with mail service at Forestville.

This office was located in the present community of the same name in the northwest quarter of section 23, Town 26 North, Range 24 East, Town of Brussels.

The origin of the name "Kolberg" is uncertain. It may be an Americanization of Colburg, the capitol of Prussia. There were many German settlers in the area. Kolberg is also a fairly common German family name; perhaps one of them was honored with the village name.

Conrad Guth was the postmaster for the life of the Kolberg post office. His application to the Post Office Department estimated that the proposed office would serve "about fifty families."

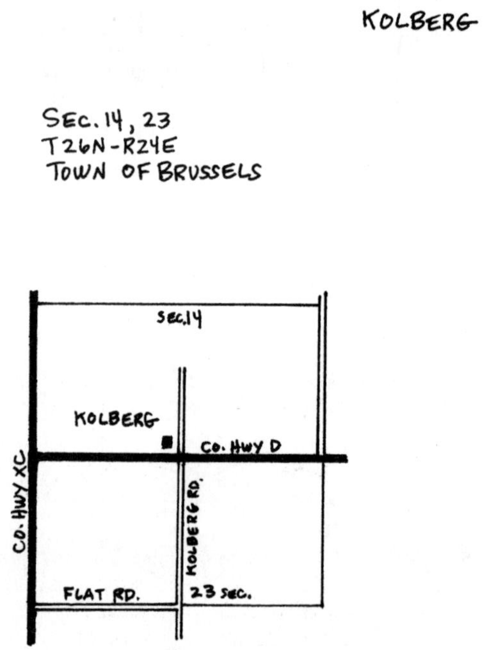

Leccia

Established April 15, 1880.

Discontinued December 9, 1885, with mail service at Brussels.

Location: Next to St. Michael's Catholic Church on County Highway C south of the village of Brussels in the northwest quarter of section 28, Town 26 North, Range 24 East, Town of Brussels.

The Leccia and Minor (q.v.) post offices were products of the religious unrest from 1870 to 1890 in the Belgian community of southern Door County that produced both a Spiritualist and an Old Catholic movement. The Leccia office was established for and named in honor of Father Erasmus Leccia, who started an Independent Catholic Society based on rejection of papal authority, and who was involved in the building of St. Michael's Church in 1860. Upon

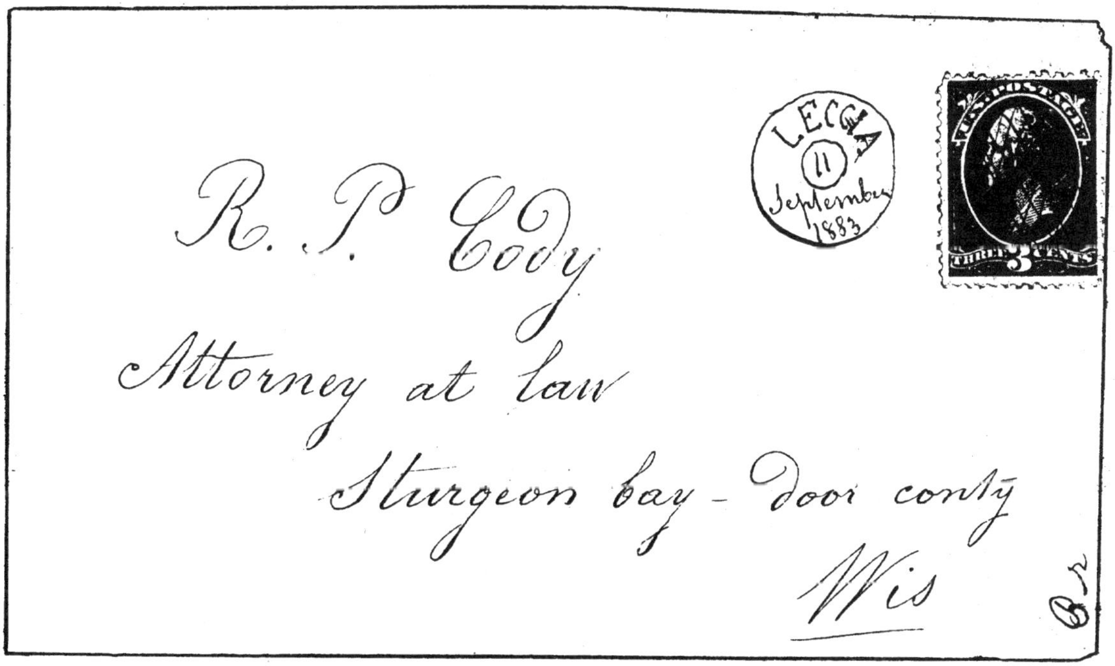

The Leccia post office apparently used only hand-drawn postmarks, such as this 1883 example.

his reconciliation with the Roman Catholic Church, some of his indignant parishioners secured the Minor post office in protest against the continuation of the office bearing Father Leccia's name.

Proposals in 1880 to name the new post office Misere or Masse were turned down by the Post Office Department in favor of Leccia. It was estimated that the new office would supply 200 people.

✉

Leccia Postmasters and Dates of Their Appointments
- Adrien Francois - April 15, 1880
- Pierre J. Reiner - August 11, 1885

Annual Salaries of Adrien Francois as Postmaster

1883	$8.13
1885	$7.98

LECCIA

MINOR

SEC. 28
T26N R24E
TOWN OF BRUSSELS

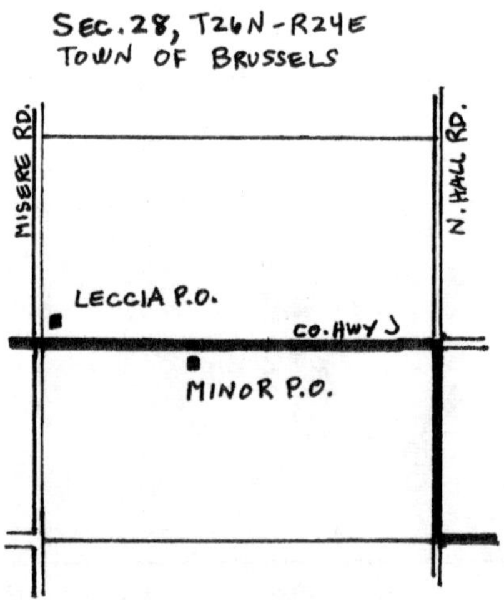

Lily Bay

Established May 6, 1879.

Discontinued October 5, 1882, with mail service at Sturgeon Bay.

The Lily Bay post office served the settlement of the same name on the Lake Michigan shore in section 6, Town 27 North, Range 27 East, Town of Sturgeon Bay. However, the application for the post office indicated its location to be in the northeast quarter of section 1, Town 27 North, Range 26 East. This site is about a half mile west of Lily Bay in the middle of a cedar swamp, which seems an unlikely location for a post office. Perhaps the applicant for the office misread his map in making the application.

Lily Bay was a busy lake shipping point in the 1870s and 1880s, with a mill, pier, dam, store, blacksmith shop and several dwellings. For some years it served as a port for Sturgeon Bay in winter. It was originally called St. Joseph in honor of Mr. Joseph, one of the owners and partner of William H. Horn (see Horn's Pier). When Mr. Joseph retired from the partnership, the name was changed to Lily Bay after Mr. Horn's daughter, Lily.

In 1879, the name St. Joseph was proposed for the post office but was denied by the Post Office Department. It was estimated that the new post office would serve a village with a population of "about twenty-five" and a total population of "about 200."

✉

Lily Bay Postmasters and Dates of Their Appointments
Benjamin Minsker - May 6, 1879
Henry H. Reynolds - April 2, 1880

Benjamin Minsker served as postmaster at Clay Banks both before and after his term at Lily Bay.

LILY BAY

SEC. 1 T27N R26E
SEC. 6 T27N R27E
TOWN OF STURGEON BAY

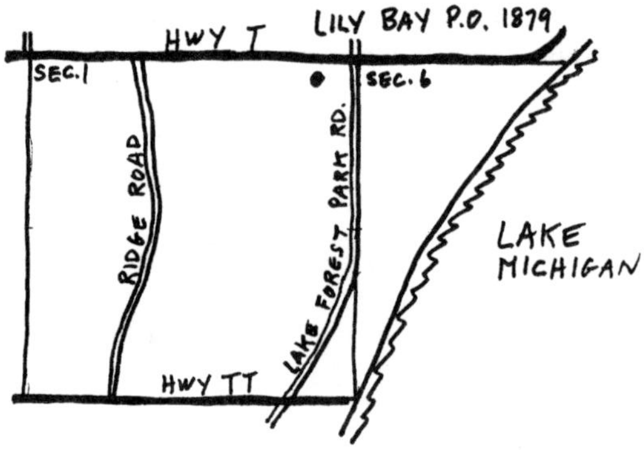

Little Sturgeon

Established November 12, 1860. Discontinued August 1, 1893, with mail service at Stevenson's Pier.

Reestablished August 16, 1893. Discontinued for the last time on April 29, 1905, with mail service at Brussels.

The Little Sturgeon post office had at least three different locations in the Town of Gardner (Town 27 North, Range 24 East). It was first established at the Little Sturgeon settlement which was named for the Bay on whose shores it was located. This was in the northwest quarter of section 2. An 1893 site document of the Post Office Department lists the same location. In 1897, when August Bosman became postmaster, the office was moved to the northwest quarter of section 9. In 1899, the Door County plat book showed the office to be in the northwest quarter of section 17, still bearing the Little Sturgeon name, but about five miles by road from Little Sturgeon Bay. Other locations may have been used as the postmastership changed hands over the years, but they are not a matter of record.

In the 1870s and '80s, Little Sturgeon had a shipyard, sawmill, shingle mill, grist mill, pier, store, post office and several houses.

> *With all this business, Little Sturgeon was a most active place. Many old settlers claim that it was more of a business place at the time of the (civil) war than Sturgeon Bay. 'Sturgeon Bay was the county seat,' they claim, 'but Little Sturgeon had the business.' (H.R. Holand,* History of Door County, Wisconsin *I:433, 1917)*

By 1900, business at Little Sturgeon had declined to near zero and has so remained since.

✉

The *Door County Advocate* in the 1870s commented occasionally on postal matters at Little Sturgeon:

> *September 22, 1870 - Complaints are made that the Green Bay mail contractor fails to supply the Little Sturgeon post office according to the contract. He carries the mail over the central road giving Little Sturgeon folks the go-by. It should be remedied.*
>
> *July 15, 1876 - Our Little Sturgeon neighbors are now served with semi-weekly mail service instead of only once a week as heretofore. The people of that place have clubbed together and will defray the expense of the additional trip by private subscription. The P.O. department should increase the service to three times a week as soon as possible. There are a large number of intelligent people*

residing at and in the vicinity of Little Sturgeon who receive their mail at that place and who are put to great inconvenience by this primitive style of mail service. Once a week was sufficient for all ordinary purposes twenty years ago, but in these progressive days it is entirely inadequate.

December 20, 1877 - The post office at Little Sturgeon has removed to the residence of Joseph Delmont, and the latter is appointed assistant postmaster by A.M. Spear, who moved and was unable to retain his office.

March 26, 1874 - Congress has established a new mail route between Ahnapee and Sturgeon Bay, and returning by way of Forestville.-Ahnapee Record. The new route spoken of is between Ahnapee and Little Sturgeon Bay.

✉

Little Sturgeon Postmasters and Dates of Their Appointments

James C. Gardner - November 12, 1860
William Baptist - January 30, 1865
Peter Merriman - February 6, 1873
B.F. Washburn - June 12, 1873
Robert W. Bero - December 9, 1874
John M. Burritt - July 19, 1875

1864 combination of handstamp and manuscript postmarks.

Albert M. Spear - December 16, 1875
Joseph Delmont - December 26, 1877
Reinhard Lyon - January 11, 1888
Peter J. Lendon - August 16, 1893
John P. Tobin - May 22, 1894
Louis Drebelow - September 21, 1896
August J. Bosman - April 15, 1897
Charles Jenquinn - February 19, 1903

Postmasters' Annual Salaries

1864-65	James Gardner	$ 26.48
1864-65	William Baptist	$ 8.25
1871	William Baptist	$ 24.00
1873	B.F. Washburn	$ 24.00
1877	Albert Spear	$ 33.00
1879	Joseph Delmont	$ 21.11
1883	Joseph Delmont	$ 43.74
1885	Joseph Delmont	$ 60.30
1887	Joseph Delmont	$128.87
1889	Reinhard Lyon	$ 45.63
1891	Reinhard Lyon	$ 45.67

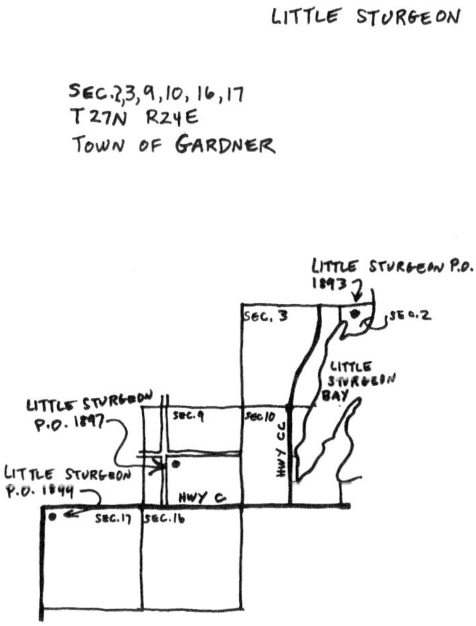

Malakoff

Established June 18, 1874. Discontinued March 4, 1879.

Reestablished July 1, 1879, and finally discontinued December 22, 1881.

Location: On the south side of the present curve in State Highway 57 in the southwest quarter of section 26, Town 28 North, Range 26 East, Town of Sevastopol. The office was in the home of the postmaster.

The postmaster for the life of the office was Henry B. Stephenson, who had come to Door County in the late 1850s. In 1874 he wrote a short history of the Town of Sevastopol which was published in the *Door County Advocate* on January 14, 1875. In it he said

> *In the spring and summer of 1874, two post offices were established in the town, one at George Bassford's corners called 'Sevastopol,' and the other at H.B. Stephenson's and called 'Malakoff,' and located nearly in the center of the town. So you see we have a Malakoff here in Door County and it is a very formidable one, too.*

The existence of two post offices located 2 1/2 miles apart, both bearing Russian names related to the Crimean War, and both starting up within five months of each other, does not seem to have been totally explained. Sevastopol post office (q.v.) opened first, in February, and was named for the Town, which in turn had been named for the Russian city. Malakoff post office followed in June, and was given the name of the famous Russian General Malakhov. This indicates a certain amount of rivalry between the two postmasters, because there were no Russian settlers or other place names in the town.

✉

Mr. Stephenson's application for his post office in 1874 stated that it would serve "about 150 persons." Another document he submitted to the Post Office Department in 1879 lowered his estimate to "fifty persons."

✉

> *After considerable delay another post office has finally been established in the town of Sevastopol. It's name is Malakoff and H.B. Stephenson blushingly wears the honors as Postmaster. (*Door County Advocate*, July 12, 1874)*

✉

The Malakoff postmaster's annual salary in 1877 was $7.21. Such small sums, which reflected the amount of business transacted by the office, undoubtedly led to its temporary closing, as reported by the *Door County Advocate* on March 13, 1879:

The P.O. department has ordered the Malakoff post office in the town of Sevastopol discontinued. We understand one of the reasons was that about the only person who received mail there was the postmaster.

MALAKOFF

SEC. 26
T28N R26E
TOWN OF SEVASTOPOL

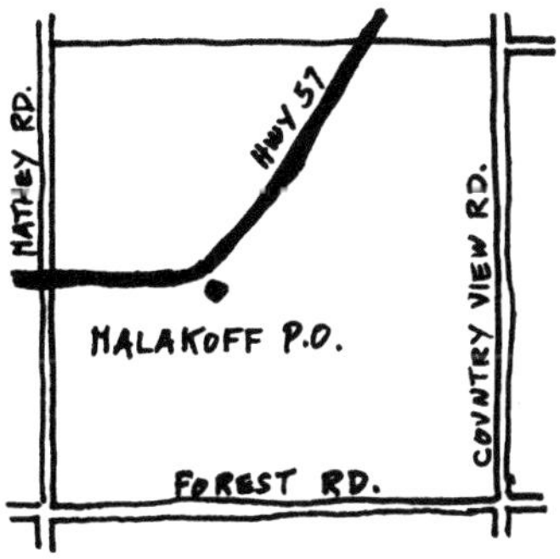

Maplewood

Established February 17, 1874. Discontinued April 30, 1904, with mail service at Sawyer.

Reestablished April 28, 1914, and is still in service. Zip Code - 54226.

The Maplewood post office has had several locations in Town 26 North, Range 25 East, Town of Forestville. It originally was on an old stage road in section 10. In 1970, the first post office building was still standing on a farm owned by Jennings Schmeling in the northwest quarter of section 10, where it had been moved from its original location south of the Schmeling farm.

Post Office Department documents in 1894 and 1899 showed the office located at the railroad crossing of Idlewild Road in the northeast quarter of section 4.

In 1918 the office was located on the west side of State Highway 42 south of the railroad tracks in the northeast quarter of section 8. Since 1949, the location has been on Highway 42 just north of the railroad in the southeast quarter of section 5.

The post office was named for the village of Maplewood, which name was given to be descriptive of the local countryside.

⊠

An item from the *Door County Democrat* of May 8, 1897:

The post office at Maplewood has been changed back to the Jos. Deffoe, Sr., place, and Mr. Deffoe appointed postmaster instead of Mrs. Katie Goetz, widow of the late Wm. Goetz. The change has caused much dissatisfaction among patrons of the office. On the other hand, of course, a few are pleased at the change.

Maplewood post office about 1935.

⊠

Mrs. Veronica Russell, Maplewood's tenth postmaster, served in that capacity for thirty-five years, fourth longest of any Door County postmaster, and longer than any of the county's woman postmasters.

In October, 1988, Postmaster Robert Zirbel was interviewed by the *Green Bay Press-Gazette* about his office:

It's not exactly a demanding position, although Zirbel is the entire U.S. Postal Service for Maplewood...(He) has forty-five customers, and there is no home delivery. They all have to come to the post office that shares a building with an implement repair shop...and Zirbel isn't sorting mail twenty-four hours a day, either. In fact, it takes less than an hour to sort the 200 or so pieces of mail that come in every day...Most of Zirbel's day is spent sitting alone in the office, possibly reading manuals or bulletins. People checking their mail break up his day, but there are even drawbacks to that.

'It's the same conversation fifteen times a day, like the weather, Packers, the Brewers,' he said. But the big excitement comes when someone mails a package overseas, Zirbel said.

Yes, things are that slow in Maplewood.

Zirbel doesn't mind.

'I've lived here all my life, so I like it here,' he said.

1894 registered cover.

Maplewood Postmasters and Dates of Their Appointments

James H. Lockhart - February 17, 1874
Robert Lockhart - December 3, 1887
Joseph E. DeFaut - May 16, 1890
William M. Goetz - November 15, 1893
Joseph E. DeFaut - April 14, 1897

William J. Lawson - March 23, 1900
Charles Hoeppner - April 28, 1914
Mrs. August Hoeppner - September 24, 1929
Roy J. Hoeppner - December 13, 1929
George Feller - August 15, 1933
Mrs. Veronica Russell - November 7, 1949
Robert L. Zirbel - December 22, 1984
Susan DesJardins - December, 1994 (clerk in charge)

Postmasters' Annual Salaries

1877	James Lockhart	$10.26
1879	James Lockhart	$ 8.64
1883	James Lockhart	$10.52
1885	James Lockhart	$25.31
1887	James Lockhart	$28.02
1889	Robert Lockhart	$20.46
1891	Joseph DeFaut	$32.81

Internally dated 1933; an unusual postmark type.

MAPLEWOOD

SEC. 3,4,5,8,9
T26N R25E
TOWN OF FORESTVILLE

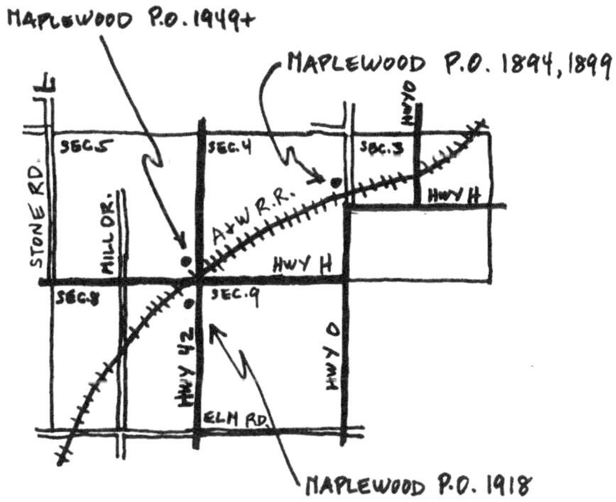

Marcus/Forestville

Established as "Marcus" on September 16, 1858.

The name was changed to "Forestville" on April 10, 1863. The office was discontinued on November 27, 1868.

Forestville was reestablished on January 27, 1870, and is still in service. Zip Code - 54213.

Location: In the present village of Forestville on State Highway 42 in the Town of Forestville. U.S. Post Office Department records show that in 1865 the Forestville office was in the northwest quarter of section 33; in 1870 it was in the southwest quarter of section 20; and since 1918 it has been in the northeast quarter of section 32. All these locations are in Township 26 North, Range 25 East. The exact location of Marcus post office is not known, but was probably in section 32 or 33.

The Marcus post office was named for its first postmaster, Marcus McCormick, who was one of the very early settlers of the area. In December of 1857, the Door County Board set off Forestville as a township. At that time it was the third town to be established in the county and included what is now the Town of Clay Banks as well as the present Town of Forestville. Clay Banks became a separate township by County Board action in 1859. On November 3, 1857, the first meeting to organize the Town of Forestville was held at the house of Marcus McCormick, who ten months later became the first postmaster of Marcus.

Forestville post office was named for the village and township, which name was locally descriptive of the countryside.

Postal matters at Marcus and Forestville seemed to be somewhat unsettled in the 1860s. The *Door County Advocate* made notice of the situation several times:

> *June 25, 1863 - The Post Office at Forestville has changed its Post Master name. It will hereafter be known by the name of 'Forestville.' J.M.L. Parker is the new postmaster, at whose house the Post Office will be kept. We understand the entire change gives great satisfaction to the people of Forestville.*
>
> *December 17, 1868 - The post office at Forestville has been discontinued. This will be a serious annoyance to the people in that vicinity. Their nearest post office now is at Ahnapee, about nine miles from the one discontinued.*
>
> *October 8, 1874 - A letter to the Editor from 'Philo' at Forestville said in part that 'Our mail facilities are greatly improved over those of the past few years. We*

are now served with a mail once a week from Ahnapee to Little Sturgeon by way of Forestville and Tornado, tapping the Green Bay and Sturgeon Bay mail at Tornado; thus we receive the Advocate five days earlier than by the old round-about way. Thanks to Hon. Philetus Sawyer, our able and efficient representative [in the U.S. Congress]...

✉

The *Door County Advocate* of March 1, 1962 noted that "Kenneth O'Hern's wide Irish smile told it all Monday morning as he and postal clerk Elnora Perry have moved to new quarters, the new Forestville Post Office."

✉

When Kenneth O'Hern retired in 1989 after twenty-nine years as Forestville's postmaster, the *Door County Advocate* of March 10 that year published a feature by Keta Steebs on his career. Included in it were Mr. O'Hern's recollections of his first days on the job:

When Ken...first reported for duty, he didn't have the faintest idea of what was expected of him. He remembers standing out in the post office lobby for what seemed like an eternity before an inspector, engrossed in taking inventory and making sure every stamp and money order was accounted for, finally let him in the office.

Once inside the hallowed domain, Ken says he still stood around feeling help less. By now the postal inspector had left, the inventory was intact and Ken O'Hern was in charge of the store.

'I stood there watching other people work,' he says, shaking his head at the memory. 'The clerk was sorting the mail for the lock boxes, the rural carrier was sorting mail for the routes and no one had time for me.'

The clerk, who only worked part-time, mercifully took Ken under her wing before her two-hour shift ended. He says he was just starting to get the hang of mail-sorting when he saw her reach for her coat and prepare to leave. Although grown men don't often grovel, Ken practically got down on his knees begging her to stay longer.

In this case, begging didn't help nor did Ken's promise of extra pay aid his cause. Rules are rules, the clerk told him, and her schedule was made out for two hours in the morning and two hours in the afternoon-nothing more—nothing less.

'So there I was, the postmaster, and I didn't know a thing about the place,' he says ruefully. 'The clerk taught me what I had to know in the little time she could spare, but it was quite a while before I felt comfortable with the job.'

Ken's name went into the postmaster-candidate hat in 1960, a year that still saw powerful patronage committees deciding who their man would be. Ken says he was so totally uninvolved in politics at that time, he didn't know the job was a political appointment...

Of the sixteen applicants writing the test that year, Ken was the top scorer but his job was far from assured. Fortunately, when he was asked to introduce himself to the patronage committee, Ken's apolitical nature stood him in good stead. He hadn't helped any of the members, but he hadn't hurt them either, so he at least had a fighting chance.

After mulling things over, the committee eventually sent Ken O'Hern's name to the U.S. Senate for confirmation... 'My name was thrown out of the hat,' he says. 'The party in power could call for a new exam, hire anyone it chose or renominate me. I was lucky enough to have someone from the opposite party renominate me and the senate, fortunately, confirmed my appointment.'

'...The system is so much better today,' he confides. 'It's a totally different environment. Today's postal employees are career people-chosen from within the system—and trained to handle every aspect of the business.'

The all-powerful patronage committees, most of whom expected largesse for their efforts, are also a thing of the past. Ken doesn't regret their passing, but he does say the Postal Reorganization Act of 1970 cut his budget so close to the bone he no longer has a clerk—even a part-time clerk—to help out when he's busy...Rural carrier Edson Stevens and substitute carrier Joanne Bongle are the only other Forestville Post Office employees...

Postmasters and Dates of Their Appointments

Marcus McCormick - September 16, 1858
James M.L. Parker - April 10, 1863
John Stoneman - January 27, 1870
Richard Perry - February 28, 1870
John Fetzer - March 28, 1881
William Duwe - June 13, 1889
Richard Perry - April 21, 1891
Catherina M. Duwe - May 26, 1891
Harlow H. Fuller - February 26, 1892
Lizzie Sloan - April 6, 1892
John Fetzer - May 24, 1894
Martin Schmitz - February 5, 1896
Bernard Awe - January 18, 1898
Edward M. Perry - January 27, 1915
John H. Poh - August 28, 1934
Raymond H. Dix - September 1, 1947

Eugene P. Naze - October 1, 1948
Kenneth J. O'Hern - September 2, 1960
Ralph Haroldson - June 17, 1989

Postmaster's Annual Salaries

1860-61	Marcus McCormick	$ 4.24
1864-65	James Parker	$ 8.97
1871	Richard Perry	$20.00
1873	Richard Perry	$34.00
1877	Richard Perry	$18.00
1879	Richard Perry	$26.40
1883	John Fetzer	$52.59
1885	John Fetzer	$99.07
1887	John Fetzer	$99.73
1889	John Fetzer	$96.44
1891	Catherina Duwe	$89.46

Note: Forestville Postmaster John Fetzer was the same man for whom Fetzer Post Office (q.v.) was named.

MARCUS
FORESTVILLE

SEC. 20, 29, 32, 33
T26N R25E
TOWN OF FORESTVILLE

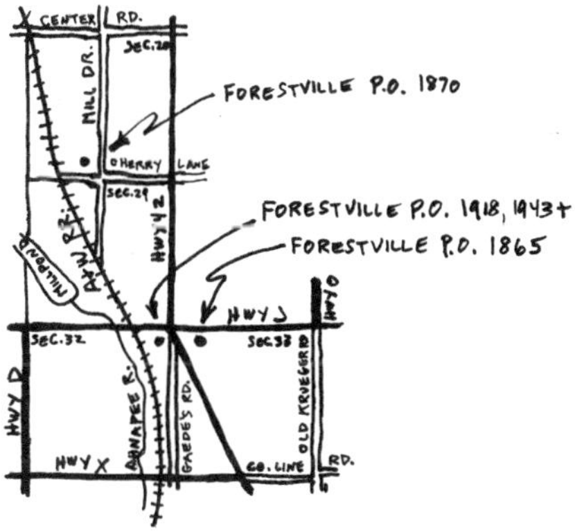

Minor

Established July 31, 1882.

Discontinued October 3, 1882, with mail service at Sturgeon Bay.

Location: On the south side of County Highway J in the northeast quarter of the southwest quarter of section 28, Town 26 North, Range 24 East, Town of Brussels.

As noted in the history of Leccia post office (q.v.), Minor post office resulted from religious differences among the patrons of Leccia post office based on their perceived interference with their mail by the pastor of St. Michael's Catholic Church, where Leccia was located.

The group of dissidents petitioned for their own post office, which was granted, and had it named for Edward S. Minor, Sturgeon Bay entrepreneur and politician, who helped them secure the office.

Mr. Minor came to Door County in 1858 and became a farmer, served in the Civil War, became a merchant, timber and stone dealer, tug operator, and superintendent of the Sturgeon Bay and Lake Michigan Ship Canal. Beginning in 1878, he served three terms as an assemblyman and one term as a senator in the state legislature. In 1895 he was elected to the U.S. House of Representatives, where he served six terms as a dedicated member of the Republican party.

The postmaster for the life of the Minor post office was Desire Englebert. His 1882 application to become the postmaster estimated that the population to be served by the proposed office was 250 people.

Minor had the shortest life of any Door County post office - sixty-five days. It was undoubtedly closed when the U.S. Post Office Department woke up to the fact that Minor was located less than a mile from the established Leccia post office. There is even a possibility that Minor never actually functioned. A number of similar cases of short-lived post offices exist in Wisconsin where approvals were granted but withdrawn by the Post Office Department before the new office could begin operations. However, the *Door County Advocate* for July 27, 1882, mentioned a new post office in the Town of Brussels called Minor in honor of E.S. Minor. No documents or covers are known that would prove or disprove this possibility.

LECCIA

MINOR

SEC. 28
T26N R24E
TOWN OF BRUSSELS

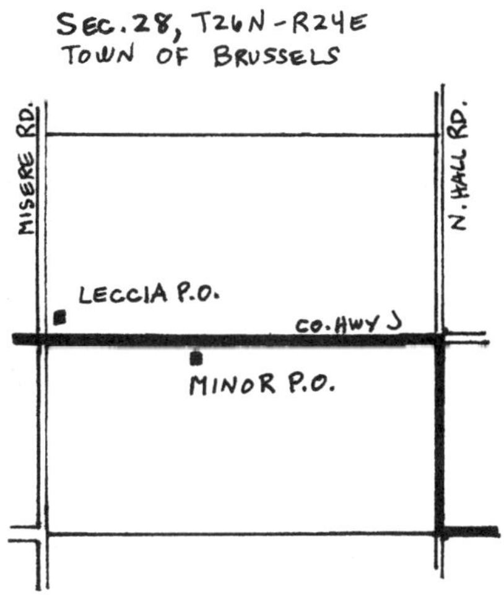

Namur

Established on June 14, 1872. Discontinued on January 21, 1879.

Reestablished on March 4, 1879. Discontinued on July 28, 1886, with mail service at Red River in Kewaunee County.

Reestablished on March 26, 1888, and finally discontinued on April 29, 1905, with mail service at Brussels.

The Namur post office had two locations in the Town of Union (Town 26 North, Range 23 East). The first, in the 1870s, was in the northwest quarter of the northeast quarter of section 28, in or near the home of the postmaster. The second location, from 1888 to 1905, was in the present community of Namur on State Highway 57 in southern Door County. The Post Office Department's site document for the 1886 office describes this location as in the northeast quarter of section 14. The office was in a building next to St. Mary of the Snows Catholic church, a location in the southwest quarter of section 12, which makes suspect the description supplied by the postmaster to the Post Office Department.

Namur was named after the city and province of the same name in Belgium by the Belgian immigrants in the community.

⊠

The Belgian settlers in the southern part of Door County were a volatile group. From 1870 to 1890 there was a period of religious unrest that involved at least three post offices, Leccia (q.v.), Minor (q.v.) and Namur. In those years religious feeling was intense. There was a Spiritualist and an Old Catholic movement. Opposing factions resorted to violence on occasion. There are stories of fist fights in churches during Mass, and of priests being chased down the road by their detractors.

Front of window from Namur post office now in the Door County Museum.

Namur had its share of problems. The *Door County Advocate* for February 18, 1879, reported that "The Namur Post Office has been discontinued by the Post Office Department because of improper handling of the mails—they weren't as 'contraband' as they should have been." The office allegedly was closed because of censorship exercised by the local Catholic priest over the mail. However, the Namur office reopened in March, 1879, presumably under new management, and lasted until 1905 when it was replaced by rural free delivery from Brussels.

1901 registered cover. (Courtesy of C.R. Kannewurf)

Estimates of people to be served by the Namur office supplied to the Post Office Department by postmasters varied considerably over the years:

1873 "about 120 families"

1879 "120 votes at the General Election"

1886 "about 500 people"

1890 "400 to 600 residents"

The *Door County Advocate* reported on May 31, 1890 that "Alex Degrandgagnage of Union died of pneumonia last week, causing the discontinuance of the Namur post office until

Back of window from Namur post office now in the Door County Museum.

someone else can be found to accept the trust." The *Advocate* reported further on August 9, 1890 that "Mrs. Alex Degrandgagnage has been appointed postmistress at Namur." Mrs. Alex D. was Johnnie Degrandgagnage in USPOD records.

⊠

Namur Postmasters and Dates of Their Appointments

Clement Geniesse - June 14, 1872
Philohene Decamp - June 24, 1889
Alexander Degrandgagnage - September 4, 1889
Johnnie Degrandgagnage - July 19, 1890
Frank Evrard - August 28, 1894

Postmasters' Annual Salaries

1873	Clement Geniesse	$12.00
1877	Clement Geniesse	$18.54
1879	Clement Geniesse	$20.97
1883	Clement Geniesse	$44.93
1885	Clement Geniesse	$62.33
1889	Clement Geniesse	$45.78
1891	Johnnie Degrandgagnage	$27.25

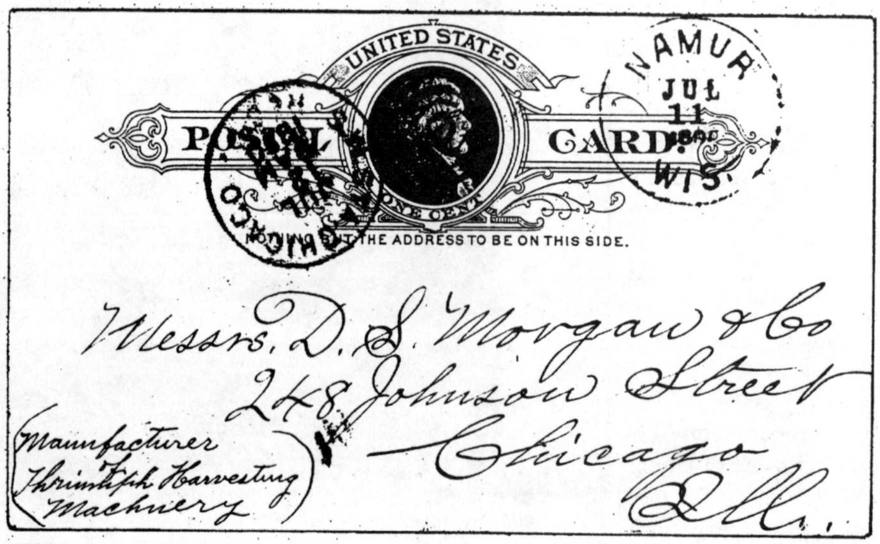

1890.

NAMUR

SEC. 11, 14, 21, 22, 23, 28
T26N R23E
TOWN OF UNION

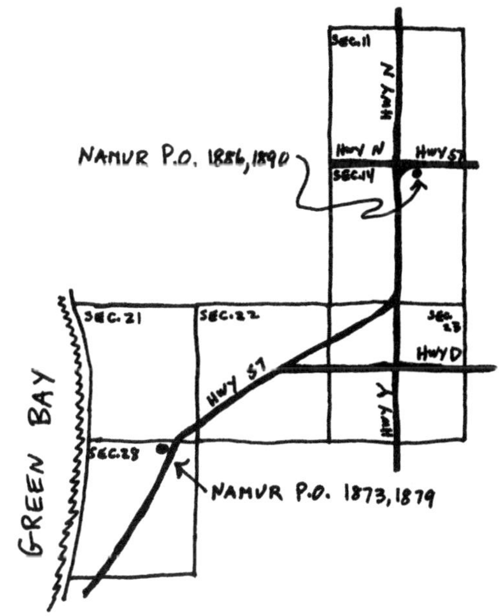

Nasewaupee

Established September 4, 1858.

Discontinued January 29, 1862.

The post office was located on the Sawyer (west) side of Sturgeon Bay in the Fuller house where Hickory street runs into the Bay. This is in the northwest quarter of section 7, Town 27 North, Range 26 East; originally in the Town of Nasewaupee, now in the City of Sturgeon Bay.

> *The word 'Nasewaupee' is of wide range and really conveys or can be used in different sense or meaning. In one way it has reference to early dawn, or that part of the day before sunrise. However, in the sense which it is connected with the township, 'Nasewaupee' is of different meaning. In 1856, Mr. Nelson W. Fuller and others, wanted a post office on the west side of the bay. As to a name for the post office to be established, the Post Office Department in Washington did not agree with Mr. Fuller and other parties here, so the whole matter concerning the name was left with the postmaster at Green Bay, who thought that 'Nasewaupee,' the name of a Menominee Indian Chief that once located thereabouts, was appropriate. Nasewsaupee Post Office flourished under Mr. N.W. Fuller's administration as P.M. At least we presume it flourished, for his net earnings the first three months were 37¢. He finally resigned the position of postmaster, in favor of his brother, Mr. E.S. Fuller, who kept up the office for a time, when the post office came to the same end as did Chief Nasewaupee—passed from existence. When the township was organized [in 1859], it was named after the deceased post office, and now the name 'Nasewaupee' lives on and only time will tell how far up the ladder of fame it will climb. (C.I. Martin,* History of Door County, Wisconsin, *pp. 68-69, 1881)*

It is not certain yet how far Nasewaupee has climbed. At least it has not fallen off the ladder, since the township is still flourishing.

Nasewaupee Postmasters and Dates of Their Appointments

- Nelson W. Fuller - September 4, 1858
- Elijah S. Fuller - March 24, 1859
- Elijah Fuller's annual salary for 1860-61 was $6.65.

NASEWAUPEE

SEC. 7, NW 1/4
T27N R26E
CITY OF STURGEON BAY (SAWYER)

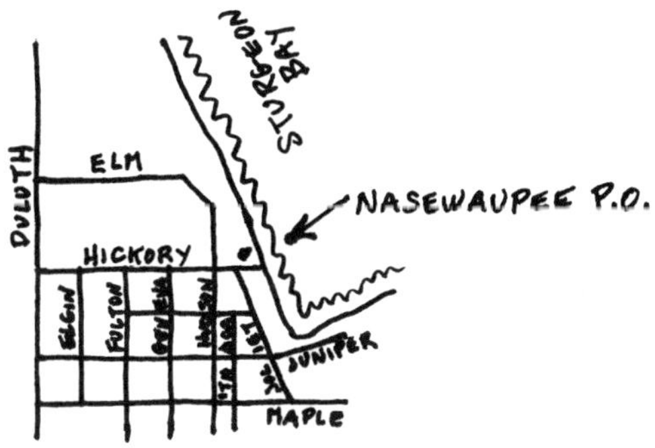

Newport

Established October 17, 1882.

Discontinued April 30, 1904, with mail service at Ellison Bay.

Newport post office was named for and located in the village of that name at the end of the road on the Lake Michigan shore in the southwest quarter of section 21, Town 32 North, Range 29 East, Town of Liberty Grove. Newport State Park, purchased by the Wisconsin Department of Natural Resources in 1966, includes the entire Newport town site and relics of its existence. A guide book for the site and its history is available at the park.

> *Newport was settled in the early 1870s by Hans Johnson, a logger, who built a dock, sawmill, and later a general store and post office. Johnson had about twenty-five men working for him in the late 19th century, but the forest was soon cut over and Johnson sold his logging interests to Peter Knudsen in 1895. Knudsen later took over the store and post office.*
>
> *In 1914, the Newport area was subdivided into plats and streets in a land speculation scheme promoted by Knudsen, but development never took place and the idea was abandoned...Newport became a ghost town. (Wisconsin DNR,* Newport State Park Visitor, *1978)*

✉

> *...Newport was once the site of a substantial pier, general store, mill and post office, and history tells us the village once boasted a barber, carpenter, justice of the peace and news dealer. Memory reminds us that up until the mid-1950s, the remains of a few log homes were still standing.*
>
> *(In 1880)...residents had a tri-weekly stage service running from Sturgeon Bay and Green Bay with fares priced at $2 and $4 respectively. Mail was sent by 'special supply'—meaning it went by whatever means of transportation was available. (K. Steebs in* Door

Newport pier about 1890.

County Advocate, *December 30, 1970)*

✉

Newport Postmasters and Dates of Their Appointments

Hans Johnson - October 17, 1882

Peter Knudsen - January 22, 1892

Mr. Johnson's application for the post office estimated that it would serve seventy-five people.

Annual Salaries of Hans Johnson as Postmaster

1883	$21.20
1885	$18.97
1887	$29.18
1889	$35.65
1891	$27.74

Newport general store and post office about 1890.

1892.

NEWPORT

SEC. 20,21
T32N R29E
TOWN OF LIBERTY GROVE

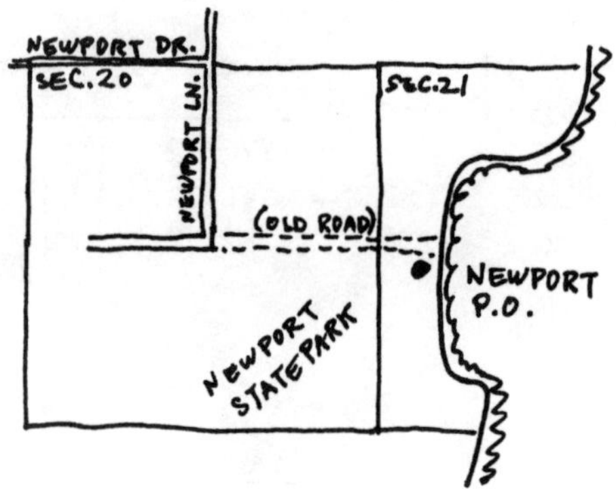

North Bay

Established February 25, 1870.

Discontinued May 19, 1873.

Location: On the east side of North Bay, Lake Michigan, in the northeast quarter of section 26, Town 31 North, Range 28 East, Town of Liberty Grove. This area is today known as Marshall's Point.

The post office was named for the bay, which was originally called Denton Harbor because fractional section 26 was owned by a fisherman, D.E. Denton. However, since it was the far thest north bay on the lake side of the county that was considered to be a good harbor for ships seeking shelter from storms, the sailors called it North Bay, the name that has persisted since.

At the time the post office was established, Denton's land was owned by G.A. Thomson, who built a large, store, barn, and dock and went into the lumbering business. The post office was apparently located at his establishment. "His store at that time was said to be the largest general store north of Sturgeon Bay." (H.R. Holand, *History of Door County, Wisconsin* II:436)

The *Door County Advocate* duly noted the North Bay post office:

> *February 24, 1870 - Bidders for the Ephraim mail route should put in bids for carrying the mail to North Bay as a post office will be established there and the route extended.*
>
> *March 17, 1870 - A post office has been established at North Bay and J.L. Ramsay appointed postmaster.*

J. Louis Ramsay was the postmaster for the life of the office. His application for the office stated that "It will supply mail to about sixteen families north of here."

Ramsay's annual salary as postmaster for 1871 was $12.00.

NORTH BAY

SEC. 22,23,24,25,26,27
TOWN OF LIBERTY GROVE
T31N R28E

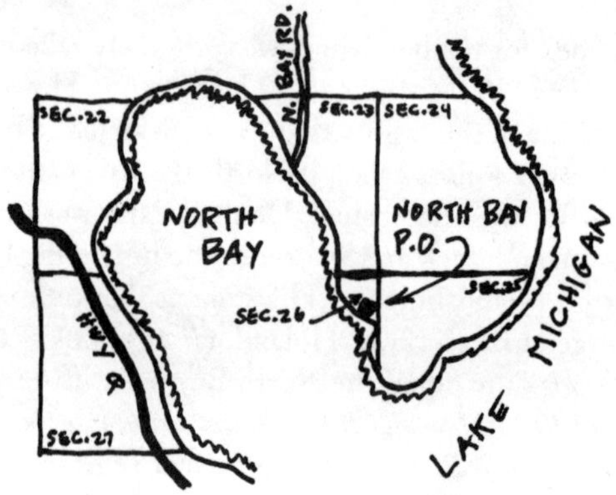

Rowleys Bay/Rowley

Established as "Rowley's Bay" On July 1, 1878.

The name was changed to "Rowley" on June 25, 1883, but changed back to "Rowleys Bay" (without an apostrophe) on January 2, 1890.

The office was discontinued August 4, 1893, with mail service at Ellison Bay, but was reestablished, still as "Rowleys Bay," on July 18, 1894.

The office was finally discontinued April 30, 1904, with mail service in Sister Bay.

Location: On Rowleys Bay, Lake Michigan at the end of the road (the present County Highway Z) in lot 4 of the southeast quarter, section 25, Town 32 North, Range 28 East, Town of Liberty Grove. In the 1878 application by Lyman Greenwood for his post office, the location is given as in section 26, apparently in error, since it would put the office a mile west of its actual location.

In this same application the population to be served was listed as 200, while in Samuel Roger's reapplication in 1894, the number had declined to 150.

Today, the Rowleys Bay post office site is part of the Wagon Trail Resort.

Rowleys Bay was named for Peter Rowley, who, as H.R. Holand described, came to Door County from Green Bay in 1838 and settled on the west shore Green Bay "away back in the early morning of Door County's history." Rowley then moved on up the county in 1840 to settle at what is now Rowleys Bay. This, too, was not to be permanent, for in 1842, he moved south with his family to just north of Two Rivers in Manitowoc County, where he spent the rest of his life. However, his name remains at Rowleys Bay.

Leonard Peterson, writing in 1991 about the history of the Wagon Trail Resort at Rowleys Bay, noted that the post office was in the building that is now the resort's bakery. He also described some of Samuel Roger's experiences as postmaster. While Rogers had come to Rowleys Bay in 1876, he did not become postmaster until 1881. Then in 1893, the Post Office Department decided to close his office, to which he raised strong objections.

> *S.A. Rogers was not to be defeated in his quest to have a post office in his store because he had 150 people who relied on the service it provided. He again petitioned the 'Appointment Division of the Office of the Fourth Assistant Postmaster General" to establish a 'Special Office' to be supplied with mail from some convenient point on the nearest mail route by a special carrier. In other words, the mail*

for Rowleys Bay constituents had to be transferred from Ellison Bay by a carrier 'for a sum equal to two-thirds the amount of the salary of the postmaster at such office which will be paid by the department.'

His request also states that the name should remain the same as spelled without an apostrophe, and not be a shorter, different name because Rowleys Bay is a lake port and is known by all seamen and shown on government charts, while a new name will not be known.

The signature of Peter Knudson, the postmaster of the Newport Post Office, was used to certify the correctness of the answers on Mr. Roger's forms. Mr. Knudson very likely was having the same problems and the two colonists probably collaborated to keep the identities of their own communities. It didn't last too long because both post offices were discontinued on the same date in 1904.

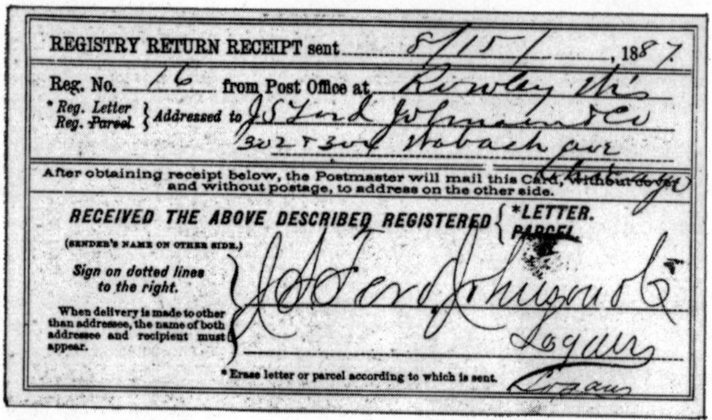

REGISTRY RETURN RECEIPT sent 8/15/ , 1887.
Reg. No. 16 from Post Office at
*Reg. Letter / Reg. Parcel } Addressed to
After obtaining receipt below, the Postmaster will mail this Card, without cover and without postage, to address on the other side.
RECEIVED THE ABOVE DESCRIBED REGISTERED { *LETTER. PARCEL.
(SENDER'S NAME ON OTHER SIDE.)
Sign on dotted lines to the right.
When delivery is made to other than addressee, the name of both addressee and recipient must appear.
* Erase letter or parcel according to which is sent.

A return receipt for a registered letter originated at the Rowley post office in 1887.

*...A letter I found, still in its original envelope, has this return address: 'Return to Mrs. S.A.R., Rowleys Bay, Wis. if not delivered in twenty days.' The postmark is Rowleys Bay, Mar 2, but the year is not legible. The post office was discontinued in 1904, which also was the same year S.A. Rogers and his wife moved back to New York, so the letter would have had to be written before that time, or probably about 1890. A 2¢ stamp was used. The letter is addressed to Mr. S.A. Rogers, Gower, Missouri, Clinton County. (*Rowleys Bay - Reliving the Heritage of Northern Door County, *pp. 60-106, 1991)*

✉

Rowleys Bay Postmasters and Dates of Their Appointments

Lyman A. Greenwood - July 1, 1878

Samuel A. Rogers - November 21, 1881

Postmasters' Annual Salaries

1879	Lyman Greenwood	\$17.13
1883	Samuel Rogers	\$35.61
1885	Samuel Rogers	\$41.23
1887	Samuel Rogers	\$44.96
1889	Samuel Rogers	\$40.47
1891	Samuel Rogers	\$46.38

ROWLEY
ROWLEYS BAY

SEC. 25, 26
T32N R28E
TOWN OF LIBERTY GROVE

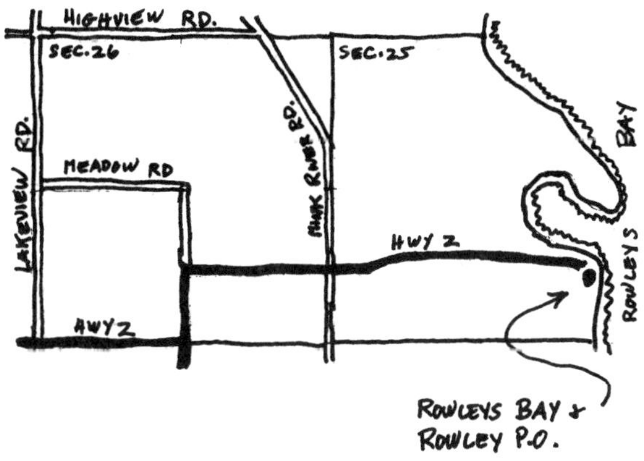

Salona

Established August 1, 1881.

Discontinued January 30, 1904, with mail service at Sawyer.

This office was located in the northeast quarter of section 5, Town 26 North, Range 26 East, Town of Clay Banks.

Salona had something of an identity problem. William Warren, who applied to the Post Office Department as the proposed postmaster, had to submit three names to get one accepted. His first choice was Haven, the second was Garfield (after the U.S. President), and the third and winning name was Salona. Why Salona was chosen is unclear. It still persists as the name of a local women's club which has never been able to satisfy its curiosity as to where the name came from. Possible connections are the Salona post office in Racine County, Wisconsin from 1841 to 1842, a Salona post office in Pennsylvania, and the cities of Salona in Greece and Austria.

1886, with postmaster's name in the handstamp.

Salona post office had close connections to the Warren's Corners office (q.v.). William H. Warren was the first postmaster at both offices, and the first location of each was, as the *Door County Advocate* put it, "at Mr. W.H. Warren's place on the Clay Banks road."

Mr. Warren's application for his office estimated that it would be serving "about 400 or 500" people.

Salona Postmasters and Dates of Their Appointments

William H. Warren - August 1, 1881
Julius Warren - April 25, 1884
James E. Spalsbury - August 30, 1893
Eugene Madoche - December 14, 1894

Postmasters' Annual Salaries

1883	William H. Warren	$13.56
1885	Julius Warren	$37.77
1887	Julius Warren	$66.62
1889	Julius Warren	$39.70
1891	Julius Warren	$34.23

SALONA
WARREN'S CORNERS
HORN'S PIER
CHEESEVILLE

SEC. 3, 4, 5
T26N R26E
TOWN OF CLAY BANKS

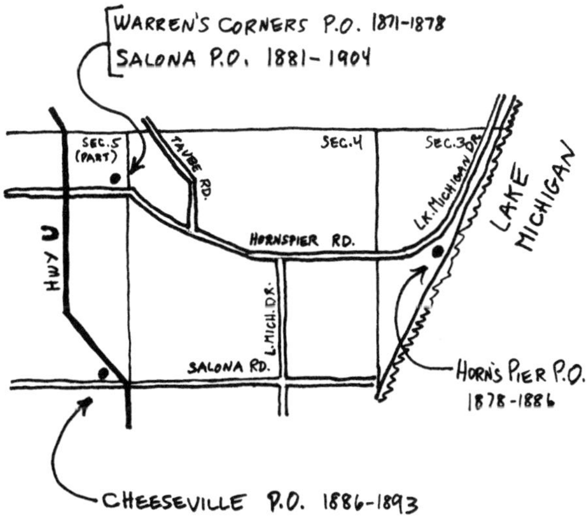

Sawyer

Established July 13, 1874.

On April 30, 1938, the Sawyer post office was discontinued and made a Station of the Sturgeon Bay post office. The location of the facility was not changed at this time (see below).

On March 1, 1948, it was made into Contract Station A of Sturgeon Bay, operated by private contractors who supplied quarters and furnishings. Remaining post office employees were transferred to the Sturgeon Bay office.

Lloyd Londo had the first Contract Station in his barbershop at 50 South Madison Street in the building between Woerfel's Drug Store and the West Side Hardware Store. He operated Station A there until March 1, 1956, when the Wisconsin Department of Health would no longer permit him to operate a post office in his barbershop.

Station A was next moved to Mac's Sport Shop, 27 South Madison Street, where it was located from March 1, 1956 to July 1, 1957. On the latter date it was moved to Hagen's Welding Shop at 22 East Pine Street, where it remained until August 21, 1986.

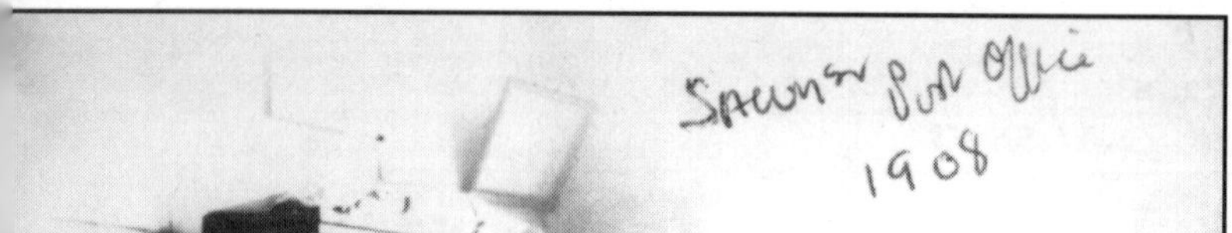

Interior of Sawyer post office, 1908.

The next location was at the West Side Branch of the Bank of Sturgeon Bay, where it was kept from August 21, 1986, to January 2, 1987, on which date it was moved to the West Side Branch of the First National Bank. This location was used until it closed on December 31, 1989. For lack of bids, no contractor was engaged until August 1, 1990, when Station A reopened in the Bay Plaza Laundry at 229 Bay Plaza.

On July 27, 1994, the Contract Station was moved to the S Stop Convenience Store at 922 South Duluth Avenue. The station again was moved on

January 30, 1995 to Wiess Cleaners, 231 Green Bay Road.

The Sawyer post office was and is located in Section 7, Town 27 North, Range 26 East, City of Sturgeon Bay. Sawyer included all of the city on the west side of Sturgeon Bay.

Based on information supplied by Stanley Greene and Arden Robertson of Sturgeon Bay, the various locations of the Sawyer post office are as follows:

Sawyer RFD carrier about 1910.

1874-1876 (Postmaster Haines) At the foot of Maple Street on the south side, next to the ferry dock.

1876-1889 (Postmaster Goettleman) - In the hotel at the corner of Oak and Madison Streets.

1889-1893 (Postmaster Anderson) - In the Hoslett building (later Trodahl's store and the Zephyr Oil Company) at the corner of Maple and Madison Streets.

1893-1894 (Postmaster Cochems) - The location is uncertain; he was postmaster for only ten months. Possibly it was in the same location as the Anderson office.

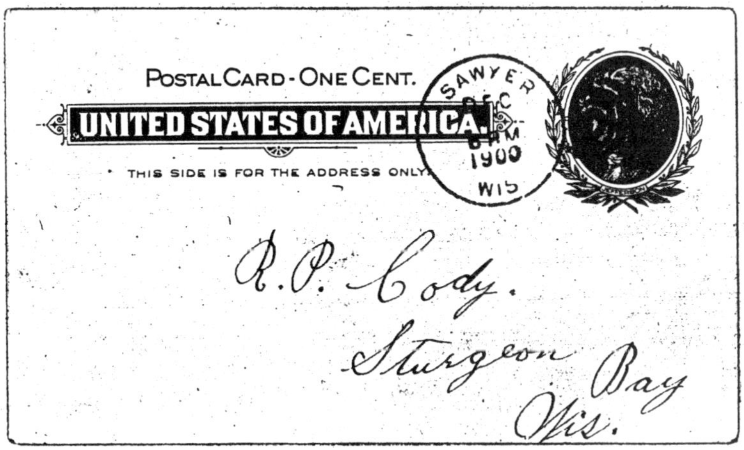
POSTAL CARD - ONE CENT.
UNITED STATES OF AMERICA.
THIS SIDE IS FOR THE ADDRESS ONLY.
SAWYER DEC 1900 WIS
R. P. Cody.
Sturgeon Bay
Wis.

1900 postal card.

1894-1898 (Postmaster Dechesne) - In the building now housing Andre's Food and Spirits at 23 West Oak Street.

1898-1917 (Postmaster Anderson) - In the same location as during his 1889-1893 term, the corner of Maple and Madison Streets.

1917-1922 (Postmaster William Stephan) - At Anderson's location on the corner of Maple and Madison Streets.

1922-1934 (Postmaster Langemak) and 1934-1938 (Postmaster Walter Stephan) - At 26 East Oak Street.

⊠

Sawyer was originally platted in 1872 and named Bay View by Joseph Harris, Sr., founder of the *Door County Advocate* and one of the organizers of the Sturgeon Bay - Lake Michigan Ship Canal. He wanted to provide facilities for the population boom anticipated when work started on the canal. He was unable to get approval of Bay View as the name for a new post office, since there was already an office of that name in Milwaukee County, so he had the office named in honor of Congressman Philetus Sawyer of Oshkosh, Wisconsin. Congressman Sawyer, alleged to have been unable to read and write, employed Mr. Harris as his secretary when Congress was in session and was one of the strong supporters of the canal project. He was instrumental in securing a 200,000-acre grant of timber lands, mostly in Marinette County, Wisconsin, for the canal company to use in financing canal construction.

⊠

The *Door County Advocate* made frequent mention of goings-on at the Sawyer post office:

> *October 12, 1889 - The post office in Bay View was turned over to Capt. Anderson last week. The office was created in 1873 through the efforts of the late Joseph Harris and named Sawyer in honor of Philetus Sawyer, member of congress from this district. Mr. Goettleman was made postmaster.*
>
> *August 11, 1894 - Postmaster Deschene announces the following time for opening and closing the Sawyer post office: During week days from 7:00 a.m. to 8:00 p.m.; Sundays from 9:00 a.m. to 10:00 a.m. Positively no mail delivered outside of these hours. Money order department closes after the last outgoing mail.*
>
> *August 11, 1894 - Both the Green Bay and Ahnapee mails are being carried by single rigs, business having fallen off to such a degree that there*

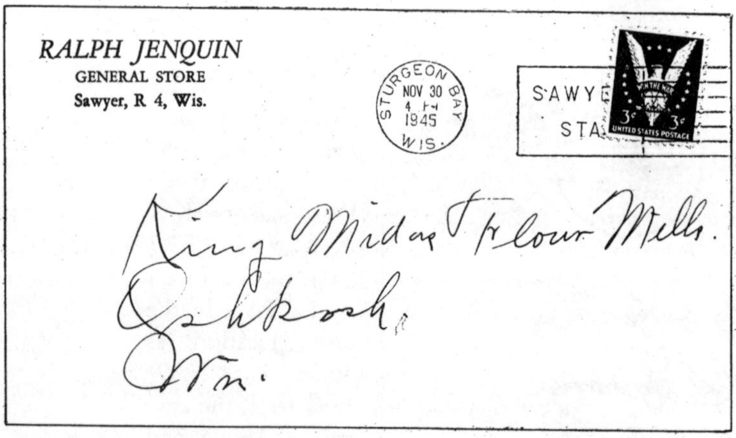

Sawyer Station postmark after Sawyer was attached to the Sturgeon Bay post office.

isn't money enough to make a double outfit pay running expenses.

February 4, 1899 - Write it Sawyer and drop Bay View. That will put an end to the confusion of names.

November 28, 1938 - Taking the only step possible to obtain a city carrier, parcel post deliveries and local postage rates for first class mail, 300 Sawyer residents have petitioned the post office department to make the Sawyer post office a substation of the Sturgeon Bay office. Another convenience will be to use "Sturgeon Bay' as the address because in the past Sawyer was merely a post office and not a city.

Sawyer postmaster Erik Anderson and friends, 1908.

April 29, 1938 - An error in postal orders indicating that mail would not be sacked directly to Sawyer under the new consolidation with Sturgeon Bay brought a flurry of protests, but the error had already been corrected and Substitute Carrier Walter Urdahl will be taking mail to all patrons who have complied with regulations.

January 16, 1948 - Lloyd H. Londo, west side barber, is the successful bidder for operation of the Sawyer branch post office. He has made arrangements with Alex Witz to use the same building that has served as the Sawyer post office for years and will move his barber shop there. He will dispose of the pool tables in the rear of his present shop in the building owned by Hallie Rowe. Londo's bid for the contract office was $2,600.

July 27, 1990 - Postmaster Phil Hoslet announces the awarding of a contact for a postal station on the west side of Sturgeon Bay. The contract has been awarded to Bay Plaza Launderette, 229 Bay Plaza, effective August 1, 1990. (Note: The closing of the previous Station A in the First National Bank building on January 31, 1990, came at the request of the contractor, not the U.S. Postal Service)

Since 1990, the contract postal station on the west side moved to 922 South Duluth Avenue on June 27, 1994 and to 231 Green Bay Road on January 27, 1995. The firm that operated the station went out of business on January 31, 1996 and the station was closed by the Sturgeon Bay Post Office at that time.

Sawyer Postmasters and Dates of Their Appointments

Melvin Haines - July 13, 1874
John Goettleman - May 19, 1876
Erik N. Anderson - September 17, 1889
William Cochems - September 5, 1893
Leon Deschene - June 29, 1894
Erik N. Anderson - October 1, 1898
William R. Stephan - September 28, 1917
Arnold E. Langemak - March 14, 1922
Walter P. Stephan - August 20, 1934

Postmasters' Annual Salaries

1877	John Goettleman	$ 59.97
1879	John Goettleman	$102.57
1883	John Goettleman	$147.64
1885	John Goettleman	$ 77.58
1887	John Goettleman	$199.77
1889	John Goettleman	$237.71
1891	Erik Anderson	$256.46

Sawyer rural mail carriers, 1916.

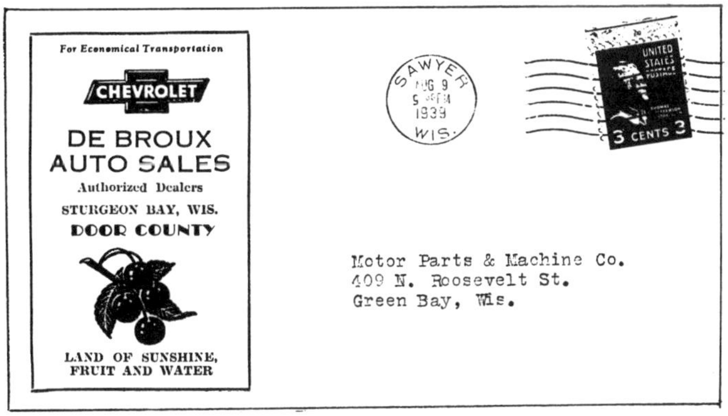

Illustrated advertising cover, 1939.

SAWYER

SEC. 7
T27N R26E
CITY OF STURGEON BAY (SAWYER)

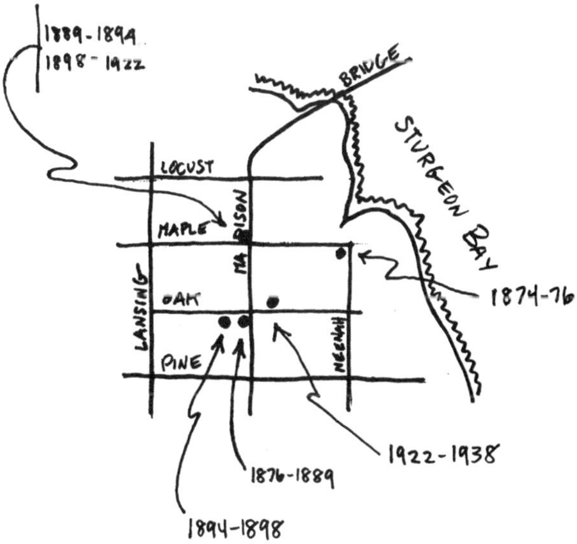

Sevastopol

Established February 17, 1874.

Discontinued October 15, 1902, with mail service at Sturgeon Bay.

The office was located in the southwest corner of section 15, Town 28 North, Range 26 East, Town of Sevastopol, just east of the present intersection of State Highway 42 and County Highway P.

The Sevastopol post office was named for the township in which it was located. The naming of the town was a matter of some controversy. Established in 1859, it was first named Laurieville after the Laurie family, pioneer residents of the town and prominent in the county's history. The name did not sit well with the farmers of the town, and in 1860 they petitioned the County Board for a name change, which was granted. The chosen name was Sebastopol, for the fortress city on the Black Sea of such importance during the Crimean War a few years earlier. The name was spelled with a "B" (Sebastopol) at the time it was adopted, but it became spelled with a "V" (Sevastopol) almost immediately thereafter. Martin, Holand, and other historians attributed the changed spelling to some sort of clerical error, but this cannot be proven. There are "B" spellings for towns in California, Georgia, Illinois and Louisiana, and a "V" spelling in Indiana as well as in Wisconsin. A possible alternative is a transliteration of the Russian cyrillic letter which looks like a "b" but is pronounced like a "v."

The Bassford house, site of Sevastopol post office (1991 photo).

The first Sevastopol post office was in the log home of the postmaster, George Bassford. He had moved to Door County in 1856, and was one of the first residents inland in the township. His house was where the meeting of pioneers was held to form Sevastopol township in 1859. By 1859 he had become the largest landowner in the town and was active in local politics. Among other activities, he built a halfway-house and stage stop to replace his original log house. This building also held the post office and still stands on its original site at the intersection of P and 42.

In 1966, the Bassford log building that housed the first Sevastopol post office was moved to the "The Farm," where it... "stands as an appropriate monument in tribute to the pioneers of this area." (fide Orville Schopf)

1887 manuscript postmark.

In February, 1874, the proposed Sevastopol post office was estimated to serve 200 people. In March of that year, Henry B. Stephenson applied for a post office at a location two and one-half miles away to be called Malakoff (q.v.); it was estimated to serve 150 people. It is questionable whether the neighborhood was that densely populated at the time. Ultimately, the Malakoff office did very little business and closed in 1881.

Even before they had their own post office, people in Sevastopol were complaining about their mail service. A letter signed "Played-Out-Reporter" appearing in the *Door County Advocate* of January 18, 1874, had this to say on the subject:

> *...Speaking of wood reminds me of what most of the farmers are doing this winter; that is cutting a little cordwood to help pay their subscription to the papers published at Sturgeon Bay. Speaking of papers reminds me that there are a great many persons in this town that complain about our Postmaster at Sturgeon Bay. Most of our citizens are subscribers to papers published in Chicago, Milwaukee and other places, and the complaint is, they can't get more than one paper in the course of three or four weeks, and they think the fault is with the postmaster; but this scribbler thinks the fault is their own, because the Postmaster [William Dresser] is a very fine man, and he is accomodating too. He has a nice lot of boxes for sale, and if the growlers would buy a box, they would be very likely to get all their mail every week. I think the Legislators ought to pass an act to compel every person taking mail from the Sturgeon Bay office to purchase a box (and pay for it in advance). It is not to be expected that a postmaster can keep track of every persons mail when he has no paid-up box to put it into.*

Sevastopol Postmasters and Dates of Their Appointments

George Bassford - February 17, 1874
Henry Martin - January 21, 1879
William Moeller - November 6, 1893
Mary L. Batchelder - April 15, 1895
Anna M. Bassford - November 28, 1898

Postmasters' Annual Salaries

1877	George Bassford	$13.20
1879	George Bassford	$16.67
1883	Henry Martin	$33.45
1883	Henry Martin	$57.34
1887	Henry Martin	$51.90
1889	Henry Martin	$57.45
1891	Henry Martin	$62.82

SEVASTOPOL

SEC. 15
T28N R26E
TOWN OF SEVASTOPOL

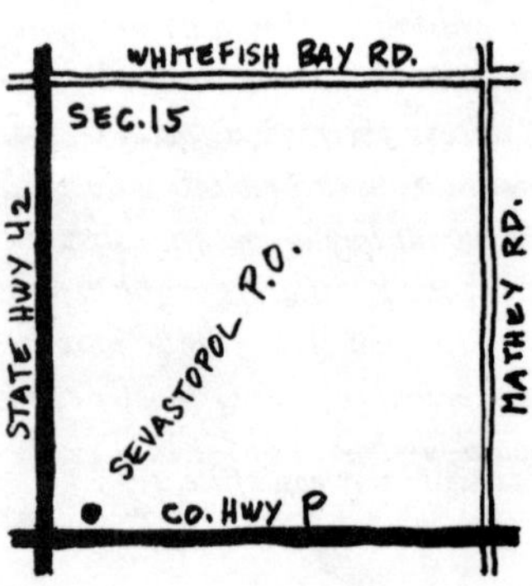

Sister Bay

Established February 21, 1875. The office is still in service. Zip Code - 54234.

The current office is in the Village of Sister Bay in the northeast quarter of section 5, Town 31 North, Range 28 East, Town of Liberty Grove. In his application for the first Sister Bay post office in 1873, Alonzo Henderson, the proposed postmaster, listed the location in Lot 4, southwest quarter of section 5. He also stated in the application that Sister Bay "is not a village," and that his office would service "forty families of actual settlers."

The post office was named for the bay of Green Bay on which it is located. The bay in turn was named for the Sister Islands which are near the village. Increase Claflin, recognized as Door County's first white settler in 1835, is credited with naming the Sister Islands because they look so much alike. However, another source of the name was given by Malcolm Vail in his book *Tails of Ephraim Waters* (1956). He wrote that "The Sister Islands, lying off the present village of Ephraim, were named for the two daughters of an old Goodrich Line Captain."

✉

The village of Sister Bay in 1962 celebrated its fifty years of existence with a booklet, *Sister Bay Golden Jubilee, 1912-1962*, which contained information on postal service in the village:

> *The first postal service was tended to by Margaret (Maggie) Roeser...This was a weekly service cared for by her in the Roeser homestead basement. Jim Hanson had the first general store in the village in 1880, later moving to Ephraim and selling out to Wenzel Bunda in 1887. Both of their stores were maintained in the basement of the Roeser home. (p. 6)*

Sister Bay post office, 1907.

1895 registered cover.

...Mrs. Wenzel Bunda operated the store along with the post office until the tragic fire of 1912 when the store and many other buildings burned to the ground. (p. 18)

Sister Bay is the name by which...it has always been known, although called Big Sister Bay at one time, [and] was named in connection with the Sister Islands that flank the harbor opening to Sister Bay. (p. 2)

The mail deliveries to Sister Bay have come by boat and horse. Then with the invention of the automobile, by truck. In 1904, rural delivery service was started in Sister Bay. The first to carry mail were Andrew Johnson and Adolph Soderburg. The arrival of the mail from the south came by Walter Olson and Anton Waller. Passengers were also carried on the stage, as it was called in those days. The post office moved from place to place depending on who the postmaster was. Martin Jischke is the only living postmaster who served the Sister Bay office. The present postmaster, Henry Eckert, has been on the job since 1951.

Retired rural mail carrier Andrew Magnette is the only living rural carrier. The present rural mail carrier Merrill Maahs has been serving the route since his appointment in 1955.

The post office building has been maintained in the new post office building and fire station since the building was erected in 1947. (p. 22)

✉

Alonzo S. Putman...in 1892 took the contract for carrying the mail to Sister Bay...He ran an excellent stage service all over the northern part of the county...and to the time of his death (May 22, 1917) he still carried the mail throughout the locality both winter and summer, though he used horses during the cold season. (H.R. Holand, History of Door County, Wisconsin *II:219, 1917)*

M.J. Jischke is the postmaster of the village of Sister Bay, where he is also actively engaged in business in connection with his father, who is proprietor of a meat market...He is filling the position of postmaster, to which he was appointed on the 24th of February, 1915...[and] is making an excellent record. (op. cit., II:227)

Sister Bay post office, about 1950.

Sister Bay Postmasters and Dates of Their Appointments

Alonzo Henderson - February 21, 1873
Hiram Elison - October 26, 1874
Alonzo Henderson - December 13, 1875
Thomas W. Hunt - December 11, 1876
Calvin Gray - August 16, 1877
Theodore Maybohm - June 16, 1879
Jonathan E. Hoyt - July 23, 1879
Andrew Roeser - August 4, 1886
Anna B. Dickson - May 17, 1893
Wencel Bunda - September 16, 1893
Frank Bunda - August 26, 1899
Mary Bunda - January 10, 1905
Martin J. Jischke - February 6, 1915
Stannie Sigurdson - May 13, 1935
Walter L. Larson - November 15, 1949
Henry G. Eckert - June 27, 1951

Daniel J. Heuvelmans - February 9, 1980
Theresa C. VanPay - January 9, 1982
Clarice F. Berns - October 13, 1984
Linda Smith - October 6, 1993
Karen E. Sunstrom - September, 1995

Note that Sister Bay had seven postmasters in the first six years of its existence. No other Door County post office has had so many changes in so short a time.

Postmasters' Annual Salaries

1873	Alonzo Henderson	$ 12.00
1877	Thomas Hunt	$ 51.38
1879	Calvin Gray	$ 86.83
1883	Jonathan Hoyt	$208.07
1885	Jonathan Hoyt	$273.42
1887	Andrew Roeser	$188.79
1889	Andrew Roeser	$157.64
1891	Andrew Roeser	$172.56

1894.

SISTER BAY

SEC. 5
T31N R28E
TOWN OF LIBERTY GROVE

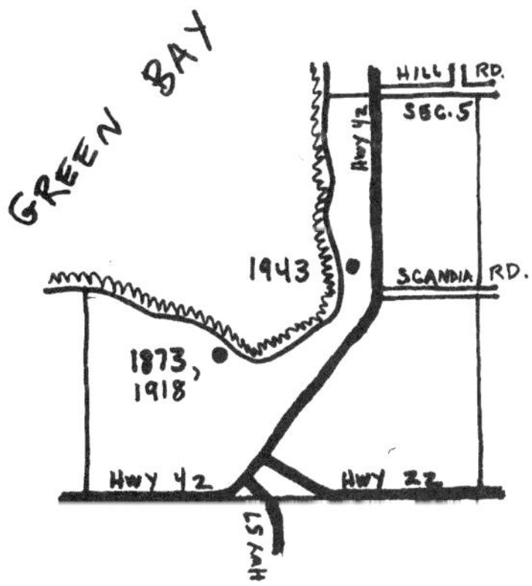

Stevenson's Pier

Established January 30, 1882.

Discontinued April 29, 1905, with mail service at Brussels.

This post office had two locations. The application for the post office, dated January 3, 1882, placed the office near the shore of Little Sturgeon Bay, off Green Bay, in the southwest quarter of section 11, Town 27 North, Range 24 East, Town of Gardner. The 1899 plat book of Door County showed the office to be on the east side of Stevenson's Pier Road in the southeast quarter of section 14. This location was between the present County Highway C and Riley's Bay Road about one and one-half miles south of the 1882 site. The change in location probably occurred when the postmastership changed hands in 1884.

Backstamped 1890.

The office was named for the Stevenson family who operated a pier at Little Sturgeon Bay.

Two postmasters served Stevenson's Pier. Albert B. Stevenson was appointed January 30, 1882, and was succeeded by Anton J. Eichinger on March 28, 1884.

In 1882, Mr. Stevenson estimated that his proposed post office would serve "over forty families."

✉

Postmasters' Annual Salaries

1883 Albert Stevenson	$4.98
1885 Anton Eichinger	$32.56
1887 Anton Eichinger	$35.64
1889 Anton Eichinger	$20.64
1891 Anton Eichinger	$25.20

STEVENSON'S PIER

SEC. 11, 14
T27N R24E
TOWN OF GARDNER

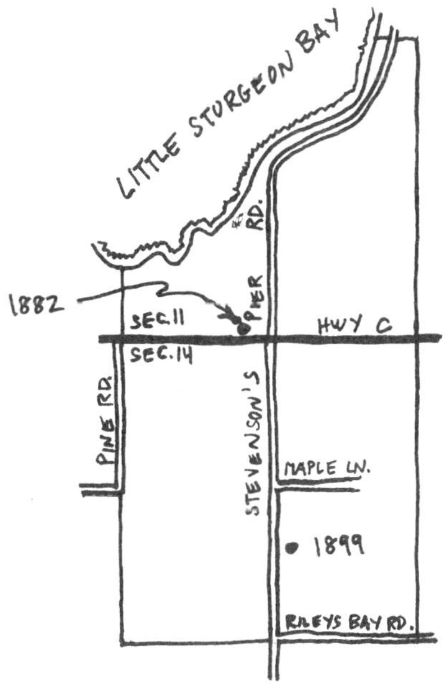

Stokes

Established January 4, 1883.

Discontinued July 14, 1903, with mail service at Sawyer.

This office had two locations near the intersection of what is now State Highway 42/57 and County Highway O. In 1882, Post Office Department site documents listed the site as in the southeast quarter of the northwest quarter, section 22, Town 27 North, Range 25 East, Town of Nasewaupee. This was on the northwest side of Highway 42/57 opposite the end of Highway O. In 1894, the location was described as in the southwest quarter of the northeast quarter of section 22, and mapped on the southeast side of Highway 42/57 just east of Highway O.

The post office was named probably for the first postmaster. It was originally proposed to call the office Stokesville, but this was denied by the Post Office Department.

In 1883, the population to be served by the proposed office was listed as 400.

⊠

Until the spring of 1991, the log cabin in which the Stokes post office was first located stood at the site described above. Reconstruction of the state highway required that the old cabin be removed from the site. An effort was made to move the structure to another site, but its wood was so rotten that it could not be moved and instead was torn down. All that remains is a photograph of the cabin published in the *Door County Advocate* of March 1, 1991.

⊠

Stokes Postmasters and Dates of Their Appointments

- Charles Stokes - January 4, 1883
- Wenzel Soukop - July 18, 1894
- Anna Soukop - June 18, 1895
- Joseph Jindra - April 23, 1897
- Caroline Ludwik - November 24, 1899

Annual Salaries of Charles Stokes as Postmaster

1883	$13.26
1885	$32.82
1887	$48.82
1889	$53.25
1891	$48.32

STOKES

SEC. 22
T27N-R25E
TOWN OF NASEWAUPEE

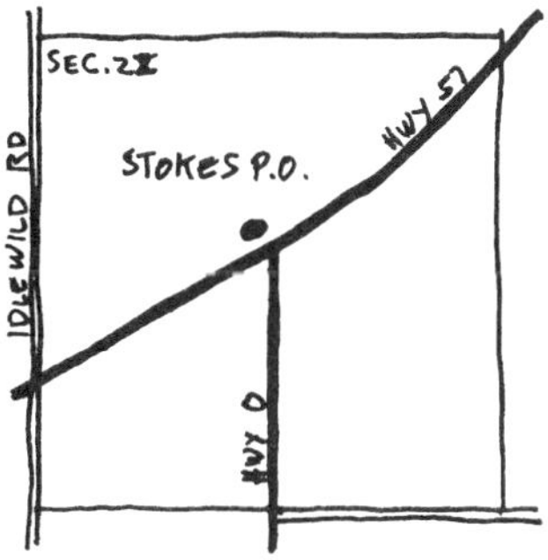

Sturgeon Bay

Established October 22, 1855. The office is still in service (Zip Code - 54235). It is located in the City of Sturgeon Bay, Town 27 North, Range 26 East.

The post office bears the name of the city and former village where it always has been located. The city in turn bears the name of the arm of Green Bay which it bridges.

Sturgeon Bay has been known by this name at least as far back as the Jesuit Father, Claude Allouez, who visited the bay in 1676. The Menominee Indians are said to have given the name because the bay is shaped like a sturgeon and because sturgeon were plentiful in its waters. In its early years, the village was known first as Sturgeon Bay, then Graham (after Robert Graham, an early settler, who platted the village in 1855), then Tehema (an Indian name that never really caught on), then Otumba (an Aztec tribe in Mexico), and then back to Sturgeon Bay again.

"Otumba" was chosen because Lyman Bradley, one of the founders of the first sawmill on the bay, saw the name in a newspaper. The sound of it so impressed him that he enlisted the help of his brother-in-law, Assemblyman Ezra B. Stevens, who had a bill passed by the state legislature in the late 1850s to give the name to the new town created in central Door County. The U.S. Post Office Department, however, by calling its office Sturgeon Bay, brought about the final change in name.

Postmaster Frank Tachovsky (left), Mayor Orville Austad and P.O. clerk Mrs. Marcella Giesseman, 1973.

The water itself was known as Big Sturgeon Bay to prevent confusion with Little Sturgeon Bay to the south. The simplification used by the Post Office Department rapidly caught on. Little Sturgeon remained as a place name (and had its own post office for a time), but Sturgeon Bay, minus the "Big," became in 1860, by action of the Door County Board, the name of the township. In 1874, Sturgeon Bay became the name of the incorporated village and the official name of the bay.

For many decades, postmasters were required to provide a building and equipment with which to operate their post office. Most Sturgeon Bay postmasters were storekeepers who operated their office where they did business. This meant that post office locations changed whenever a new postmaster was appointed. Sturgeon Bay was no exception; fifteen locations, all on the east side of the bay, were in use between 1855 and 1936 when the office became permanently located in the present federal building. The intensive researches of Stanley Greene have identified these locations as follows:

1855 - In Robert Graham's store about seventy feet north of the northwest corner of Second Avenue and Pennsylvania Street.

1858 - In the McIntosh and Strawn store at what is now the northeast corner of Second Avenue and Michigan Street.

1862 - In the Sittig residence, now 42 South Second Avenue, a building then used as offices for the County Clerk and Register of Deeds.

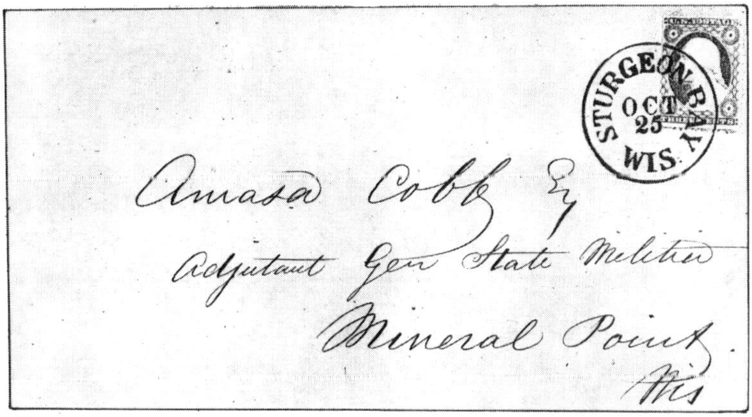

About 1860.

1864 - In the county office building on the southeast corner of Second Avenue and Michigan Street, fronting on Second Avenue. In 1868 the office was in the same building, but fronted on Michigan Street.

1871 - In the Dresser store, now 111 South Third Avenue.

1876 - In the T.C. Hayley Company store which was on the south portion of the site that is now 163 North Third Avenue.

1881 - In the Peschon Block, the northern portion of a building now listed as 23 North Third Avenue.

1883 - In Dreutzer's store, now 164 North Third Avenue.

1887 - In Shimmel's store, now 212 North Third Avenue.

1890 - In the Lawrence Building, now 120 North Third Avenue.

1894 - In the Wagener Building, now 239 North Third Avenue.

1906 - In the Falk Building at 239 North Third Avenue where the Donna Theater is now located.

1911 - In the Pinney Building at the intersection of Third Avenue and Michigan Street, now 11 North Third Avenue. The post office entrance was at the rear of the building and entered from the Michigan Street side.

1927 - In the Wiesner Building, now 235 North Third Avenue. The office eventually occupied the entire building.

1936 - The present location at 359 Louisiana Street. This is the first and only building built by the U.S. Government to house the Sturgeon Bay post office.

During the period from 1862 to 1871, postmaster William Dresser was also a Door County official, and had the post office where his county offices were. When he became a merchant, the post office followed to his store.

Arden Robertson (left) and Darrel Starr at work in the Sturgeon Bay post office, 1969.

The carrying of mail between post offices was contracted to the lowest bidder.

One of the early carriers, a redoubtable gentleman named David Houle, carried mail sixty-five miles from Sturgeon Bay to Two Rivers once each week and still had energy left over to fiddle for dances...

...Jessee Birmingham, a sailboat owner and operator with a regular run to Green Bay and back, easily secured the first contract and happily carried mail in addition to freight and passengers. His willingness to take the job may be that the amount of cargo space required was almost nil. An empty cigar box substituted for the traditional mail pouch.

Mailmen, like the before mentioned Houle, didn't have it as easy. Their job, with a knapsack replacing the cigar box,

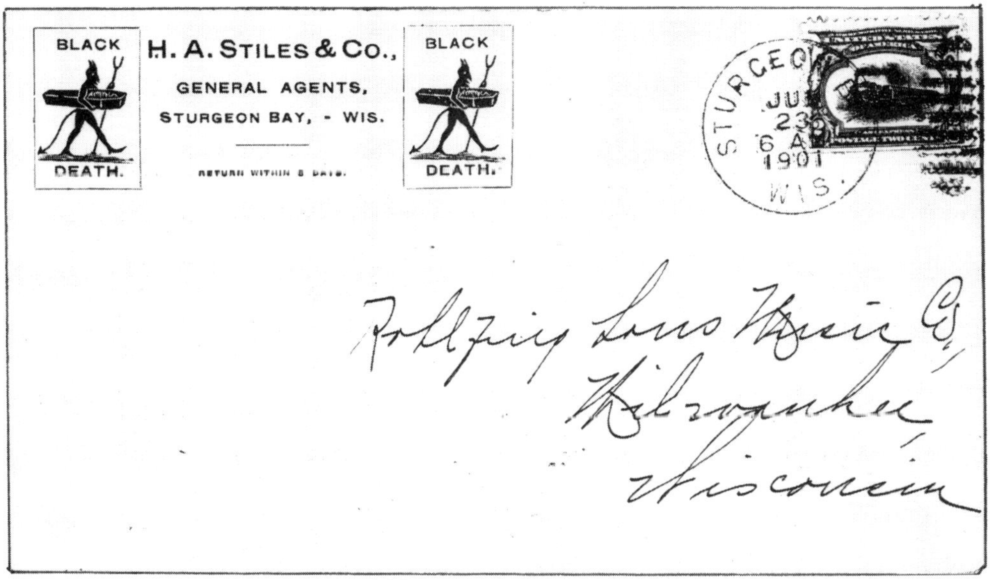

1901; "Black Death" was an orchard pesticide.

> *was to hike through swamps and creeks following the tortuous Indian trail from Bay Settlement north. The round trip of 120 miles took three days to make (although Houle only took two) and even then settlers grumbled about the slow service.*
>
> *By 1859, road conditions were improving and the mails graduated from foot to mule to stage. The first stage, actually an open wagon built to haul freight and passengers, was much slower than other means of transportation. Passengers paid...[a fare] and had, we are told, the privilege of walking behind the wagon most of the time or giving it a hefty shove when it got stuck.*
>
> *After twelve years of service, the village was still only getting two deliveries per week from Green Bay, but the post office's financial condition was definitely improving. In 1867, about $32,000 was handled in postal money orders, a not inconsiderable amount for the post-Civil War period. (*Door County Advocate, *June 10, 1976)*

About the time Sturgeon Bay became a city in 1883, the post office was designated a Presidential Office under an 1876 Act of Congress. The postmaster was then paid $1,100 per year and the services of a clerk, which led to a more stable operation.

The state of the post office in Sturgeon Bay was frequently the subject of news stories and editorial comments in the *Door County Advocate.* Some items just passed along routine information, some were complimentary, and some offered vitriolic criticism, but they were seldom dull. Here is a sampler from the ongoing opus of the *Advocate* vs. the U.S. Post Office Department:

> *July 15, 1862 - Mr. William K. Dresser, the new Postmaster of Sturgeon Bay, has been duly installed into office; serves him right! If he hadn't served the public well and faithfully in other public positions, he wouldn't have got into this scrape.*
>
> *January 29, 1863 - 'U.S. Mail Express.'—Sleighing has commenced; (rather late but better late than not at all) and Robert Graham, our mail contractor, alive to the wants of the people has commenced running his express conveyance to Green Bay. He will carry passengers and freight to and from Green Bay twice a week, starting from here on Monday and Thursday mornings at 6:00 a.m. Orders should be left at his office on Sturgeon Bay.*
>
> *December 24, 1863 - 'Great Storm and Blockade.'—A heavy snow storm commenced raging here on Saturday night last, and it has been snowing and blowing all the week since and still continues. The lumbermen say it is two and a half foot deep in the woods on a level, while here in the village and on the roads and in the clearings the high wind has drifted the snow into banks of from four to ten feet deep. We understand that the mail from Green Bay, which left here on Monday morning, did not reach there until Wednesday. The return mail has not yet arrived, now two days behind time - we are blockaded in - the Michicott mail started out this morning, but could not get through and returned here - we can't get out and our mails can't get in, so we are without any late news and can't give our readers the latest arrivals. If the snow storm continues much longer, it will seriously interfere with our lumbermen in the woods. There is an abundance of snow for a good winters logging if we could only control the clerk of the weather and have him 'shut off' the supply.*
>
> *February 18, 1864 - Ole Lawson, the mail contractor on the route from Sturgeon Bay to Ephraim, is running a team for the accommodation of travelers between the two places. All who wish to travel on that road would do well to give Mr. Lawson a call, as you will undoubtedly find his terms satisfactory.*
>
> *November 25, 1864 - Senator Harris ought to have a post office and mail conveyance of his own. We pity Mr. Postmaster Dresser, as the Senator piles work on him every mail day without mercy. Last Saturday night he handed in to our post office over two hundred letters on the Ship Canal business alone, and through the late campaign has mailed on an average about one hundred letters on each mail day, the fruits of which may be seen in the returns of the Union votes at the late election in Door County. Truly the Senator is 'some' on letter writing; so much so that he astonished the Senators and Postmaster of the Senate at Madison last winter.*

January 26, 1866 - The late snow blockade for a short time stopped our communications with Green Bay, and in doing so played havoc with the arrival of our mails. During the last week we have done without them altogether, we hope for the last time. As the roads are in good condition now, we suppose our troubles with the non-arrival of the mails are at an end

August 16, 1866 - Post Master Dresser has received the necessary information and blanks, and is now ready to furnish money orders to any of our citizens wishing them. It is a convenience that will be appreciated by everybody here who desires to send money through the mails. Any amount not exceeding $50 can be sent by one order at the following rates: For any sum not exceeding $20... 10 cts.. For any sum from $20 to $50... 25 cts.

Sturgeon Bay post office about 1940.

January 31, 1867 - Revenue Stamps.—The Senior (Advocate Editor) in company with our excellent Representative in Congress, Hon. P. Sawyer, lately waited on the Commissioner of the Interior to ask him to establish a depository for the sale of Internal Revenue stamps at the post office in our village. They were received very courteously by Commissioner Rollins who, on having explained to him the growing importance of our county and its isolated position rendering it difficult to procure a supply of stamps from outside, at once granted the request...This will be a great convenience to our people whose wants will soon be supplied by our worthy postmaster. In the course of time, all our wants will be supplied. Next spring when work begins on the canal we shall need a bank and that will follow in due time in the march of improvements fast developing around us.

October 3, 1867 - Our citizens have many things to make them happy. One of these blessings in disguise is the beautiful regularity and promptness with which the Green Bay mail is carried. Semi-occasionally or oftener during the season, the boat has broken down, or the mail is left, or the boat don't run at all for a week, and our people can enjoy the luxury of 'waiting and watching over the border' buoyed up by the expectation that if the boats are not all right in a week or two, the mail will make its appearance through the woods. If the 'powers that be' would only give our mail contractor a dose of physic to regulate the carriage of the mail 'how happy we would be.'

August 13, 1868 - The people of this town and county are peculiarly blessed with the mail service between Green Bay and this point. Every little while the mail carriers are changed, the horses give out, the wagon breaks down, or some other accident happens which delays the arrival of the mail from half a day to three or four days. The contract for the mail service was let at such a low figure that the mail contractor finds it impossible to fulfill the contract and make money. So, by running it to suit himself, and without regard to the contract time or the convenience of the people which it supplies, he manages to get along. We submit that if an experienced man is greedy enough to bid down to such a figure as to render the prompt carriage of the mail unprofitable, that he should suffer for it, and not foist the disagreeable consequences on the people. As the matter stands now, the mail contractor is the Post Office Department as far as the Green Bay mail route is concerned.

June 30, 1870 - Mr. T.C. Russell, who has carried the mail from here to the entire satisfaction of our business men, has closed his duties in that capacity. Not once during the time of this service has he been behind time with the mail, and nearly every time he is from one to three hours ahead, and occasionally he has served up our mail to us the night before due. This extreme punctuality is very remarkable and commendable, considering the state of the roads much of the time. In fall and spring egregious mud holes alternate with thumping corduroys and flooded swamps; in winter the snow falling, at times, three to four feet deep and piling in mountainous drifts, would be regarded

Site of Sturgeon Bay post office, 1911-1927, at corner of Third and Michigan.

as impassable barriers to any but the most energetic in the discharge of duty. We hope the new contractor will be successful in securing him to continue on the route. This would be the most convincing assurance he could give, that we were to have our mail punctually delivered.

July 17, 1870 - The new mail contractors commenced carrying the mails last week under their contracts. Victor DeGrandgagnage on the Green Bay route; T.W. McCullough on the Bailey's Harbor route; Carl Hempel on the Fish Creek and Ephraim route; and the old contractor, W. Calhoun, on the Kewaunee route. The retiring carriers, Messrs. T.C. Russell, Green Bay; M.M. Carrington, Bailey;s Harbor; and Carl Nelson, Ephraim, have all proved model mail carriers, delivering the mail with carefulness and commendable promptness. We but echo the sentiments of all our citizens when we express the wish that the new carriers will be as good as the old ones.

December 1, 1870 - Enough red tape has at last been untied to admit of the tri-weekly mail between this place and Green Bay over the Central State road going into operation. The post offices at Duchateau and Little Sturgeon will be supplied from the post office at Brussels twice each week. The mail will arrive here Mondays, Wednesdays and Fridays at 7:00 p.m. and leave Tuesdays, Thursdays and Saturdays at 6:00 a.m. The service will commence next Monday. The business of this place has long demanded the increase which will prove a welcome accommodation to our business men.

December 8, 1870 - The frightful state of the central road prevents the carrying of the tri-weekly mail from Green Bay until the snow flies. Here is a convincing argument that the road should be fixed at once.

February 2, 1871 - We are indebted to the courtesy of Postmaster Dresser for the following items concerning Uncle Sam's business here:

Detailed Statement of the Business of the Sturgeon Bay P.O. for 1870.

Am't of prepaid postage on mails sent from this office	*$687.32*
Am't of unpaid postage on mails sent from this office	*18.38*
Total	*$705.70*
RECEIPTS	
From sale of stamps and envelopes	*$576.32*
From unpaid postage collected	*41.19*
From box rents	*22.25*
Total	*$639.76*
REGISTERED LETTERS	
Whole No. of registered letters received	*293*
Whole No. of registered letters sent	*352*

Of which two were temporarily delayed on their passage but none were finally lost.

M.O. BUSINESS

109 money orders issued amounting to	*$29,224.57*
191 money orders paid amounting to	*4,816.16*
8 money orders repaid amounting to	*155.91*
3 money orders were lost in the mails and duplicates were issued therefor amounting to	*63.50*

260 mails were received and the same number dispatched over five different routes. Mail contractors were four times behind time, twice on the Kewaunee route and twice on the Ephraim route, about an hour each time...

February 19, 1871 - The Green Bay mail stage has donned a cover which makes it considerably more warm and comfortable for passengers.

March 24, 1871 - The late severe storm failed to put any of the mails at this place behind time, which speaks well for the pluck of carriers.

July 13, 1871 - Postmaster Dresser is having a building put up on Cedar St., just south of the Sturgeon Bay House, which he intends to occupy, when finished, as a post office. It is eighteen by twenty-eight feet, one story high, and will be a decided improvement on the present close quarters to which he is confined.

March 16, 1871 - The Green Bay mail carrier reports that the central road will be impassable in a few days and he will have to bring the mail over the old route. The road should have been fixed last fall and certainly should be now before the swamps thaw out. Appropriations were made by the county Board of Supervisors last fall to mend the bad portions of the road between this place and Williamson's shingle mill and from that place to Frank Pierre's tavern [Brussels]. It is very important that the appropriations should be expended at once and the road made passable.

October 5, 1871 - The Green Bay mail due here Monday evening did not arrive until Tuesday afternoon, being delayed by large quantities of timber thrown across the central road by the fires.

November 23, 1871 - The post office has been removed to the new quarters prepared for it by Postmaster Dresser on Cedar Street next door to the Sturgeon Bay House. With more comfortable and roomy quarters, the P.M. is prepared to disperse mail matter, town orders and justice impartially.

April 11, 1872 - The mail stages are enjoying the beauties of our roads just now. The Green Bay mail came through on wheels, for the first time last week.

April 18, 1872 - The Green Bay mail due here Friday evening did not arrive until Saturday afternoon. It was delayed by a blockade in the road through the burnt district. The extraordinary heavy gales of Friday and Saturday had thrown about two hundred trees across the road, which took considerable time for their removal.

December 5, 1872 - An exchange discourses on noise in the post office thusly: We suggest to our young friends who are in the habit of visiting the post office at mail time, that it would be more becoming in them, as well as more agreeable to their elders, if they would avoid all unnecessary loud talking, boisterous laughter, or anything which draws the attention of, or disturbs others. As young people grow older, they discover that it is very easy to distinguish between what is natural and unassumed, and what is unnatural and affected. That fits the young fry that hang around our post office exactly.

December 24, 1872 - The internal arrangement of the post office has undergone some changes lately. The back room wherein the waiters for the mail kept the stove warm has been partitioned off the same as the front part, shutting us off effectually from the warm embraces of the aforesaid stove. The front part is to be used as a telegraph office and news room and the back part for the post office.

Sturgeon Bay post office about 1938.

August 14, 1873 - Much complaint is made about the Green Bay mail service... We understand that the horses are run down and not fit for the service, and if the contractor would put on new animals, fit for the work, the carrier could and would make good time. Our people have been long suffering in this matter and it is time that their well grounded complaints should be heard and heeded.

December 11, 1873 - The Kewaunee Enterprise, speaking of mail matters, says: 'There are, we understand, three petitions in circulation for daily mail service along the lake shore from Two Rivers north—one for a daily mail from Two Rivers to Kewaunee, one for a daily from Two Rivers to Ahnapee [Algoma] vis

Kewaunee, and one for a daily mail from Two Rivers to Sturgeon Bay via Kewaunee and Ahnapee...' With an energetic mail contractor and proper relays of horses, we think a daily mail could be run between Two Rivers and this place on time most of the season...Petitions asking for a daily service on this route have been sent forward to Washington and we think bids will be asked for in the March advertisement in conformity with those petitions...

March 26, 1874 - The arrangements for a daily mail service between this place and Green Bay are finally settled, to commence on the first of July next. John Hendricks, the successful bidder for three times a week will carry the daily at $1140 per year.

November 5, 1874 - The Green Bay mail was detained several hours last Thursday night, the conveyance having broken down and compelled the mail carrier to foot it fifteen miles before he could get his rig repaired. We must expect such mishaps on that route until the road is frozen up.

May 14, 1885 - Now that we have a daily boat between here and Green Bay, would it not be a good scheme to have the mail conveyed back and forth this way? This would give us rapid communication with the outside world.

September 17, 1887 - The contract to carry the mails between this city and Ephraim has been let to J.W. Carmody of Egg Harbor for $7,000 a year. The route is a daily and the distance is about thirty miles.

Ahnapee and Western Railroad depot at Sturgeon Bay about 1920.

March 8, 1890 - Monday's mail from the south was the largest received here in about a week as last week's storm forced the accumulation of three days of deliveries. Emil Baumgartner came through with the mail from Green Bay, but reported roads blocked with fallen trees and pieces of fences. Friday's mail from the south came through about 4:00 p.m. Saturday, and there was little of it as railroads from south and east were blocked by the weather.

May 31, 1890 - Hart Brothers bid $3 per day to carry mail by steamer between here and Green Bay, plus the expense of delivering the bags to and from the steamer. The amount seems to be more than the post office is willing to pay and doubtless the project will fall through.

February 21, 1891 - James Dunn of Sevastopol was awarded the contract for carrying the mail from this city to Ellison Bay for four years. He bid $800 to make six 38-mile trips per week. John Spencer, the current contractor, has run the route for about eight years.

February 6, 1892 - Routing mail by rail from Green Bay to Menominee, Michigan and across the bay by horse and sleigh to Sturgeon Bay will cut five hours off the delivery time.

July 30, 1892 - A.S. Putnam of Evergreen has the contract to carry the Ephraim mail for $700 per year; Baumgartner Brothers have the contract for carrying the mail between Sturgeon Bay and Green Bay, but details couldn't be obtained.

✉

In 1873, a second newspaper in Sturgeon Bay began to publish under the editorship of George Pinney. The newspaper was called the *Expositor* and seemed to be opposed to any position the *Door County Advocate* took on an issue. Name-calling and mud-slinging of the lowest order went on in print for two years until the *Advocate* changed hands and editorially ended the quarrel. The *Expositor* became nicknamed the "Hurdy-Gurdy" and was always called by that name in the columns of the *Advocate*. A typical example of the *Advocate's* invective appeared in the November 6, 1873 issue and concerned an argument over mail routes:

> *We are constrained to admit that the truly good editor of the HurdyGurdy is an adept at misrepresenting facts. It may be owing to the bad associates by whom he is constantly surrounded, and whose bad example has warped a noble nature into such moral deformity as to make it resemble in shape, somewhat, the ungainly casket in which it is contained. The last number of our truly good man's sheet has a two-column article all about the mail between this place and Green Bay, Bailey's Harbor, Fish Creek and other places, which is as fine a piece of artistic lying as we have lately had the pleasure of reading. It goes on to give what it calls a rearrangement of the mail routes by which the Green Bay mail route is to be extended to Bailey's Harbor, the mail route to Egg Harbor, Fish Creek and Ephraim discontinued and a daily mail between this place and Green Bay rendered forever impossible. If true, it is, indeed, a dreary outlook. But fortunately it is untrue. It is true, however, that Mr. Moses Kilgore did make, and is now making, an effort to change the mail routes mentioned, in this way: To have a daily mail from*

Green Bay to this place; a tri-weekly mail from here to Bailey's Harbor, from there across to Egg Harbor, Fish Creek and Ephraim and back on the same route, making two routes in the place of the three now used, doubling the mail facilities between this place and Green Bay and adding one-third to the mail facilities now enjoyed by all points north of us. Whether Mr. Kilgore will succeed or not is unknown, but if he should it is presumed that the people will not complain much of this manner in which they have been robbed of their mail facilities. It is also true that Mr. Kilgore has an idea of bidding for the Green Bay mail contract, although he did not do it at the previous letting, the HurdyGurdy to the contrary notwithstanding, and if he should be successful in his bidding and obtain the contract, we also presume that the people would not grumble much thereat, for even the Hurdy-Gurdy says he 'is an excellent mail carrier,' although how it came to utter that truth is past our comprehension unless it was an error of the proof-reader.

Site of Sturgeon Bay post office, 1911-1927, at corner of Third and Michigan.

If the truly good man of the Hurdy-Gurdy, instead of 'looking forward to the time when we should have a daily mail to Green Bay,' would join hands with those who are working for that consummation instead of looking forward to it, he would be in a better frame of mind and be better prepared to free himself from the bad associations of his wicked companions.

The famous sixty-hour blizzard that stormed into Door County in the first week of March, 1881, was a disaster of the first magnitude. The *Door County Advocate* gave it extensive front-page coverage in the March 10, 1881 edition:

THE STORM KING

He Rages Violently for
Nearly Sixty Hours
Immense Snow Drifts Formed by
the Terrible Northeast
Every Avenue and Thorough-
fare Completely Blockaded
No Mails From Green Bay for
a Period of Ten Days

...Up to Tuesday evening, no mail had been received from Green Bay and points south of there since a week ago Saturday—a period of ten days. It is reported that the mail which left here for Green Bay last Wednesday had got as far as Frank Pierre's, where it still remained at last report...

The mail from Bailey's Harbor and Ahnapee has arrived twice—last Wednesday and Tuesday evenings.

It was confidently expected that a mail from Green Bay would arrive here Tuesday evening, but we have been disappointed in this respect, and there is no telling when it will get in now...

No mails from Ephraim, Fish Creek and Egg Harbor since the 25th of February—nearly two weeks...

The only mail received at this office from outside from the 26th of February to the 8th of March—a period of ten days—was the Kewaunee Enterprise of the 25th ult...

The non-arrival of the mails from south has caught our brewers without an adequate supply of [revenue] stamps, hence they came pretty near shutting down on furnishing the saloonists with the beverage...

William Cooper, who brought the mail over from Ahnapee on Tuesday, reports that the storm was still more severe over there than at this point. The northeast had a full sweep from the lake, which drifted the snow in a manner heretofore unknown...

Kilgore, the Bailey's Harbor mail contractor, managed to get through to this place with the mail last Wednesday p.m. He was soon followed by Capt. Harking, the Ahnapee carrier. Both stages left again Thursday morning...

The Ephraim mail finally arrived here from that and intermediate points last Thursday evening. It did not leave again until Saturday morning, and our friends up there were just two weeks without a mail.

The Green Bay mail finally got in here last Wednesday p.m. It had left the Bay Tuesday of the week before, and been lying over at Red River for a week. Thursday afternoon, another mail came in from the same place and since then everything in this line has been running with its customary regularity.

✉

In the winters of 1892-1993, he [Nicholas Arnold Wagner] was postmaster of the State Senate at Madison, Wisconsin, and in 1894 was appointed the postmaster of Sturgeon Bay (H.R. Holand, History of Door County, Wisconsin *II:173, 1917)*

✉

The *Door County Advocate* has continued its reporting of news about the Sturgeon Bay post office:

May 30, 1919 - After waiting three years, the Sturgeon Bay post office has received a modern canceling machine which cancels stamps and places the mailing date of the letters on the envelopes. it is a great improvement over the hand method used for so many years past.

October 28, 1927 - The Sturgeon Bay post office will be moved into the new Ogden building next Monday night so as to start operations there without interruption of service promptly at 8:00 Tuesday morning.

January 29, 1932 - An inspection by George Ridenbach determined that changing mail delivery in Sturgeon Bay from rural carriers to the city delivery system 'would be extravagant,' according to a report received by Postmaster Garland.

December 29, 1944 - Sturgeon Bay Postmaster J.C. Weitermann reports record postal receipts of $81,657.43 in 1944. There was also a record 38,053 cancellations on December 18 and a record 232,878 cancellations for the year.

A Sturgeon Bay mail carrier in winter, 1994.

December 24, 1969 - Rumblings in the press tell of projected changes in the U.S. postal system. Machines, they say, will engulf vast quantities of letters and parcels, sorting, routing and spewing them out to be swiftly whisked away to their destinations. But it would be unthink-

able to consider a machine doing all this at Christmas. Santa's proxies have many faces. No machine can equal the sights and sounds of your friendly neighborhood post office at this hectic season. (by Henry Shea)

December 21, 1972 - This Christmas season the Sturgeon Bay office will handle over 306,000 pieces of mail from December 1 through 23. Approximately 30,000 pieces per day pass through the post office. This is about three times the regular mail load. According to Postmaster Tachovsky, the total is up about three percent from last year.

...There is no automation at the Sturgeon Bay post office, so the estimated mail flow is determined by the number of canceled pieces and the metered postage machines used by businesses around town. A large percentage of mail that is canceled but not sorted goes by bulk load to the Sectional Center Facility (SCF) or the Area Mail Processing (AMP) center in Green Bay.

The Green Bay SCF gets all the daily mail left over from the one hundred area post offices... 'Door County mail, other than Sturgeon Bay mail, is often sent through AMP to centralize mail for speeding up the process through mechanization in order to reduce costs,' Tachovsky said...

The Sturgeon Bay post office complement of postal workers will be reduced this year from twenty-six to twenty-three...(by Linda Adams)

June 10, 1976 - From September 30, 1963 to March 14, 1966, the Sturgeon Bay post office, which was being enlarged and remodeled, did not have a postmaster. Wendell Fuller was in charge.

April 6, 1988 - it looked more like Christmas than the day after Easter at the Sturgeon Bay post office this Monday as customers formed long lines, waiting to purchase 3¢ stamps. The increase in first-class postage effective Sunday accounted for more than a doubling of business at the city's post office with Monday sales at almost $6,700. Regular daily revenue is between $2,000 and $3,000...There are nine big rural routes out of Sturgeon Bay...Sturgeon Bay is one of the largest city delivery offices in the Green Bay district. Only a few like Manitowoc, Marquette and Iron Mountain are larger. Sturgeon Bay employs twenty-one persons, fifteen carriers and six clerks in addition to nine rural substitute carriers, the assistant postmaster and the postmaster...

May 18, 1990 - Sturgeon Bay Postmaster Phil Hoslet announces that a new Customer Service Station (Station B) will open Monday (May 21) at the Piggly Wiggly store in the Cherry Point Mall. All domestic services except Express Mail and money orders will be offered. The new station is handicapped accessible...[Station B closed in the summer of 1992 when the Piggly Wiggly store went out of business].

October 6, 1992 - ...Five Postmen with combined experience, plus military time, totaling 125 years...worked their last day Friday [October 2, 1992 at the Sturgeon Bay post office] before taking the retirement window offered by the U.S. Postal Service. A national restructuring of the postal system meant retirement opportunities for Postmaster Phil Hoslet, Ralph Zirbel, Tom Fowles, Don Harding and Jerry Bauer...Retirement affected three of the other ten post offices in Door County. Amount the retirees are Wayne Rupiper of Washington Island, Pat Peterson at Ellison Bay and Evelyn Kerscher Abts at Brussels.

✉

The recollections of retired mail carriers, clerks and other postal people add important personal touches to the history of any post office. One such person was Walter Urdahl, who retired in 1968 after thirty-nine years as a mail carrier in Sturgeon Bay. A story about his career appeared in the *Door County Advocate* for September 5, 1968:

...During his career with the Postal Service, he walked more than 130,000 miles. His routes averaged from twelve to eighteen miles a day.

The reporter asked how many times he had been bit by a dog. 'Only four or so,' Urdahl said. Then he laughed, 'The last time it was a dog with no teeth.' Then there was a collie on Memorial Drive that was tied to a log and took after Urdahl at full tilt with log trailing behind. Urdahl escaped by the shoreline route.

He once made the wire services with a Herb Reynodls picture of a dog that followed him on his mail route. Urdahl recalls that the dog had no calendar and would wait in vain at the usual corner on Sundays. The dog even followed Urdahl to his desk at the post office, which the postmaster of that time did not appreciate.

When Urdahl started, Casey Gleasner told him that to be a real mailman, he had to have a cud of chewing tobacco in his mouth. The potent juice made Urdahl reel on this route.

Urdahl began his career in the Postal Service in 1929 as temporary employee. At that time Nat Garland was the postmaster at the Sturgeon Bay office and Arnold Langemak at the Sawyer post office.

For the last three years, since the retirement of Elmer Fidler, Urdahl was the carrier on the city route that includes the east side business section. However, during his years of service, he has at different times carried every city letter route. Following the consolidation of the Sawyer and Sturgeon Bay post offices on April 30, 1938, he was the first city carrier on the west side operating out of the present Sturgeon Bay office.

At that time the city had only three letter routes, one on the west side and two on the east side. Presently, there are five letter routes and a combination route with one and a half letter routes on the west side and three and one-half on the east side. The combination route includes parcel post delivery and small parts of both the east side and west side for letter delivery.

While in Postal Service, Urdahl served for ten years as president of the National Association of Letter Carriers, Branch 3035...

The late Arden Robertson served the Sawyer and Sturgeon Bay post offices for 43 years prior to his retirement in 1973. He wrote about life around the post offices at Christmas time in the 1930s that

...Extra funds were given postmasters to hire extra seasonal help during the Christmas rush, usually college boys home on vacation and happy to earn the extra money.

Mail usually arrived during business hours. When the train whistled, everyone heard it and came rushing to the post office to wait for their mail. The windows were closed so that all employees could help distribute the incoming mail to the proper sections and the rural carriers. This would take about one hour.

Pictorial envelope used in 1904.

By then the lobby was jammed. Everyone knew one another so one could hear local gossip and about the gifts that were being ordered to be sent through the mail. When the windows opened, clerks were busy selling stamps, handing out mail and weighing parcels on an old-fashioned scale while looking up the zone and figuring out the cost. There was no modern equipment like postal meters or computing scales...

Postal employees were busy waiting on patrons during the day, leaving little time for hand canceling letters and cards and stamping parcels so during the Christmas rush this often had to be done after closing hours with the work continuing until midnight to get caught up with the outgoing mail deposited at the post office and brought in by the rural carriers in time for the early morning dispatch.

Mail was dispatched according to train lines and dispatching clerks had to know the location of all the offices in the state to make correct connections and avoid delay. Bags of parcel post and first class mail had to be locked and could only be opened with a special key at the post office or the railway mail car...

*Christmas is still a busy time at the post office even if it seems much of the old time Christmas spirit has given way to the commercial aspect. Old-timers can remember what a thrill it was for both young and old alike when Santa arrived on the train, opened the mail car door and stepped out onto the depot platform. (*Door County Advocate, *December 17, 1981)*

Weathered faces of eight men peer down from a wall at the Sturgeon Bay post office...Posted in 1938,...they...are the work of Santos Zingale who, after the Depression, was a Milwaukee artist on relief.

It was the era of FDR's Works Progress Administration as part of his New Deal. Fine arts were placed in the category of The Section whereby artists competed to create murals and sculpture for new federal buildings...In the four years that The Section was in effect, 2,200 projects were commissioned. About 500 of those are murals in midwestern post offices.

The plan was to bring fine art to small towns, to illustrate an American theme along either national or local lines or show an era of postal history.

Zingale won the commission to paint 'The Fruits of Sturgeon Bay' in his Milwaukee studio. The fishermen in the mural depict the bustling commercial fishing trade that still occupies a noble share of Door County residents... (Cheri Harris in the Door County Advocate, *December 21, 1984)*

The painting was cleaned and restored in 1984 by Anton Rajer.

Sturgeon Bay Postmasters and Dates of Their Appointments

- Robert Graham - October 22, 1855
- David C. McIntosh - October 11, 1858
- David A. Reed - March 24, 1862
- William K. Dresser - May 30, 1862
- Gustav A. Dreutzer - March 17, 1876
- Chris Daniels - February 28, 1879
- Gustav A. Dreutzer - March 11, 1879
- Gideon W. Allen - January 20, 1887
- Joseph Harris, Jr. - March 20, 1890
- Arnold Wagener - April 5, 1894
- FitzJames Hamilton - November 1, 1898
- Edward S. Minor - March 11, 1911
- Hubert A. Wagener - August 14, 1915
- Nathaniel C. Garland - February 24, 1927
- Harry R. Jones - August 16, 1935
- John C. Weitermann - March 16, 1942
- Francis J. Tachovsky - March 25, 1966
- Elmer W. Tilque - May 21, 1977
- Phillip R. Hoslet - July 30, 1988
- J. Kenneth Liebert - October 3, 1992
- Kenneth Chriske - February 22, 1993

Postmasters' Annual Salaries

1860-61	David McIntosh	$ 81.98
1864-65	William Dresser	$ 195.61
1871	William Dresser	$ 380.00
1873	William Dresser	$ 490.00
1877	Gustav Dreutzer	$ 906.80
1879	Gustav Dreutzer	$ 679.88
1883	Gustav Dreutzer	$1,100.00
1885	Gustav Dreutzer	$1,100.00
1887	Gideon Allen	$1,000.00
1889	Gideon Allen	$1,000.00
1891	Joseph Harris	$1,100.00

Tornado
see Williamsonville

Burning of the Tornado post office, 1974.

Burning of the Tornado post office, 1974.

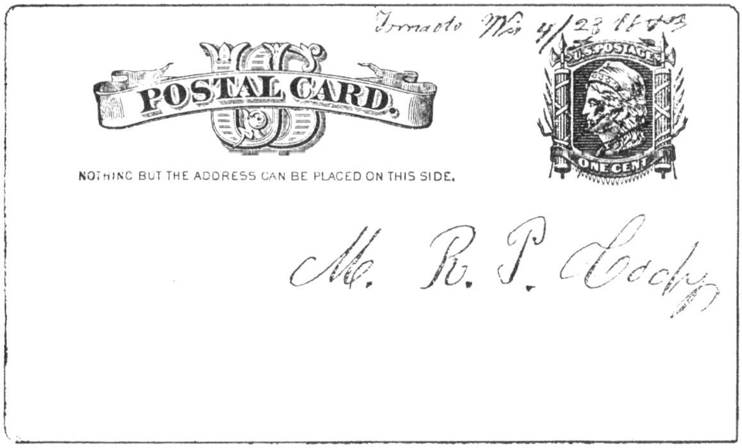

Message on back of card dated 1883.

WILLIAMSONVILLE
TORNADO

SEC. 1,2 - T26N R24E - TOWN OF BRUSSELS
SEC. 35,36 - T27N R24E - TOWN OF GARDNER

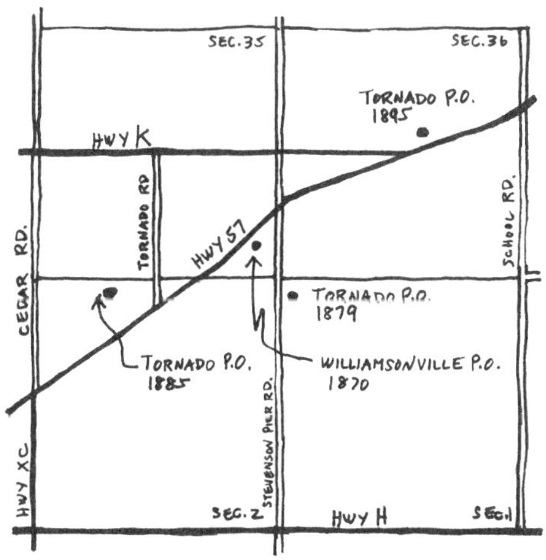

Valmy

Established July 1, 1899.

Discontinued December 31, 1903, with mail service at Institute.

This office was located in the present community of the same name on State Highway 57 in the Town of Sevastopol (the southeast quarter, section 7, Town 28 North, Range 27 East).

The source of the name has not been confirmed. Possibly it is connected with the Battle of Valmy, France, in 1792. In this decisive conflict, the Prussian Army withdrew from the French Army, an action that prevented the Prussians from advancing on Paris to put down the French Revolution.

In 1899, the proposed post office was estimated by Postmaster-to-be Ella Simon to serve "about 300 people in county and village."

✉

Valmy Postmasters and Dates of Their Appointments
Ella Simon - July 1, 1899
John Bunda - September 26, 1900

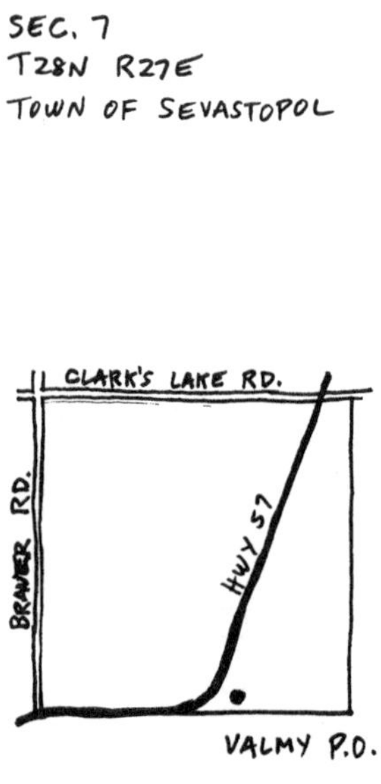

Vignes

Established November 10, 1891.

Discontinued January 30, 1904, with mail service at Sawyer.

Location: At the southwest corner of the intersection of the present County Highway OO and Shiloh Road in the southeast quarter, section 17, Town 26 North, Range 26 East, Town of Clay Banks.

The origin of the name "Vignes" was determined in a letter from the Reverend Phillip A. Fretheim, Pastor of the Tanum-Forest Evangelical Lutheran Congregation at Vignes to J.B. Hale in 1977. He wrote that "everyone contacted is quite sure the name of Vignes is of Norwegian origin. No one is quite sure as to why, but it is believed that it was a place or name. Upon looking at a map of Norway, we found a place called Vigdenes - could possibly be named after this. In translating Vignes, we find Vig - meaning inlet, creek, entrance, etc. - and Nes - meaning head land, flat land, landing place. Vignes is located about one and one-half miles from Lake Michigan on the flat land above the rolling area between the lake and the flatter country side. Of course, we have no idea if this had any bearing on it or not. Also, the little creek that winds near Vignes does come out in the lake near where one of the first settlements was (Clay Banks)...Most of the first settlers in this area were from Norway, many from the Valders area of Norway."

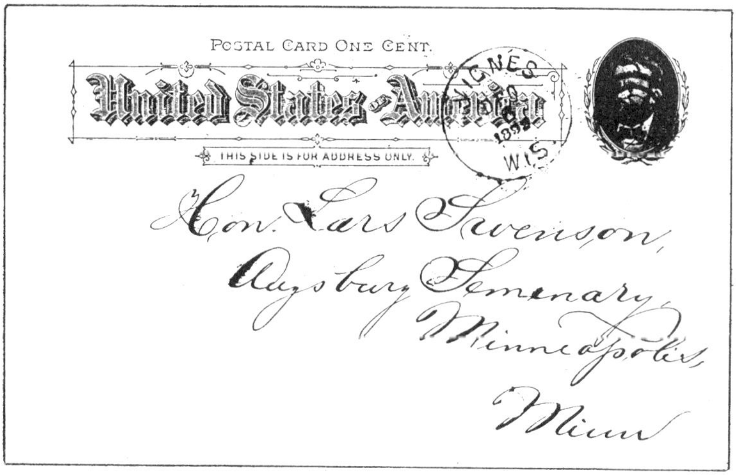

1892.

When Mathias Nygard applied for his postmaster position in 1891, he stated that the population to be served by the proposed Vignes office was "about 200 people."

Vignes Postmasters and Dates of Their Appointments

- Mathias Nygard - November 10, 1891
- Wenzel Jirtle - July 30, 1894
- William Birdsall - September 27, 1894
- Mathias Nygard - May 4, 1895
- Paul E. Kampine - May 9, 1898
- Ole H. Roalkram - January 4, 1899
- Ole C. Rye - August 17, 1901

VIGNES

SEC. 17
T26N R26E
TOWN OF CLAY BANKS

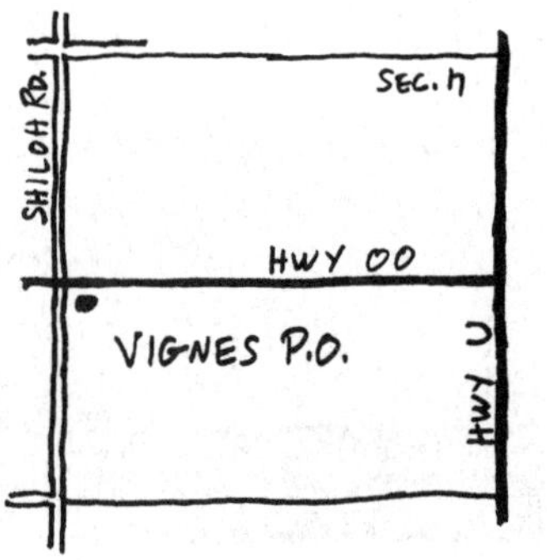

Voseville

Established September 27, 1881.

Discontinued October 31, 1902, with mail service at Sturgeon Bay.

Voseville post office had three sites in Town 28 North, Range 27 East, Town of Sevastopol. The first was in the northeast quarter of section 18 from 1881 to 1883, and the second was in the northwest quarter of section 18 from 1883 to 1896, both of which were at the village of Valmy. In 1896, the post office was moved two and a half miles east to Whitefish Bay where the office was located about a block from Lake Michigan on Whitefish Bay Road in the northeast quarter of section 16.

Voseville was named for its first postmaster, although its locations were at Valmy and Whitefish Bay, which were names used from the beginnings of settlement.

In 1881, the name "Whitefish Bay" for the proposed post office was denied by the Post Office Department. The population to be served at that time was estimated at 200; but in 1883 the estimate had risen to "about 400."

✉

The *Door County Democrat* noted unhappiness with the location of the Voseville post office:

November 7, 1896 - Thos. Vose having resigned the office of postmaster at Voseville, it has been moved two miles east to the lake shore, and Chas. Mashek appointed postmaster. The change makes it more convenient for the people in the extreme eastern part of the county, but is somewhat of an inconvenience to the farmers in the vicinity of Institute and in the neighborhood of where the office was formerly. An effort was made to have the office remain in the same locality, but it failed. The Baileys Harbor

Voseville post office site at Valmy prior to 1896 (1991 photo).

Voseville post office site at Whitefish Bay, 1896-1902 (1991 photo).

stage will have a several miles longer route now and will no doubt be entitled to considerable of an increase in pay. Mr. Vose resigned the office because the mortgage on his farm has been foreclosed and he has been obliged to move therefrom.

November 21, 1896 - The new location of the Voseville post office, being so far off the main stage route line, it is said that the department may find it necessary to establish a 'side line' to supply the office. Our subscribers complain of the change on the grounds that the present location is inconvenient to them as compared to the former location. Many farmers in the vicinity of Voseville would like to see Mr. Mashek move his store and the office part of his business to a point on the old Thomas Vose farm. It would make the store a convenient trading place for a large additional number of farmers, and be a benefit all around.

✉

Voseville Postmasters and Dates of Their Appointments

Thomas Vose - September 27, 1881
Thomas V. McCullough - September 4, 1883
Thomas Vose - December 7, 1883
Charles V. Mashek - October 24, 1896
Mathias Peffer - September 18, 1897

Annual Salaries of Thomas Vose as Postmaster

1883	$ 64.30
1885	$ 91.02
1887	$102.87
1889	$ 98.81
1891	$ 87.12

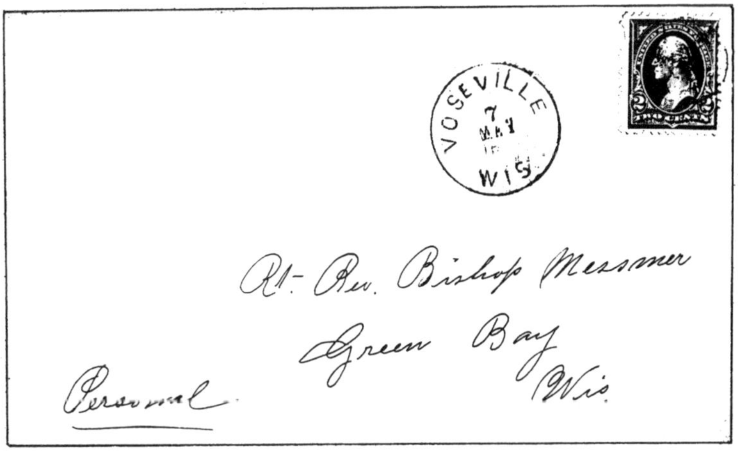

Backstamped 1896.

VOSEVILLE

SEC. 16, 17, 18
TOWN OF SEVASTOPOL
T28N R27E

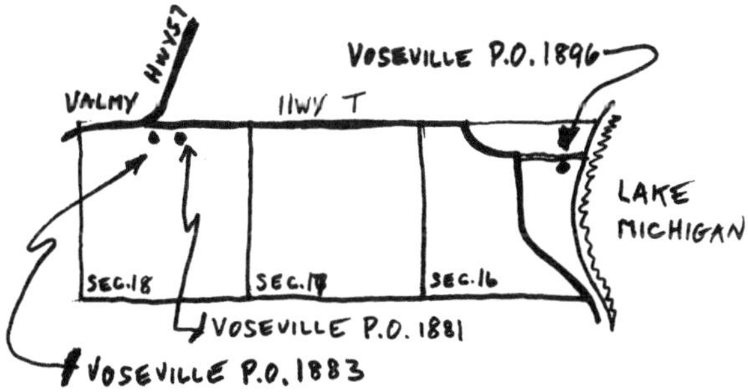

Warren's Corners/Horn's Pier/Cheeseville

Established as "Warren's Corners" on August 11, 1871.

Discontinued on May 28, 1872, but reestablished on June 17, 1872. Warren's Corners was located in the northeast quarter of section 5, Town 26 North, Range 26 East, Town of Clay Banks.

On June 17, 1878, the name was changed to Horn's Pier and moved to the Lake Michigan shore at the end of what is today Hornspier Road in the northwest quarter of section 3 in the same township.

On August 11, 1886, the name again was changed, this time to Cheeseville, and the location of the office moved to McDermott's store at Madosh's Corners, which was at the intersection of what is at present County Highway U and Salona Road. This site was in the southeast quarter of the southeast quarter of section 5, Town 26 North, Range 26 East, Town of Clay Banks, about two miles west of Horn's Pier.

Cheeseville post office was discontinued on August 4, 1893, with mail service at Salona. The Salona post office (q.v.) at that time was located at the former site of Warren's Corners post office. William H. Warren was the first postmaster at both Warren's Corners and Salona.

Warren's Corners was named after the first postmaster. Horn's Pier was named after the business and industrial complex on the Lake Michigan shore owned by William H. Horn. He and his partner, a Mr. Joseph, also owned piers at St. Joseph (Lily Bay) and Whitefish Bay. Cheeseville was named because of its location next to a cheese factory; the office itself was in McDermott's store.

> *A new post office has been established at Mr. W. H. Warren's place on the Clay Banks road, about half way between this place and the Clay Banks post office. The name of the new office is Warren's Corner and Mr. Warren has been appointed postmaster.* (Door County Advocate, *August 24, 1871)*

On June 13, 1872, the *Advocate* reported that "the post office at Warren's Corners has been discontinued, Mr. Warren having sent in his resignation and no one appointed in his place." This state of affairs did not last long; a new postmaster, J.L. Phillips, was appointed on June 17, 1872.

✉

> *In the northeastern corner of the town (of Clay Banks), at a place now hard to find as it is buried in swamps and sand drifts, was Horns Pier. W.H. Horn of Manitowoc located here in 1864 and built a very long pier in 1866. Two thousand cords of wood could be stored on it. In September, 1871, the pier, warehouse,*

store and other buildings were destroyed by a forest fire which did great damage in the town of Clay Banks. It was, however, rebuilt at once and did a very big business, shipping about two cargoes of forest products daily. It was a regular stopping place for the lake steamers that plied between Chicago and Buffalo. According to published reports in the Door County Advocate in January, 1873, there was shipped from this pier during the preceding year 100,000 cedar posts, 10,000 railroad ties, 5,000 cords of wood, 1,000 cords of hemlock bark and 5,000 telegraph poles.

William H. Horn...came from Manitowoc where he had considerable property. He was a keen man, rather too sharp in business dealings...In company with a Mr. Joseph, he also built a large pier a few miles north of the canal...The village that grew up there was called by them St. Joseph [Lily Bay, q.v.]. When the people of Sturgeon Bay and the northern towns were unable to get the telegraph line extended beyond Sturgeon Bay, Horn & Joseph personally extended it from Horn's Pier to St. Joseph, Whitefish Bay, Jacksonport, and Baileys Harbor, at all of which points they installed operators. When the timber cutting came to an end in the latter '80s, Foscoro, Clay Banks, Horn's Pier and St. Joseph ceased to be shipping points and W.H. Horn moved to other parts. (H.R. Holand, History of Door County, Wisconsin *I:442–443, 1917)*

Mr. Horn apparently returned to Manitowoc or Chicago, as the *Door County Advocate* of May 8, 1891, mentioned that he had recently purchased several pieces of property in Chicago and ventured into lumbering and shingle-making in Menominee County, Michigan.

In the *Advocate* for September 9, 1886, it was noted that "The post office at Horn's Pier has been removed to Madosh's corners." This was the new Cheeseville post office location in McDermott's store.

✉

Being burned out didn't discourage W.H. Horn of Clay Banks from rebuilding his extensive holdings. Having lost his new store, saloon and a log shanty the last week in September (1871), Horn was gamely planning on opening soon a new saloon and store. The Advocate noted that his losses came to something like $10,000 and congratulated the doughty businessman for his unshaken faith in the future. (Keta Steebs in the Door County Advocate, *September 28, 1971)*

✉

Populations estimated to be served by the proposed post offices:

Warren's Corners in 1871 - "65 families"
Horn's Pier in 1878 - "about 500"
Cheeseville in 1886 - "about 200"

Postmaster and Dates of Their Appointments

Warren's Corners:

William H. Warren - August 11, 1871
Jared L. Phillips - June 17, 1872
Julius Warren - January 31, 1876

Horn's Pier:

William H. Horn - June 17, 1878

Cheeseville:

Francis McDermott - August 11, 1886

Postmasters' Annual Salaries

Warren's Corners:		
1871	William Warrent	$ 12.00
1873	Jared Phillips	$ 12.00
1877	Julius Warren	$130.24
Horn's Pier:		
1879	William H. Horn	$ 71.60
1883	William H. Horn	$130.19
1885	William H. Horn	$ 51.55
Cheeseville:		
1887	Francis McDermott	$ 38.33
1889	Francis McDermott	$ 45.01
1891	Francis McDermott	$ 37.51

SALONA
WARREN'S CORNERS
HORN'S PIER
CHEESEVILLE

SEC. 3, 4, 5
T26N R26E
TOWN OF CLAY BANKS

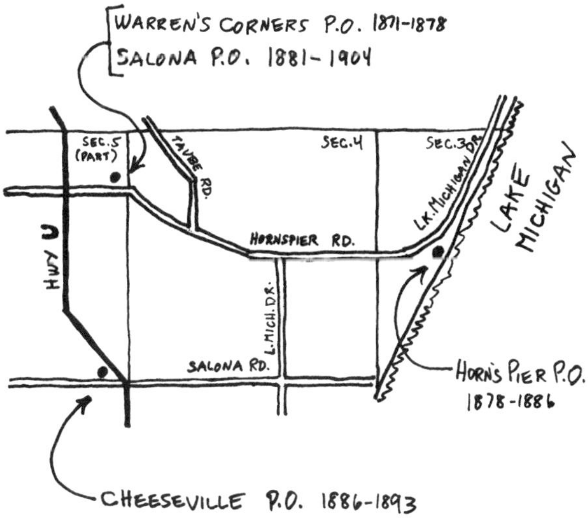

Washington Harbor

Established June 22, 1854.

Discontinued January 31, 1916, with mail service at Detroit Harbor.

Location: At the north end of Washington Island on the Lake Michigan harbor of the same name. The office had at least three sites in sections 25 and 26, Town 34 North, Range 29 East, Town of Washington.

In 1816, the U.S. Government sent several ship-loads of troops and provisions from Mackinac Island, Michigan, to Green Bay to establish a military post. The command ship was the schooner *George Washington.* During the trip the vessels became separated and the *George Washington* put into what is now Washington Harbor for two days to wait for the others. The officers, supposing their vessel to be the first to enter the harbor, gave her name to it and later to all of Washington Island. Thus, despite published comments to the contrary, Washington Island (and Washington Harbor) were only indirectly named after President George Washington.

✉

Henry D. Minor stated in his 1869 site report to the U.S. Post Office Department that "We get mail from Green Bay, ninety miles, weekly in summer, seven months, on Buffalo and Green Bay Propellers, 50¢ a mail. We get mail twice a month in winter from Ephraim, twenty-six miles, $6 to $10 each mail."

Backstamped 1888.

✉

Henry D. Miner, who settled on Washington Island in 1844, became a legend for the many years he spent risking his life to bring mail and supplies to the island before the government established a regular postal service. H.R. Holand told his story:

...He was an eccentric man of deep religious convictions, with a most bur-

densome outfit of rules, precepts, habits and other ironclad regulations of life and daily conduct...Mr. Miner was a man of sterling qualities who had braved the dangers of the ice in the service of his fellowmen more than any other man in the county. Two or three others in the early days attempted to carry the mail and lost their lives in their first or second attempt, but H.D. Miner for thirteen years successfully carried the mail between Green Bay and Washington Island. This is a distance of one hundred long miles and was usually covered in three days as follows: The first day from Washington Harbor to Ephraim; the second from Ephraim to Robert Stephenson's at Little Sturgeon Bay; the third day from Stephenson's to Green Bay. The fourth day was spent in making the necessary purchases and then followed the home run with a loaded pack sled. Time after time and year after year this dauntless mail carrier used to push through his perilous journey of 200 miles on the ice...Mr. Miner was not inclined, however, to boast of his experiences on the ice and we have but meager glimpses of his hardships. He was once asked to give an account of his hardest trip and this account is given below. It is but a bald and terse report, however, of his experience, and it is only between lines that we catch a glimpse of the dreary loneliness of the ice, the paralyzing fatigue, the bitter cold and the intrepid spirit that conquered in this heroic adventure.

In the winter of 1856, William Nolan came to me with $20 to pay for a trip to Green Bay for the mail. The following Monday morning I started at 4:00 with the temperature at twenty-three below zero (it was a very cold winter). I took a lunch of plenty of fat pork and molasses as I had found fats and sweets indispensable in a long journey on the ice. I reached Ole Larson's house near Ephraim at 4:00 in the afternoon. The next day I reached Bob Stephenson's at Little Sturgeon and on the third day I made Green Bay. The next day, Thursday, it blew a gale and snowed heavily. During the day I picked up at various stores quite a large sleigh load of calicoes, muslins, fishhooks, tobacco and other things. I also got the accumulated mail for three months for the island, including some very old papers. I also bought a few new ones so as to try to catch up a little with the times. Friday morning it was cold and clear with the wind from the north cutting like a razor. It was thirty degrees below zero and my friends in Green Bay urged me to stop as they did not think it was possible to endure the extremely cold weather. But as I was anxious to reach Ephraim by Saturday night—the only place in the county where they had religious service—I started out at 6:00 a.m. By 10:00, I wanted a lunch but the cold was so great I did not dare sit down to eat but nibbled a little as I walked on. I had planned to reach Sherwood's at Sawyer Harbor but by noon I saw that I would be fortunate if I could reach Stephenson's. At 4:00 I took *another lunch which braced me up. I had been ten hours on the ice, pulling a heavily loaded sled against the wind and my knees were aching and trembling. I saw that it would be impossible for me to reach Stephenson's that day but I had heard of a Belgian family which had moved in the fall before. I therefore turned in toward the shore to hunt them up. The snow was deep here and soon I stumbled and fell. I was so completely exhausted and sleepy that I was not able to get up. However, I crawled up and lay across the sled and began to kick and claw in the snow until I was able to get up. I now dragged along for a long time until it got dark, when I again fell down. The wind still blew but it seemed now like something soft and gentle cooing me to sleep and I wanted to shut my eyes and rest forever. Far away, however, I saw a light flash up and I staggered to my feet and made for the light. When I reached the place I found the inmates engaged in a fierce quarrel and they would not let me in. Two young men, however, took my sled and accompanied me through the woods to another Belgian family. It was a very small hut, just erected, but they received me very kindly and in a few minutes, after a grand supper of bear meat, I lay on the floor sound asleep. Three days later I was back in Washington Harbor with my sleigh load of calicoes. (*History of Door County, Wisconsin *I:287-290, 1917)*

For many years quite as much of Door County's history was enacted on the water as on land...The passage through the Door was particularly dreaded...I have before me the diary of the lighthouse keeper of Pilot Island from 1872 to 1889. It appears from the entries in this journal that their daily diet consisted of winds and roaring seas with a shipwreck at least twice a week...Frequently the keeper or one of his assistants leaves the station to get the mail from Washington Harbor and is unable to return for three weeks. (H.R. Holand, History of Door County, Wisconsin *I:254, 1917)*

During the period between 1871 and 1940, in the winter, mail was carried (as well as supplied) to and from the mainland on the ice... We have records of Jessie Miner carrying mail to and from Ellison Bay in 1873 and 1874. He walked, and where the ice was smooth, he skated, sometimes with thirty pounds of mail and books on his back...Mail delivery was once or twice a month, December to May, and in summer by steamboat once a week from Green Bay. This was from May to November (Mary C. Richter in Washington Island Insights, *p. 30, 1988)*

The story of Henry Miner has been touched upon by almost everyone who has written about the history of Washington Island. Anne Whitney had this to say about him:

What finally became a Saga is the story of how some of the women on St. Martins Island chided their men about letting an old man do what they could do themselves. One of the men said she should not worry, because Mr. Miner was an exceptional man and could walk on water. Mr. Miner was let in on the conspiracy and made to promise not to tell on them.

So one day the men called to the women, 'The mail is in.' As she stood in the doorway watching the mailman approach, very definitely walking on the water, she exclaimed in an awed voice, 'If I hadn't seen it with my own eyes, I never would have believed it.' He was justified, for it was spring and the weather was promoting a thaw.

Henry H. Miner carried the mail until he entered the [Civil] War, where he served for nearly two years, returning to take up his regular work at his cooperage and to carry the mail...

The old Miner home still stands with its 'lean-to' Post Office (leaning greatly with age) and the little half window where the fortunate ones were handed their mail with orders to 'mind you don't fall off the path into my good moss rose.' For years the good people of Washington Island enquired concerning the condition of that pet rose...

When Henry Miner bought land for his home with the Post Office, the land was purchased in three parcels. But when the house was finished it was found to sit 'plum' on the line of the piece he had not purchased, so the third parcel had to be invested in order to make the home legally his. An unusual proceeding in the early days. (Let's Talk About Washington Island *1850-1950, pp. 30-31, 1973)*

1909.

✉

Henry Miner's son, Jesse, succeeded his father as a Washington Harbor mail carrier. His career was in the harrowing style of his father. One of Jesse's acquaintances, Charley Noble, wrote about him in the *Door County Advocate* of June 18, 1973:

Jesse Miner was the first mail carrier Door County ever had. In 1911 he used to fascinate me with stories of his exploits. He was also a great practical joker. He carried the mail from Green Bay to Saint Martin's Island, for there were more settlers on Saint Martin's than on Washington Island at that time.

When I first knew him in 1911, he must have been over seventy-five, so a little subtracting will show what years he was working. He made the trip with a horse, riding sometimes if the mail was light, and by dog sled in the winter, and always said as we still do now, 'We don't have any winters now like we did years ago.'

...Mr. Minor only carried first class mail, and from the area he covered there were not many people who could either write, or didn't write.

At one time he told me about a harrowing experience he had with wolves. In the winter he and his dog team would stop wherever darkness overtook him. This was a particularly hard winter, so he stopped early that night. He built a lean-to so as to catch the reflected heat of the fire, and as soon as it got dark the wolves were tearing at the pine branches trying to get in. He couldn't tell if they were after him or the dogs, but he said he was not anxious to find out.

The dogs were cowering between his feet, and the wolves were getting bolder all the time, so he took a snow shoe and scooped live coals at them. He said that kept them at bay for awhile, but it did not allow him any time to sleep. He said that was hell on the snow shoe, and he had to make the trip without any, for you can't flounder around in deep snow with only one. His guests departed with daylight, when he could have got a shot at them, for he carried a musket also, an old smooth bore.

One round trip a week, thinks of it, Green Bay to Saint Martin's Island. He had a small sailboat with a center-board, and two runners, so when the ice was bad in the spring and not solid enough to hold his weight, he would sail when he could, and then drag the small boat up on the ice and pull it until the next patch of open water.

✉

Water is fickle and its idiosyncrasies need watching with an appraising eye before attempting the risky. On St. Patrick's Day of 1914, the mail came over in a motor boat. But there were others who wanted to reach the mainland, so kept their eyes on the weather signs...Not so many years ago, Claude (son of J.W.) Cornell walked over on the 17th of April. One could (perhaps) have walked over on the 17th of April, 1950, for a Centennial Attraction, except that on the 15th a thaw made it unattractive. (Whitney, Let's Talk About Washington Island *1850-1950, p. 33, 1973)*

✉

According to some of Jesse Miner's writings, the first two U.S. mail carriers across the Door were a Mr. Larson from Ephraim and H.D. Miner from Washington Island. This route was established in the year 1869. I provided for two trips a month, beginning in November to April 1st, and once a week during the summer months.

The mail had been carried for many years by Washington Island men, going to Green Bay and carrying it back to the island. This was paid for by the islanders donating what each could afford. This generally had to amount to $20 or more a month...

Henry Miner was one of these early mail carriers in the 1850s. He tells of Patsy Flanagan and Joseph Folwell, who were carrying mail from Ephraim to Washington Harbor. This was the winter of 1865. The mail was now coming by way of Ephraim. These two men were coming across the Door on floating ice, but managed to make a landing on Plum Island. If they had not made the island, they would have drifted right out into Lake Michigan.

No one was living on Plum Island at the time, and they had no lunch with them. They had to live on basswood buds for two or three days before they could safely get away. Patsy said he would never carry the mail again—not even if he got a hundred dollars a trip. He lost his appetite for basswood buds. (R. McDonald, Four Islands: A History of Detroit, Rock, St. Martin's and Washington Islands, *pp. 144-145, 1984)*

The major historian of Washington Island, Conan Bryant Eaton, included much information about the Island's postal service in his series of Island histories. The following writings about the early days of the Washington Harbor post office are from his book *Washington Island: 1836-1876*, published in 1972:

1854. People coming down from Green Bay in the spring of 1854 said a new political party had been started in Ripon; they were calling it Republican. More important - Door County's first post office was about to be established at Washington Harbor, with W. P. Ranney the probable postmaster. The Green Bay Advocate's editor saw this as a great convenience to the six or eight hundred persons living on Washington, St. Martin and Summer Islands and part of the neighboring peninsula, all heretofore 'completely isolated in winter, and in summer wholly dependent upon chance opportunities for communication...'

In October, Advocate correspondent M.E. Lyman...had gained the postmastership in place of Ranny...A week later this item appeared: 'P.M. at WASHINGTON HARBOR. - We learn that Mr. J.M. CRAW has been appointed Post Master...Vice M.E. LYMAN removed. Mr. CRAW is a straight forward business man and will unquestionably make a first rate officer.' Around Washington

Harbor in 1854 only change was certain.

1855. November found Sturgeon Bay about to get a post office, with Robert Graham post master. Island pioneers like John Boon and Henry Miner read it with interest. Graham and his Cuban-born wife, Josephine, had been their neighbors on Rock Island back in the mid-forties. The Green Bay paper hoped the government would soon establish a weekly route through Sturgeon Bay to Washington Harbor, 'a service much needed to accommodate a large, intelligent and enterprising class of citizens.'

1856. The winter was fearfully cold, the closed season for shipping interminable. For three months the island had no fresh supplies and no mail. Then Henry Miner took up William Nolan's offer of twenty dollars for a trip to Green Bay and back. After eight days spent mostly on ice battling snow, wind and cold down to thirty below, (and having pitted his life against the weather's worst fury to reach Ephraim in time for Sabbath religious services), Miner dragged his sleigh load of mail, newspapers, calicoes, bleached muslin and baby flannel, fishhooks and lines, jackknives and sundries into the Harbor...Jessee Miner once asked his father to name his hardest trip carrying the mail; Henry told him this 1856 trip 'stands alone in my memory never to be forgot.'

1857. In July, Michael Kalmbach took over the post office from J.M. Craw.

1859. In October, William Nolan succeeded Kalmbach as postmaster, becoming thereby the clearing-house for community news.

1862. The Sturgeon Bay paper kept close watch on events affecting the islands. The Wisconsin legislature, it was reported, was asking congress to extend the mail route from Green Bay through the county seat to Washington Island.

1866. Early in 1866 the Post Office Department advertised for offers to carry the mail between Ephraim and Washington Harbor monthly from November first to April thirtieth. Meanwhile, Martin (Ole) Oleson left the Island with mail on March eighth, started back from Eagle Harbor the same day, and was never heard from again. It was supposed he fell through a crack in the ice and drowned...Miner...tells us: 'The only mail carrier drowned carrying the mail was Martin Oleson who was lost in the winter of sixty-five and six carrying the mail across the Door...' J.J. Lobdell took over as postmaster.

1867. The [Door County] Advocate reported in January: 'Mr. D.E. Ranney has been appointed Postmaster at Washington Harbor in place of Mr. J.J. Lobdell, who failed to send his bond to the Post Office Department.' (By late May, the job had passed to Hiram A. Knowlton)

War Veteran Henry Miner came back from Illinois with his family and built a small cottage above the Harbor's southeast shore. It was natural that the post-

master's job (its accounts badly tangled-up by three incumbency changes within the year) should seek him out. With the annual salary now stabilized at ten dollars, people hoped things would be set for a while. No government provision was made for carrying the mail in winter; Islanders naturally looked again to Miner for that, especially for a trip before Christmas.

On the twenty-first, Miner borrowed an old canvas-patched lighthouse boat and left Detroit Harbor for Ephraim with a northeast snowstorm gathering force. By Christmas morning he was still unheard from. Then seventeen-year-old Jesse, skating on Washington Harbor's two-nights' ice, saw in the distance the flapping ear laps on his father's fox-skin cap. Henry was drawing a borrowed hand sled loaded with mail.

Someone shouted 'Here's the December mail...three cheers for Miner!' Before Henry reached the post office half the mail was handed out and on its way about the Island...In recounting these pioneer trips with the mail, Jesse generally gives his father (and sometimes himself) generous credit; considering the fearful difficulties and dangers (and the miserable recompense), no amount of credit would seem sufficient.

1869. On November 2, Jesse Miner accompanied his father on the first mail-carrying trip paid for by the federal government; and suddenly the days were past in which Islanders chipped in a dollar or so a winter for the carrier. Henceforth, the mail would move twice a month to Ephraim by carrier in winter and spring, weekly to Green Bay by steamboat in summer and fall...

1871. Postmaster (and carrier) Henry Miner was asked by some Island smokers and chewers to replenish their tobacco stock on this next trip with mail. Miner's strict moral scruples made him refuse. Son Jesse carried freight for six cents a pound, he said; they could deal with him. On Henry's next trip to Ephraim he found over one hundred pounds of tobacco in the mail. The addressees paid the government sixteen cents a pound in postage; the well-burdened mail-carrier earned not an extra penny for hauling it fifty-two miles on the ice.

1875. In early February a spirit thermometer on the Island indicated forty and one-half degrees below zero, which may have suggested second thoughts to Goodlet Goodletson. The veteran of both army and navy service in the Civil War (and former town treasurer) had just won the U.S. mail-carrying contract; for $109 he was now obliged to carry mail twice a month from Ellison's Bay to Washington Harbor, December to April.

...Just before Christmas, Henry Miner relinquished the postmaster's job (after eight years) to John Furlong (though both Henry and Jesse went on carrying the winter mail on occasion). The office moved from Miner's cottage above the south-

east shore of the Harbor to Furlong's dock on the west.

1876. Robert Severs may be one of the town's early residents most unjustly ignored in local history. Born in England in 1826, he came to America in '51 and to the islands in '52...Elected Town Clerk in 1875, he was the incumbent at his death in 1901 (having several time been assessor also). From December, 1877 to his death, he was Washington Harbor's postmaster...Described as a small, long-bearded man, 'proud as a peacock,' who often wore a swallow-tail coat, Severs was for the time and place a man of uncommon education and culture.

⊠

In 1988, Mr. Eaton added more about the later years of Washington Harbor's post office:

Already serving as town clerk and correspondent to the Door County Advocate (in 1878), Severs had recently written: 'Our veteran mail carrier cannot always on mail days cross the blasted gulf that separates us from the rest of the country.' (It should be mentioned that sporadic mail service was felt beyond the Town of Washington. A Washington Harbor Advocate column at this time reports: 'Eight men came over from St. Martin's Island today to get their mail.') By January, 1880, postmaster Severs still grumbled to the Advocate: 'Nothing but a balloon can cross the door...Hope you will receive this before dog days.'

...By mid-July the next year (1882), Washington Harbor's Severs was reporting: 'Two mails a week now.' In November he wondered in print whether fourth class offices would ever be permitted to issue postal notes. 'Every day people are trying to scare up a one or a two-dollar bill for remittance, and often...have to remit postage stamps.' Two months later service to the island had sagged to one mail a week. Still, Severs could recall, 'in days of yore we did well when we had one or two mails in winter and had to send to Green Bay through the wilderness.'

Mid-1887 saw Joseph Cornell contracting to carry mail between the Island and Ellison's Bay, one round trip weekly, for the next four years at $150 a year. John Nelson, described by Severs as ' the present faithful and efficient carrier,' had received $175, and declined to work for less. (The contractor who stood as middleman between the postal service and the local carriers lived in Missouri.)

March of 1889 saw the route shortened, with mail from Hedgehog Harbor instead of Ellison's Bay. Incoming mail now reached the Island earlier in the day, but outgoing lay at Hedgehog three days, taking a week to reach Sturgeon Bay from Washington Harbor...

In mid-April of 1904, the outside carrier is reported to have crossed Death's Door for several days past in his 'gasoline' launch.

February, 1905, saw Washington Harbor post office granted a money order office, fulfilling earlier postmaster Severs' plaintive suggestion of twenty-two years before.

November of 1915 found postmaster L.P. Ottosen laid up with rheumatism. On the day after Christmas, Jesse Miner died and perhaps the last connection with the island's earliest mail service had been severed. In January, L.P. Ottosen was reported improving, and likely to be able to attend his business in the near future, but on January 31, 1916, the Washington Harbor Post Office - Door County's oldest - was discontinued. Ottosen's poor health had forced resignation, and advertisements for an applicant had availed nothing. 'Now,' the Island column summed up sadly, 'altho the people who went to that office will receive the best service possible from the rural delivery...many will miss the little office...The very fact that there was a post office in the neighborhood seemed to lend a sort of dignity to the place and its influence meant progress...Many of us were loath to see it close.' (Washington Island Insights *1988, pp. 2-3)*

Washington Harbor Postmasters and Dates of Their Appointments

Milton E. Lyman - June 22, 1854
James M. Craw - September 29, 1854
Michael F. Kalmbach - July 12, 1857
William J. Nolen - October 28, 1859
Volney S. Garrett - April 7, 1865
J.J. Lobdell - February 27, 1866
D.E. Ranney - January 15, 1867
Hiram A. Knowlton - May 24, 1867
Henry D. Miner - October 2, 1867
John M. Furlong - December 13, 1875
Robert Severs - December 19, 1877
Lars P. Ottosen - November 1, 1901

Postmasters' Annual Salaries

1860-1861	William Nolen	$ 5.98 (2 qtrs. only)
1864-1865	William Nolen	$ 39.41
1871	Henry Miner	$ 54.00
1873	Henry Miner	$ 44.00
1877	John Furlong	$ 95.89
1879	Robert Severs	$ 49.25
1883	Robert Severs	$115.33
1885	Robert Severs	$141.68
1887	Robert Severs	$157.67
1889	Robert Severs	$218.64
1891	Robert Severs	$165.46

WASHINGTON HARBOR

SEC. 25, 26
T34N R29E
TOWN OF WASHINGTON

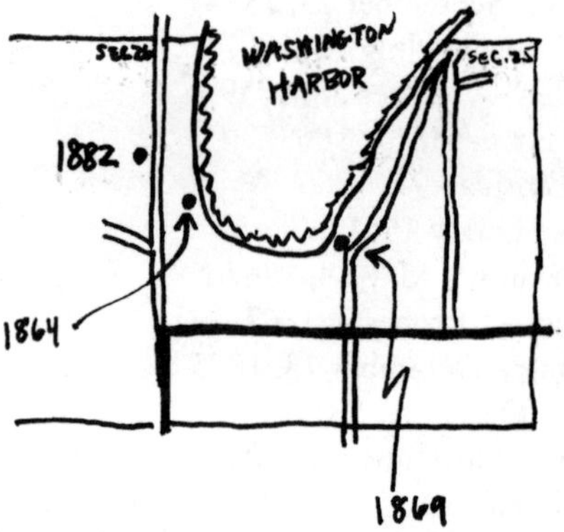

Washington Island
see Detroit Harbor

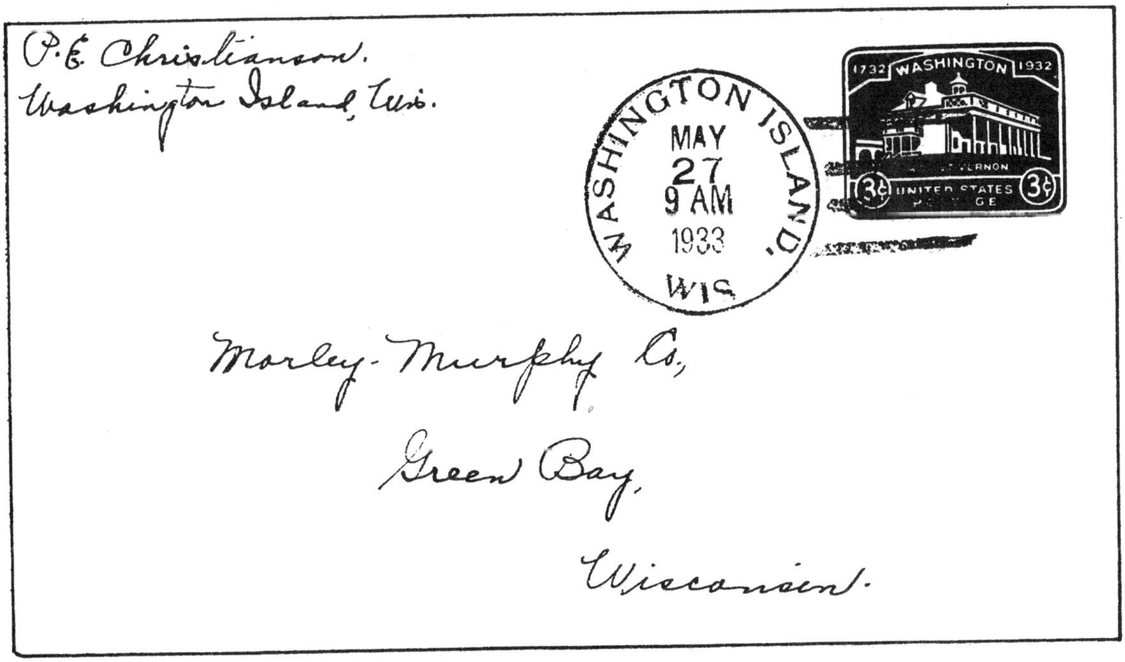

1933.

Williamsonville/Tornado

Established January 3, 1871. The name was changed to Tornado on January 29, 1872, and the office was discontinued on January 20, 1879. It was reestablished September 11, 1879, and finally discontinued February 28, 1907, with mail service at Brussels.

This post office had at least four locations. In 1870, the Williamsonville office was at the Williamson sawmill in the southeast quarter of section 35, Town 27 North, Range 24 East, Town of Gardner. In 1879, the Tornado office was in the northwest quarter of section 1, Town 26 North, Range 24 East, Town of Brussels. In 1885, Tornado was in the northwest quarter of section 2, Town 26 North, Range 24 East, Town of Brussels. In 1895, it was at the Garrett Moore property in the northeast quarter of section 36, Town 27 North, Range 24 East, Town of Gardner.

Williamsonville was named for the first postmaster, who operated a sawmill. The name of the office was changed to Tornado to commemorate the great forest fire which swept most of southern Door County in October, 1871, as well as much of Northeastern Wisconsin, including the famous Peshtigo Fire. At Williamsonville, sixty-one of the seventy-eight residents lost their lives in the fire, including the postmaster.

In 1879, a proposed post office name of Williamson's Mill was denied by the U.S. Post Office Department, while the name Tornado was approved. In 1879, the estimated population to be served by the post office was seventy-five; in 1885 it was "about one hundred families."A post office has been established at Williamson's shingle mill on the State Road in the Town of Gardner. The post office is named Williamsonville and the Postmaster John Williamson. (*Door County Advocate*, January 26, 1871)

> *The new post office of Tornado has been established on the Green Bay road, three-fourths of a mile from the late Williamsonville post office. This is the site of the new mill built by Scofield & Co. (*Door County Advocate*, February 15, 1872)*

The last building to house the Tornado post office survived until March 26, 1974:

> *They put the torch Wednesday to a piece of old history sandwiched between two modern complexes in the town of Garnder.*
>
> *A dilapidated home and two outbuildings located between a mobile home court and Southern Door's gigantic educational complex were intentionally burned by the owners, Mr. and Mrs. Roy Long, to make way for a new home.*
>
> *First to go was the shingled outdoor plumbing, then the weathered woodshed and finally the house. Left to be dismantled because of its valuable weathered lumber was the barn.*

The Brussels-Union-Gardner Fire Department stood by while neighbors reminisced. Al Moore remembered when the house was a post office and a stopping place for the stage coach. Another neighbor, Elton Spaid, could not remember a time when the house looked any different than the day it was burned, with its old shingled porch and its rusty metal siding.

> *...Landmark though it was, the old house and outbuildings were an eyesore. But...it was slow to yield to the present...It had taken a long time for it to get going, as if ghosts of the past had been stamping at the flames. (Jim Robertson in the* Door County Advocate, *March 28, 1974)*

✉

Williamsonville/Tornado Postmasters and Dates of Their Appointments

Williamsonville:

John Williamson - January 3, 1871

Tornado:

John Leatham - January 29, 1872
Ephraim C. Truman - September 11, 1879
Mrs. Harriet Watson - November 21, 1884
Fred W. Rick - May 7, 1892
Garrett J. Moore - September 9, 1895

Postmasters' Annual Salaries

1871	John Williamson	$12.00
1873	John Leatham	$12.00
1877	John Leatham	$53.51
1883	Ephraim Truman	$19.91
1885	Harriet Watson	$29.66
1887	Harriet Watson	$69.38
1889	Harriet Watson	$69.05
1891	Harriet Watson	$79.08

WILLIAMSONVILLE
TORNADO

SEC. 1,2 - T26N R24E - TOWN OF BRUSSELS
SEC. 35,36 - T27N R24E - TOWN OF GARDNER

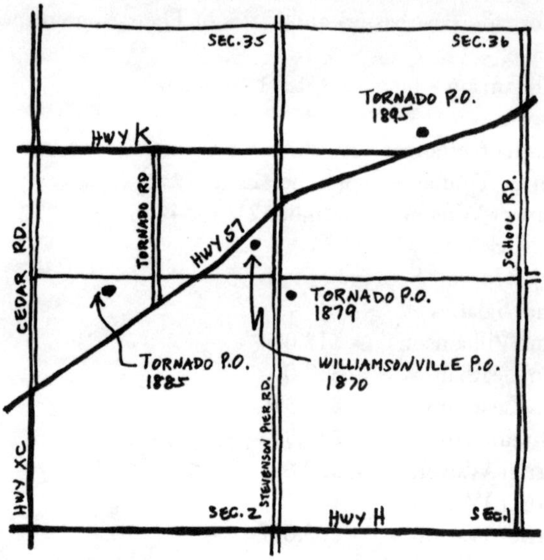

Mail on the Farm - The Story of Rural Free Delivery

In the 1890s, getting to a post office was not always easy for the rural residents of Door County. There was no home delivery and, although more than 30 post offices were operating in the county for most of the decade, the nearest office was often several miles away.

Roads were bad for at least half the year, making travel difficult. They became snowbound in winter because they were not plowed, and muddy in spring and during wet spells at other seasons because they were not surfaced. This situation was not peculiar to Door County; it was, in fact, a nationwide problem.

The U.S. Congress recognized the problem in 1893 by appropriating $40,000 to begin an experimental Rural Free Delivery program. The Postmaster General took no action immediately, but finally, in 1896, the first rural delivery routes were established out of three communities in West Virginia.

The Postmaster General also asked executives of twenty-nine states for suggestions on where to establish rural routes. His objective was to have these locations "represent territory widely divergent in physical features and in the occupation and density of its population." Sun Prairie (in Dane County) seemed to meet these qualifications for Wisconsin, but it needed four routes, rather than just one, to cover its service area. Nearly three years passed before another route was established in Wisconsin.

Rural Free Delivery at first was opposed by country store owners who operated post offices in their establishments, and by the smaller post offices, but the service became so popular with farmers that opposition was futile. By January 1, 1903, there were 550 rural routes in Wisconsin covering nearly 10,000 square miles and serving 219,600 people.

No R.F.D. postal markings exist for any Wisconsin routes prior to 1900. The explanation for this is that it was not until August 1, 1900 that the Postmaster General's Order No. 875 announced that on and after that date "rural carriers are authorized and required to cancel stamps on all letters collected by them whether intended for delivery on the route or to be mailed from a collecting office." To implement this order, a postmarking device was issued to every carrier of an operating route, and of later new routes. Thus, "R.F.D." postal markings came into general use in the late summer of 1900.

In the beginning, many carriers took their devices with them and managed to cancel their outgoing letters before returning to their offices, thus avoiding possible extra unpaid time to do it, as required by Order 875. These letters for delivery farther along on the same route, or for exchange with other local carriers, received a manuscript cancellation with indelible pencil.

R.F.D. cancellations were contrived for two reasons: First, to facilitate accurate records of mail handled on routes, and second, to publicize the growing R.F.D. system. The postmarking of mail collected on rural routes provided more publicity than the delivery phase named in its title.

The supplying of canceling devices to new routes was discontinued on July 1, 1903, although carriers were allowed to purchase their own canceling devices if they so wished. All rural route mail returned to the distributing office after this date was postmarked with regular hand or machine devices. Wisconsin R.F.D. postmarks of these types were in use until 1963. In Door County, R.F.D. postmarks are known from Forestville, Sawyer and Sturgeon Bay.

The first rural route in Door County was established in 1901 at Sturgeon Bay, with Thomas Halstead as carrier. A route also began at Sawyer early in 1902.

> *The demand for rural delivery became so great that on May 1, 1904, a total of twenty-two routes were put into operation, completing Door County service. The effective day was May 1, but because this date fell on a Sunday, Monday the 2nd*

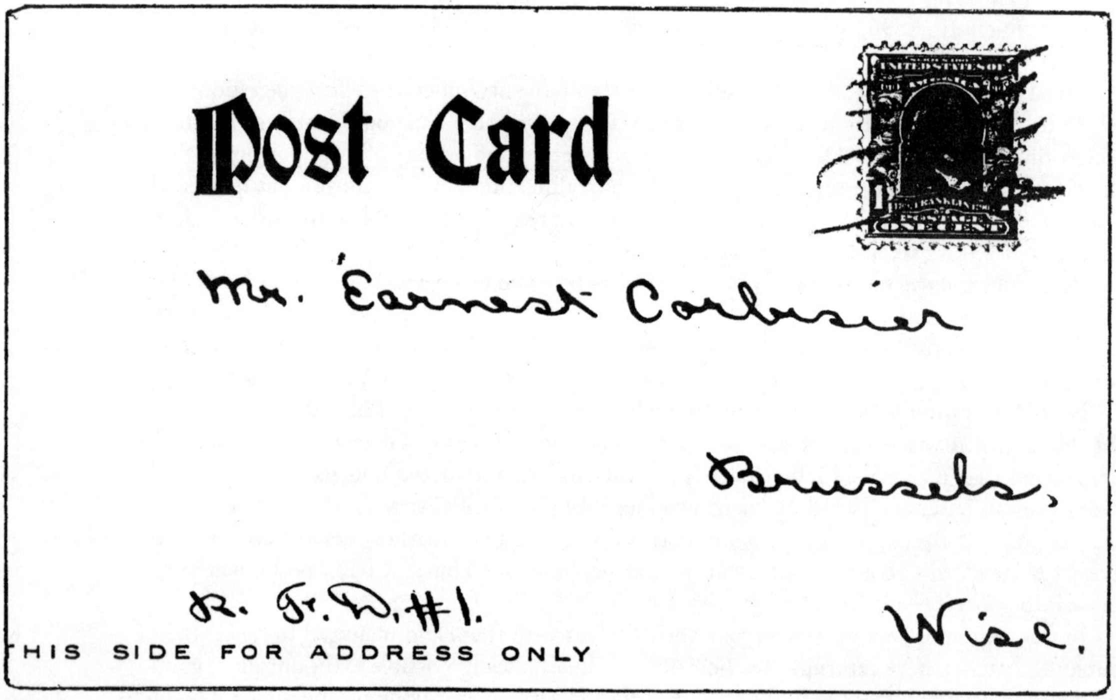

Brussels- Early 1900s postcard with manuscript postmark by the RFD carrier for delivery farther along his route on which this card was mailed.

became the first official date of service.

...Thomas Halstead was appointed to Rural Route 1 (at Sturgeon Bay). Route 2 was established in the spring of 1903 with Philip Klumb as carrier and receiving a salary of $600 per year.

...In 1902, Theodore Hanson was appointed to serve as rural carrier on Route 1 (at Sawyer) serving the areas of Hainesville, Salem, Gardner and Little Sturgeon.

May 2, 1904, saw the establishment of county-wide RFD. Franck C. Dresser was appointed to a third Sturgeon Bay route (Route 3) and Isaac Hunt and Eugene Barnard to two more Sawyer routes, Hunt to Route 2 serving the Shiloh, Vignes, Clay Banks and Salona areas, and Barnard to Route 34 serving the area of Nasewaupee, Stokes and into Maplewood.

...While farmers were delighted with rural delivery, feeling that a new world had opened up for them, it was often criticized for being impractical and expensive, mostly because mailmen had to travel over bad roads and even through for-

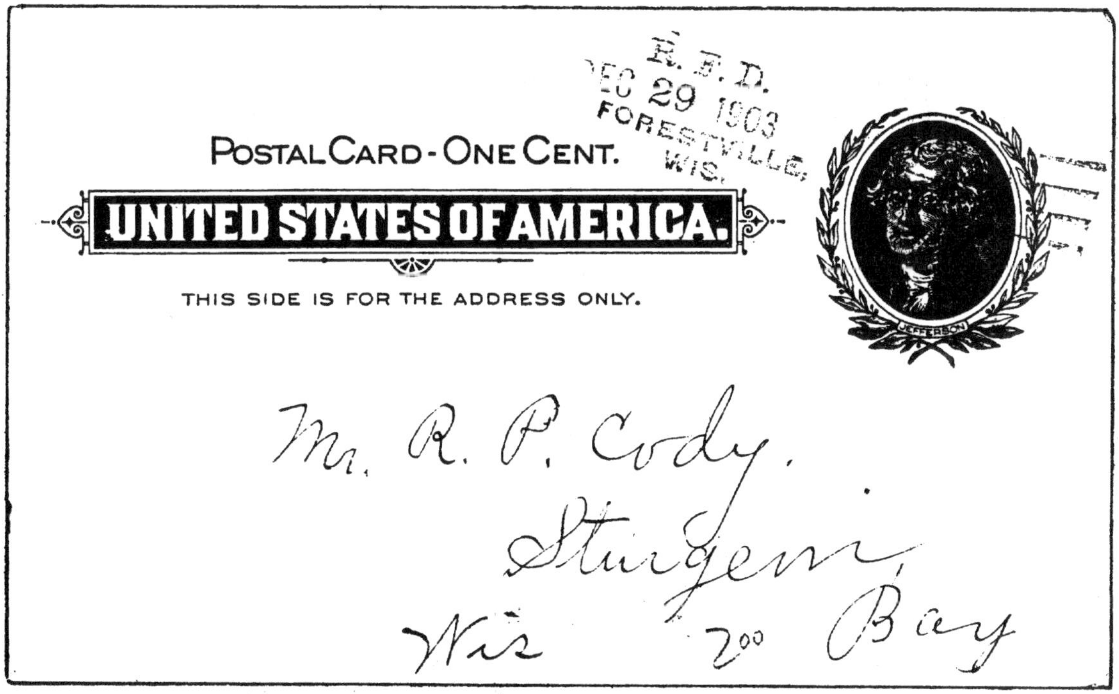

Forestville- The usual RFD carrier's handstamp on mail picked up on his route.

est to deliver mail in all kinds of weather... (Arden Robertson in Door County Advocate, *May 1, 1984)*

Between 1902 and 1910, twenty-three of the smaller Door County post offices were closed and their service replaced by Rural Free Delivery:

October 15, 1902 - Sevastopol
October 31, 1902 - Voseville
November 15, 1902 - Foscoro, Hainesville
February 28, 1903 - Clay Banks
July 14, 1903 - Stokes
December 31, 1903 - Valmy
January 30, 1904 - Vignes, Salona
April 30, 1904 - Graceport, Hastings, Newport,
Rowleys Bay, Maplewood
July 30, 1904 - Gills Rock
January 14, 1905 - Gardner
April 29, 1905 - Little Sturgeon, Stevenson's Pier, Namur
April 30, 1906 - Institute
February 15, 1907 - Kolberg
February 28, 1907 - Tornado
May 15, 1907 - Carnot

✉

Approximately 3,300 families here in the Sturgeon Bay area are served by eight rural routes.

When rural mail service began in 1896, many make-shift receptacles-including tin cans nailed to trees—were used as mailboxes.

Postal history reflects that a Kansas resident, Ira F. Collins, was among the first customers to show an interest in improving appearance and security of the mailbox.

On April 29, 1903, Collins filed a patent application for his invention of a new and improved mailbox described as follows:

This invention relates to improvements in mailboxes particularly adapted for use on rural mail-routes; and an object of the invention is to provide a mailbox of simple construction and inexpensive and so arranged as to protect the deposited mail-matter from rain or snow and which can be quickly opened and closed, resulting in a great saving of time in the collection and delivery of mail.

*This he did. (*Door County Advocate, *May 18, 1978)*

✉

On May 1, 1954, radio station WDOR of Sturgeon Bay broadcast an interview with

William Arle, a retired rural mail carrier and assistant Sturgeon Bay postmaster, about his experiences in the rural service. Edward Allen, Jr. was the interviewer, and the program was aired on the fiftieth anniversary of county-wide Rural Free Delivery in Door County.

The interview was taped, and in 1983 Edward Allen III, the WDOR station manager, kindly provided a copy of it. He deserves thanks for preserving this piece of Door County postal history. What follows here is a slightly abridged transcript of Mr. Arle's interview:

Comment by Mr. Allen: Mr. Arle served the Post Office Department for forty-three years and has come today to tell us about his experiences with rural mail service...

Response by Mr. Arle: This is the golden anniversary of complete county Rural Free Delivery Service. We had rural routes in the county before that, but it reached complete coverage on May 1, 1904. Experimental rural delivery was first inaugurated by a $10,000 Congressional appropriation about 1895. In the following year, experimental routes were established in Michigan and West Virginia. It was Congress' intention for farm boys to use the family driving horse to deliver the mail to their neighborhoods in their spare time and pick up $300 annual salary for such service.

Question by Mr. Allen: How did the farm boys like this?

Answer by Mr. Arle: It grew so fast it wasn't experimental very long. Demands came from all parts of the country. This was no spare-time job. Rural routes were established averaging twenty-four miles in length and this was considered a full-time job for a horse drawn vehicle. By 1901, this service reached Door County. On November 1, Route 1 out of Sturgeon Bay was established with Tom Halstead, son of James Halstead, veteran County Clerk as the first carrier.

Q: Where did that route go?

A: Down Bayshore Drive past the quarry. The following year, a route out of Sawyer was established with Theodore Hanson as carrier. Then Route 2 of Sturgeon Bay was established in the spring of 1903 with Philip Klumb of Sevastopol as carrier. He soon resigned the position, which at that time paid the magnificent sum of $600 per year. I took over this route on December 4, 1903.

Q: Why did he resign?

A: He was a sailor and could make more money at that than carrying mail on rural route.

Q: Then what?

A: May 1, 1904 was a Sunday, so actual rural deliveries were first made on Monday, May 2. A total of twenty-two routes were put in operation on that date from the following post offices and with the names of their carriers:

Sturgeon Bay 4 - Thomas Halstead, myself, Frank Dresser, D.D. Donovan.
Sawyer 3 - Theodore Hanson, Robert Toft, Eugene Barnard.
Brussels 3 - John Gilot, Martin Mallien, Frank Everard, Jr.
Forestville 2 - Edward M. Perry, Frank Husek.

Sister Bay 2 - Caspar Nys, Andrew Johnson.
Fish Creek 2 - Sam Churches, Joseph Duclon.
Washington Island 1 - John Malloch.
Ellison Bay 1 - Hjalmar Hoganson.
Ephraim 1 - Martin Evenson.
Egg Harbor 1 - Gust Tanck.
Baileys Harbor 1 - Jens Jenson.
Jacksonport 1 - Sam Bagnall.

Previous to rural delivery service, people had to go to the various post offices to get their mail. There were a great many of these small post offices and old timers will probably remember the names of such offices as Evergreen, Sevastopol, Whitefish Bay, Lily Bay, Voseville (later Valmy), Institute and Clay Banks.

Q: Where was the post office at Valmy?

A: Thomas Vose was the postmaster and the office was at the top of the hill toward Whitefish Bay where Mr. Vose lived. Other post offices were Vignes, Salona, Tornado, Little Sturgeon, Stevenson's Pier and others in this vicinity.

Sawyer– A manuscript postmark applied by the RFD carrier; date uncertain, but circa 1910.

Q: Do you know how many there were all together?

A: Not for sure, but there was a post office every few miles.

Q: Did each post office have their own canceling stamps?

A: Oh, yes. They were supplied by the Star Routes. All of these small post offices were discontinued with the establishment of rural delivery service. The salary of rural carriers was put on a mileage basis and fixed at $720 per year on July, 1904. They were increased from time to time and reached $1,200 at the time of World War I. These salaries included furnishing all necessary equipment, consisting of horses, buggies, cutters, and some covered wagons which were built especially for this rural delivery service, and automobiles when and where they could be used.

Q: You mean the government supplied these things to the carriers?

A: No, the carrier had to provide them out of his salary. The roads at that time were dirt, with short stretches of gravel near the larger communities. The so-called "Good Roads" program was inaugurated about 1910 and was due in large extent to the needs of rural delivery routes. The carriers advocated the program and helped to bring it about. With dirt roads in summer and snowbound roads in winter, rural carriers had some trying experiences in performing their duties, as can well be imagined. Rural carriers throughout the country organized to help themselves.

Q: You mean a union?

A: No, more of an association. The Door County Rural Letter Carrier's Association was formed on May 30, 1907.

Q: Who were the officers?

A: Frank Dresser was President, Sam Bagnall - Vice President, I was Secretary, and Edward Perry was Treasurer. With travel conditions as they were at that time, it required considerable effort to organize and get all the carriers to join, especially in the northern part of the county. To accomplish this, we held meetings at Fish Creek and Baileys Harbor to equalize travel and bring the association to carriers in those parts and we were soon organized one hundred percent. That membership record has been maintained to the present time. With improved roads and growth in population, rural delivery service has gradually developed so that practically every rural resident is served at his door. Also, due to these better roads, snow removal in winter and the use of automobiles instead of horse-drawn vehicles, routes have been increased in length. Instead of twenty-two carriers to serve the twenty-two routes of fifty years ago, much more mileage has been added and the county is now served by thirteen carriers. Routes today average about fifty miles each.

Q: Weren't customers served to their doors originally?

A: Oh, no. The law required service to at least a mile of their residence, so they erected their mail box at the nearest road corner where the carrier passed. There was not as much mail to deliver then as now. I remember going out to Brussels one time when the whole delivery for three routes would have fit in my overcoat pocket. I only had two or three daily papers to deliver on my route at that time. The two county papers and farm journals were very popular, but very few took daily papers. The Door County Rural Letter Carrier's Association became a leading force in the state association. Each year we sent delegates to the state convention. Theodore Hanson and I first attended the state convention at Oshkosh in 1908. At the Portage convention the following year, the Door County Association was recognized by my being elected state Vice-President, which office I held for two years and then became state President for the next four years. Then in 1916, the state convention was held in Sturgeon Bay. The following year in Wausau, I was elected state Secretary and continued until my transfer to assistant postmaster in 1926.

Q: How did you get to be assistant postmaster?

A: Well, the former assistant postmaster, Luke Byrne, came up to the hospital just as I was leaving after being there for five months with a broken leg from a hunting accident, and he later passed away there and never came back. This left a post office vacancy. I applied for it and got it. I was on crutches then and could no longer manage a rural route. Ike Hunt, now also retired, was appointed to replace Robert Toft as a carrier a couple of years later and became very active in the state association. He has not missed attendance since his first state meeting. In the "Looking Back" column of the *Door County Advocate* for fifty years ago just recently, it described the cold weather of January 1904, which averaged 21-1/2 degrees below zero for a period of three weeks.

Q: Boy! Did the mail get through?

A: It got through. I can remember that, but in those days we had real old-fashioned winters and were accustomed to taking such things in stride. And for snow, on the day Tom Halstead, the carrier of Route 1, returned from his route with the story that all the snow on the ice of Green Bay had drifted across the Bayshore Road near Smith's quarry until it was as high as the bluffs along the shore. He probably exaggerated a bit, but his story stood up until later when I brought in a note from the Finnegan's mail box which they left out on the main traveled highway. It told me that the snow was higher than Mike Moore's windmill and that I shouldn't attempt to come in. In those early days, cordwood was the regular fuel used in the city and farmers cut and hauled wood to the city all winter long. This traffic packed the snow that fell and drifted into the track and it was not unusual for the road to be built up six feet or more high. It formed ice. This caused great difficulty in passing and turnouts were made in places so that this passing could be done without forcing a loaded sleigh off the packed road, which would be impossible to get back on. When thawing weather came along toward spring, roads became practically impassable because horses would plunge down between or along side the icy tracks. As horses had to be sharp-shod for winter travel, they were often cut up severely. Then, too, we had chuck holes or pitch holes to contend with. These were caused by snow drifting to different depths and the continued travel over them gradually deepening the ruts.

Road crews tried to relieve these conditions by filling and lengthening the ruts, but no real solution came until the snow was completely melted in the spring. Nature finally would take care of it. Some roads drifted so full of snow that they were nearly impassable. Nearly everyone that drove carried wire clippers so they could cut the fences and take to the fields or woods to get past these places that remained closed all winter.

Q: What did the farmers think about this wire-clipping business?

A: They never kicked. They all did it themselves. After a severe blizzard, it took days to

Sawyer- 1903 RFD carrier's handstamp.

get some of the roads open for travel. Stages carried the mail north from Sturgeon Bay to Baileys Harbor on one side of the peninsula and to Sister Bay on the other side. They also carried freight and passengers. There was a half-way station at Egg Harbor where horses were changed on the Sturgeon Bay route. Another stage route was between Sister Bay and Gills Rock to supply the Ellison Bay district and Washington Island. I remember after one of the big snow storms, no farmers came to town for about a week. Finally the mail carrier got through, so they knew the road was open and then they came to town to do their shopping. They'd sit in the house with their feet propped on the window sill and then see me go by and say, "Oh, there goes Bill; we can get to town now." In the city, snow plows were used to open the streets so the people could get around and children get to school, but plowing county roads was never considered until the good-roads program was advanced considerably. You sometimes hear people longing for the "good old days." I'm sure they don't mean going back to the old roads we had in those days.

Late in 1903, imminent advent of Rural Free Delivery threatened to make superfluous one of the [Washington] Island's two post offices. 'Parties on the north side of the island' were reported in the Advocate to be moving to petition the government to abandon the change, which menaced Washington Harbor post office's existence. While some island citizens objected to the postal change, said the Advocate, all of them objected to the closing of the only barber shop, which would certainly follow if John Malloch should be chosen rural carrier. R.F.D. arrived in May, 1904, and by mid-August was reported 'working like a charm.' Neither office was discontinued at the time. (C.B. Eaton in Washington Island Insights, *1988, p. 3)*

Rural Free Delivery matters elsewhere in the county did not escape the *Door County Advocate:*

December 19, 1924 - F.J. Pies & Son (of Sturgeon Bay) are building a light bob sleigh suitable for rural carriers or delivery purposes. Sleigh building was quite an industry at the Pies shop in Sawyer some years ago, but it is several years since one was made here.

March 26, 1926 - Sawyer rural carrier Isaac Hunt put wheels on the front end of his snowmobile in place of runners the fore part of this week and is making good time. The road is bare in many places and it will not be long before the auto is in use again.

December 10, 1926 - Rural mail carriers have been compelled to give up automobiles and are now using horses. Ike Hunt of Sawyer has his snowmobile in operation and is making the best time of any of the carriers.

December 31, 1934 - Two snowmobiles have been purchased by local rural carriers who are fearing a less open winter this year. One has been received by Avery Birmingham of Route three and other jointly by Louis Solomon and Roy Marshall of Routes one and two.

February 18, 1936 - Rural mail carriers have been having such difficulty serving their patrons due to the high snow banks that Postmaster H.R. Jones has been compelled to remind the public of the post regulation which says 'patrons shell, as far as practical, keep clear the approaches of their boxes by removing the obstructions which may render difficult or impossible the delivery of mail by the carrier.'

October 4, 1940 - Isaac Hunt, Sawyer rural mail carrier, has traveled a dis-

tance equal to twelve trips around the world at the equator during this thirty and one-half years on the job. Hunt, sixty-four, retired this week.

May 1, 1984 - ...The rural carrier is a mobile post office, able to provide almost as much service as the main office. He brings both good and bad news, including bills one wishes he would forget. The patron can almost set his watch with his mail delivery and when the carrier is late most telephone calls to the post office come from rural families wondering if there is going to be a delivery because of a storm or other event.

Rural Free Delivery is one of the largest enterprises in the country, a service that is the by-product of the development of a great system of highways, country roads and communications. During recent years, more rural land being developed into housing projects has increased the role of rural delivery.

Door County Rural Free Delivery Routes, 1901-1911:

Post Office	Route #	Length	Date Est.	1st Carrier
Baileys Harbor	1	20.0 mi.	5/2/1904	Jens Jenson
Brussels	1	24.6	5/2/1904	John Gilot
	2	26.6	5/2/1904	Martin Mallien
	3	26.0	5/2/1904	Frank Everard, Jr.
Detroit Harbor	1	25.7	5/2/1904	John Malloch
Egg Harbor	1	25.8	5/2/1904	Gust Tanck
Ellison Bay	1	29.2	5/2/1904	Hjalmar Hoganson
Ephraim	1	26.2	5/2/1904	Martin Evenson
Fish Creek	1	27.6	5/2/1904	Samuel Churches
	2	26.2	5/2/1904	Joseph Duclon
Forestville	1	27.2	5/2/1904	Edward M. Perry
	2	26.2	5/2/1904	Frank Hucek
Jacksonport	1	26.0	5/2/1904	S. J. Bagnall
Sawyer	1	29.0	?/?/1902	Theodore Hanson
	2	27.1	5/2/1904	Robert Toft
	3	26.5	5/2/1904	Eugene Barnard
Sister Bay	1	27.4	5/2/1904	Casper Nys
	2	?	5/2/1904	Andrew Johnson
Sturgeon Bay	1	24.0	11/1/1901	Thomas Halstead
	2	25.7	Spring/1903	Phillip Klumb
	3	25.7	5/2/1904	Frank C. Dresser
	4	25.0	5/2/1904	D. D. Donovan

Mail by Rail on the Ahnapee & Western

American railroads have carried the mails between post offices for almost as long as there have been trains in this country. In Wisconsin, the first mail service on railroad lines was by U.S. Post Office Department "Route Agents" from Milwaukee to Waukesha in 1854. Other routes were added as railroads opened more trackage. In 1882, all Agent routes were retitled "Railway Post Office" (RPO). The last RPO train in Wisconsin carried the Chicago & Minneapolis RPO on September 18, 1970. All mail is now transported by trucks or aircraft.

Door County was the last county in Wisconsin to have a railroad, but it was not because people weren't trying. At least seven attempts were made to bring a railroad into the county, and all but one failed due to financial and political problems. A major deterrent to railroads was the strong stand of the county's shipping and lumbering business that water transportation was cheap and available, so railroads were unnecessary. In 1870, it was the Sturgeon Bay and Fond du Lac Railway Company that tried and failed. In 1881, the Wisconsin Peninsula Railway Company proposed a line from Green Bay to some point in the Town of Liberty Grove, but this, too, failed.

The *Door County Advocate* was strongly anti-railroad. A typical editorial comment on June 9, 1881, said that "A railroad running into Green Bay would interest and benefit our people about as much as though it ran in the middle of Lake Michigan. We might use it occasionally when we wanted to attend a circus or a lawsuit, but as far as regular travel or freight shipments are concerned, we would as soon think of going to New York by way of the Sandwich Island."

Other unsuccessful attempts in the 1880s to bring a railroad into the county were made by the Milwaukee, Lake Shore and Western Railway Company, the Fond du Lac, Portage and Sturgeon Bay Railway Company, the Wisconsin Railway and Navigation Company, and the Wisconsin Midland Railway Company.

Finally, in 1891, the Ahnapee & Western Railway Company convinced the people of Door County that financing a railroad from Algoma to Sturgeon Bay was a good thing. Edward Decker of Casco was the head of the railroad company. An entrepreneur of some stature, he also was instrumental in founding the Bank of Sturgeon Bay and starting the *Kewaunee Enterprise* newspaper.

Mr. Decker's company was not the last, however. In 1913, the E.E. Galle Company of Minneapolis vigorously promoted construction of a railroad from Sturgeon Bay north to Newport, but the project failed when the outbreak of World War I in 1914 reduced the company's financial capability.

Construction of the Ahnapee & Western began in 1892 when track was laid from the Green Bay and Western tracks at Casco Junction to Algoma. In 1894, construction was completed from Algoma through Maplewood, Forestville and Sawyer to Sturgeon Bay. Major obstacles overcome in this construction period were the crossing of the Maplewood swamp and the bridging of Sturgeon Bay to bring tracks to the east side of the city.

> *Three years after the project was approved the job was done and on July 23, 1894, and A&W started regular train service to Sturgeon Bay. This was followed by a gigantic celebration in Sturgeon Bay on August 9 when special trains arrived from Green Bay and Ahnapee carrying over people and special boats from Marinette, Menominee and carriages from throughout the county carried thousands more into the city for the celebration.*
>
> *The A&W offered regular passenger service until automobiles and competing bus service started cutting into its business in the 1920s...Passenger service was dropped in 1936. [After World War II] the growth in the trucking industry with semi-trailers competing in size with railroad box cars took bigger and bigger bites into the freight business.* (Door County Advocate, *June 10, 1976)*

The last regular A&W train crossed the Sturgeon Bay bridge on August 5, 1968, and the

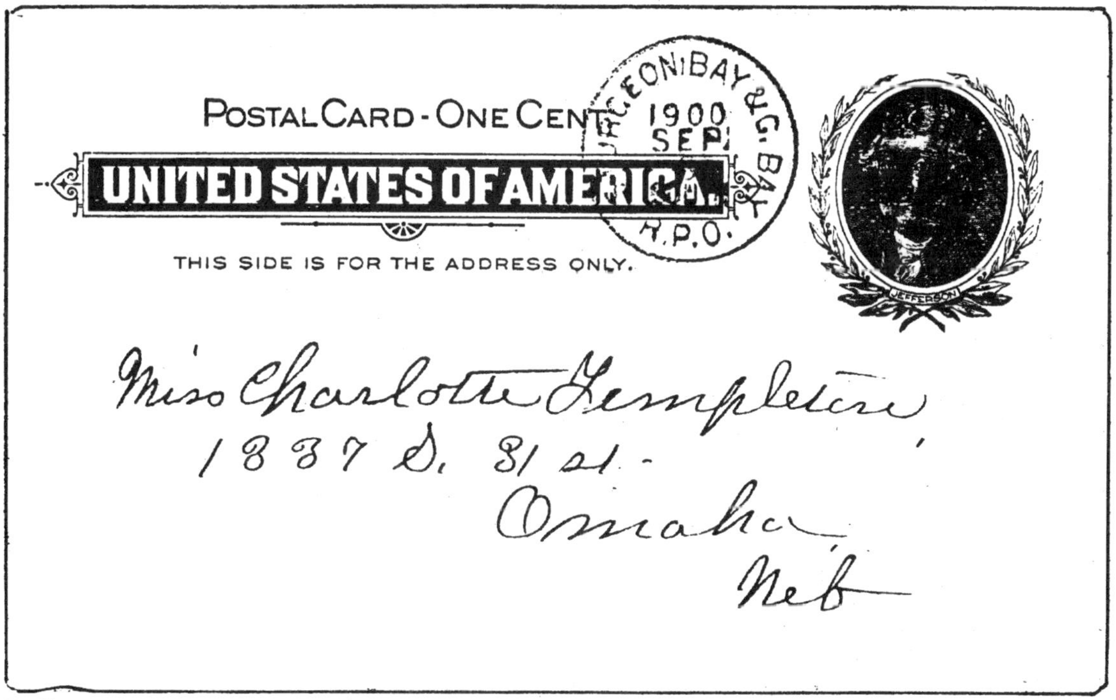

Earliest postmark type: Sturgeon Bay & G. Bay R.P.O.

last train from Sturgeon Bay to Casco Junction ran four days later on August 9. The last locomotive traveled from Sturgeon Bay's west side to Algoma on September 4, 1968.

The A&W roadbed from Sturgeon Bay to Algoma is now the Ahnapee state recreation trail, while the last Sturgeon Bay depot, built in 1914, now houses the Cherryland Brewing Company.

Mail service on the A&W began in 1895 with the establishment of the Sturgeon Bay & Green Bay Railway Post Office. This route ran on the Green Bay and Western tracks from Casco Junction to Green Bay. In Door County it served post offices at Forestville, Maplewood, and Sawyer.

Letters could be mailed at any train stop if the local post office was closed by dropping the letter in a slot on the side of the mail car which was part of the passenger train, or perhaps handing your letter to the mail clerk standing in the car door. Passenger trains for years included a car devoted solely to mail handling. Sometimes the mail section would share a car with the other baggage handling.

Over the years, three types of RPO postmarks were used on the A&W. They are told apart by the variations in their spelling: Sturgeon Bay & G. Bay, Sturg. Bay & Gr. Bay, and Stur. Bay & Green Bay.

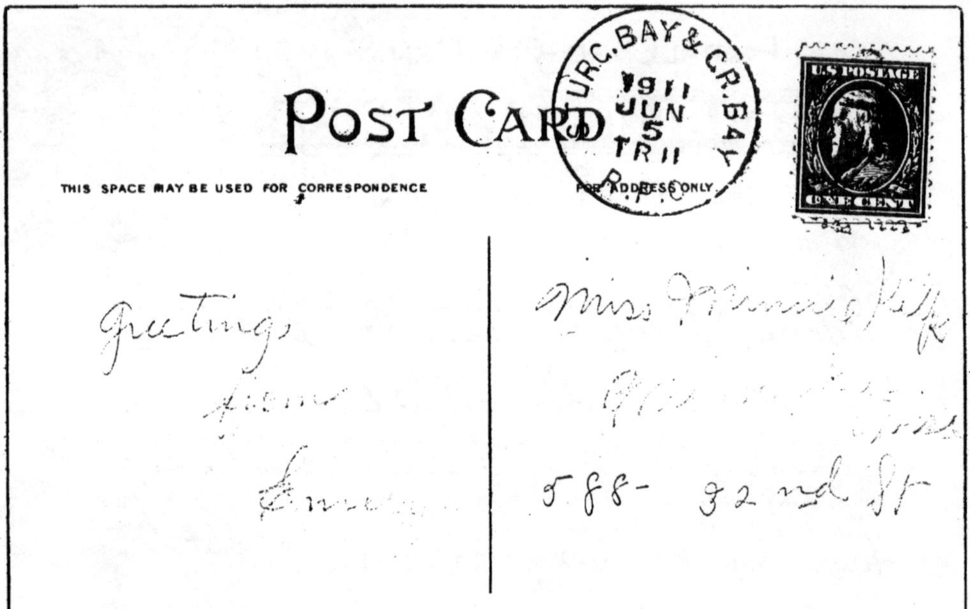

Second postmark type: Sturg. Bay & Gr. Bay R.P.O.

The Sturgeon Bay and Green Bay Railway Post Office ceased operating in 1935 when mail deliveries by truck superseded the railroad.

✉

The *Door County Advocate* for November 17, 1894 reported that "Friday (November 16, 1894), for the first time, the mail came to Bay View (Sawyer) and Sturgeon Bay by railroad. Henceforth it will depart the same way."

✉

With winter just weeks away [in 1894], A&W started its first Sturgeon Bay depot. The 28 x 100 foot combination building was constructed by Henry Poehler's crew... When finished, the depot had ash-trimmed interior and contained a telephone. Mail service came early next year. Steamer service between Green Bay and Sturgeon Bay maintained similar rates as rail traffic began to compete. No longer did the Hart line steamers handle the mails to the docks of Sturgeon Bay. Interchange between railroad and steamers for more northerly points was opened and service was curtailed only in severe weather and during lay-up of steamers. (Mailer, Green Bay & Western - The First 111 Years, *p. 132, 1989)*

✉

A momentous ice storm in February, 1922 closed the A&W between Algoma and Sturgeon Bay for four days. Forty men armed with pickaxes were required to open flanges ways and free switches. The KGB&W was also iced over from Green Bay to Luxemburg, requiring the attention of hand labor. Wednesday's mail was received the following Monday morning. (Mailer, Green Bay & Western-The First 111 Years, *p. 140, 1989)*

✉

*An unofficial report that the U.S. Post Office is contemplating the delivery of mail to Sturgeon Bay, and probably to communities north of here, by truck from Green Bay is not expected to affect the present mail contract with the Ahnapee & Western railroad. The plan is expected to speed deliveries by about three hours. (*Door County Advocate, *January 16, 1931)*

✉

The first tourists [in Fish Creek] came on the 'Chicago Boats,' excursion steamers of the Goodrich Line in the 1880s. At first they were only a trickle, and they became a flood after highways were built and motor cars became common. The railroad came later but ended at Sturgeon Bay, terminus of The Green Bay and Western (GB&W), which the locals called the 'Grab Bag and Walk Line.' (Duncan Thorp in Fish Creek Voices, *p. 195, 1990)*

Special Postal Events

Postal historians and other philatelically inclined collectors have always been fond of accumulating covers (envelopes) and postcards with stamps and postmarks appropriate to an event. Such covers may take many forms - first day of issue for U.S. postage stamps, civic celebrations, anniversaries of important historical events, openings and closings of post offices, or commemorating various national, state and local happenings. While the production of such covers may or may not have been instigated by the local post office directly concerned, it has been through the cooperation and encouragement of the local post office that collectible covers and cards have been produced.

Door County has provided its share of special postmarks and other commemorative covers. While these items are admittedly philatelic in nature, rather than produced in the normal course of the day-to-day activity of the concerned post office, they do represent a facet of postal activity important to the record of post office histories.

Over the years, many events have been commemorated; here are eighteen examples:

First day of issue for a postage stamp

A 3¢ 1934 stamp commemorated the tercentennial of the landing of Jean Nicolet on the shores of Green Bay. He was believed to be the first white to set foot on the door peninsula. The City of Green Bay was the official first day location for the issuance of this stamp on July 7, 1934. The cover shown here, while not postmarked at the Green Bay post office, has ties to both Green Bay and Sturgeon Bay since it was postmarked by the Sturgeon Bay & Green Bay Railway Post Office on the appropriate first day.

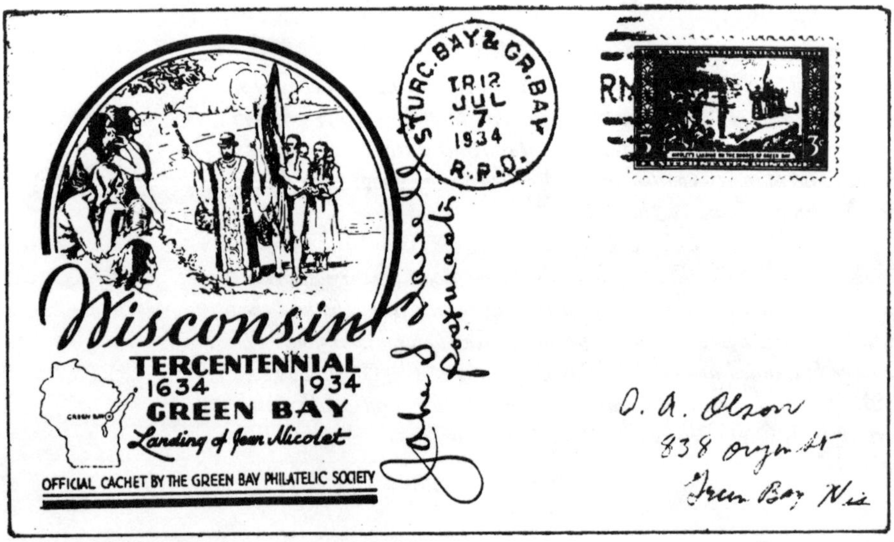

While most United States postage stamps have a designated post office for the first day of issue, there have been occasions when a stamp has been made available at every post office in the country on its first day. An example is the 1971 8¢ stamp issued to announce the change in name of the U.S. Post Office Department to the U.S. Postal Service. At Egg Harbor, the postmaster reported that fifty covers like the one shown here were postmarked on July 1, 1971.

Another example of a nation-wide first day of issue was this (below) 1973 set of ten stamps honoring U.S. Postal Service employees. Egg Harbor again provides an example of a First Day cover dated April 30, 1973.

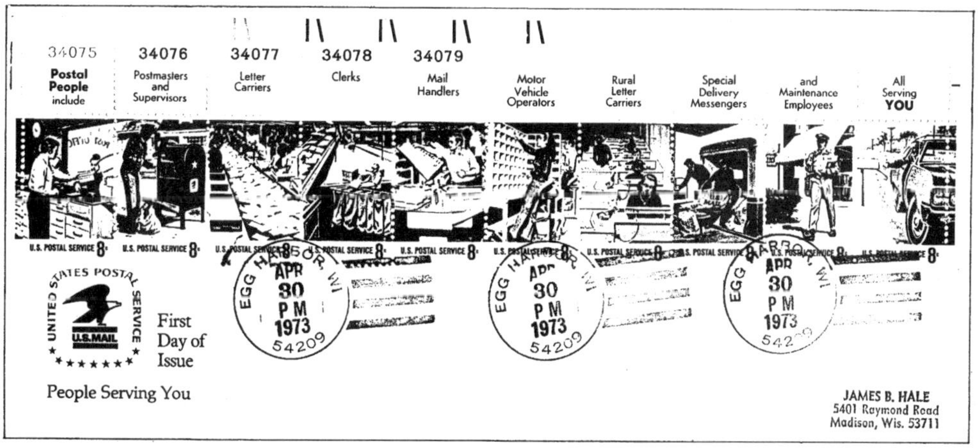

A more recent stamp first-day event was described by Linda Adams in the *Door County Advocate* of January 12, 1993: "It's a far piece from Graceland to Sturgeon Bay, but the first Elvis (Presley) 29¢ commemorative stamp sold here is already on its way to England and another of the first sold is headed to an aircraft carrier in the Persian Gulf."

> *The U.S. Postal Service limited edition "young" Elvis stamps went on sale at noon Friday [January 8] throughout the county... Sturgeon Bay Officer-in-Charge Ken Liebert reports he had an allotment of 16,000 stamps and estimates nearly 5,000 were sold Friday. Don Riewe, Washington Island's officer-in-charge, said only one person was waiting in line to purchase some of that post office's allotment of 800 stamps. In Brussels, Butch Hansen says there were a few Elvis stamp buyers, but he hasn't sold out of his 600 stamps yet...*

Post Office Last Day and First Day Covers

The final changes in the status of the Jacksonport post office provided several examples of covers in this category. The last day of operation for an independent Jacksonport post office was January 31, 1958, a cover prepared by a collector to recognize the event was postmarked on the appropriate day and autographed by Fred Erskine, the outgoing Jacksonport postmaster. (next page, top)

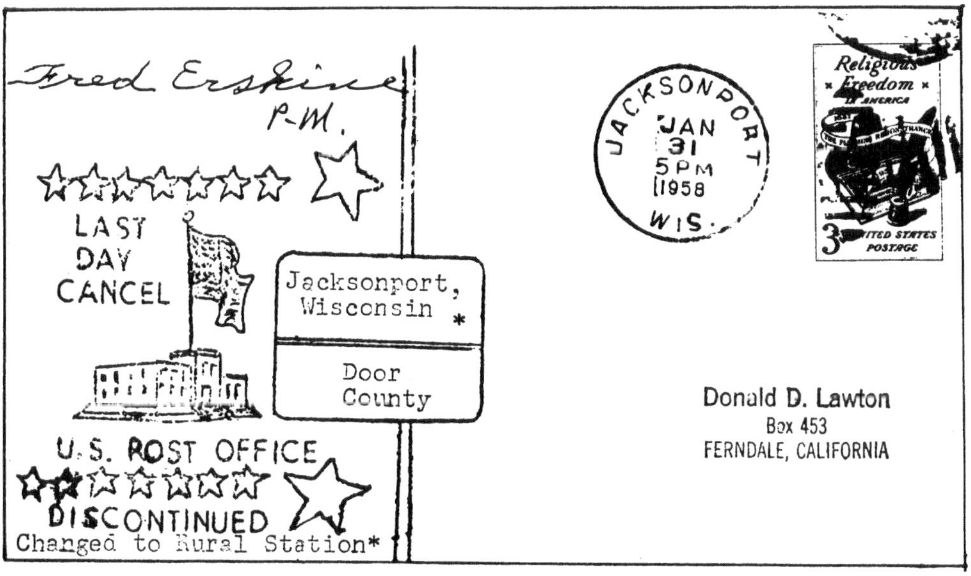

On the next day, February 1, 1958, the former Jacksonport post office became a rural branch of the Sturgeon Bay post office and covers describing the event were prepared to record the change. (next page, top)

The Jacksonport office was closed for good on May 15, 1970. Mrs. Joan LeClark, the clerk in charge at the time of the closing, reported that "thirty or forty pieces of mail were canceled on the last day, but only one of them was requested by a collector." (below)

Local and Civic Events

The *Door County Advocate* of June 9, 1989, recounted an event that began in Sturgeon Bay on June 12, 1939, under the headline "Record Glider Flight Took Off from Door County":

> *The world watched through the eyes of news-reel men and aviation editors from New York and Chicago as Ted Bellak, A Newark, N.J. glider pilot took to the skies over Door County. Bellak was after the record for the longest flight over water in a motorless plane.*
>
> *Five hundred 'letters' were flown over Lake Michigan with Bellak, who figured on a brisk demand from collectors for the canceled stamps. The envelopes included a picture of the ship and its owner and were properly notarized both here and in Frankfort.*
>
> *Thirty-five of the letters went on sale at the Chamber of Commerce office for \$1 each. New-reel shots showed Earl M. LaPlant, chamber president, delivering the mail to Bellak at the airport. The first letter was addressed to President Roosevelt, inviting him to attend the Cherry Harvest Festival here July 22 and 23.*
>
> *...Skillfully maneuvering in the air currents and the brisk west wind, the German-trained pilot and his German-made ship settled down easily at Frankfort. The fifty-four-mile flight took just sixty-six minutes, and his actual flying distance was estimated at ninety miles as the place crossed Lake Michigan near Manistee, twenty-eight miles south of his destination...The longest previous over-water flight was across the English channel April 21, 1939, a distance of just thirty-one miles...The cover shown here was back-stamped at Frankfort, Michigan on June 12, 1939.*

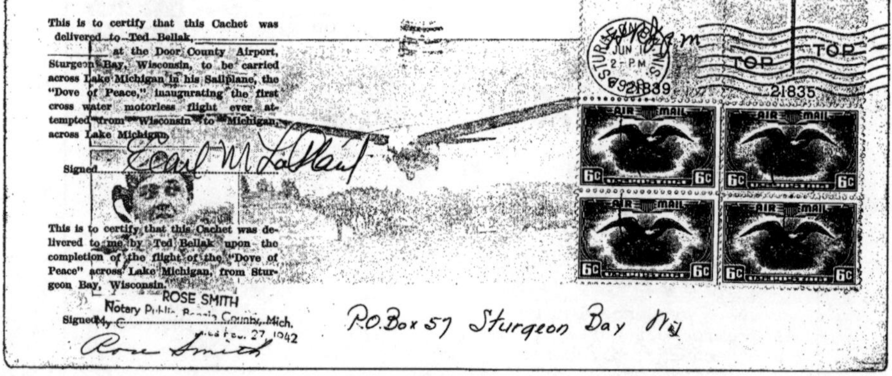

Sturgeon Bay's annual Cherry Blossom Festival was recognized in 1956 by this collector-prepared cover. The number of such covers is unknown.

The City of Sturgeon Bay's 75th Jubilee was commemorated by a local Boy Scout troop that sold "souvenir envelopes," as a money-raising project to support the troop. (below)

In 1962, the village of Sister Bay commemorated its Golden Jubilee with a special postmark provided by the U.S. Post Office Department. (below)

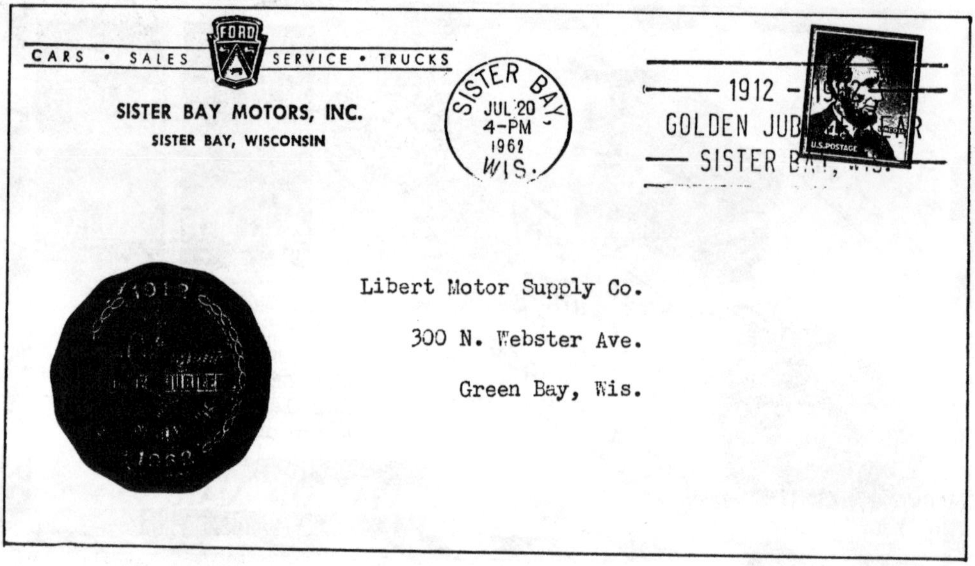

On May 29, 1971, sixteen members of the Cherryland Horsemen riding club carried the mail from Egg Harbor to Sturgeon Bay in Pony Express style. Most of the sixteen letters carried a Cherryland Horsemen label and probably ended up in scrapbooks. The mail was taken by stagecoach from Stagecoach Junction in Egg Harbor to Chief Roy Oshkosh's Trading Post where it was transferred to the first rider. Seventeen riders rode a mile to a mile and a half each after leaving Egg Harbor, and the mail reached Sturgeon Bay in about an hour. The club's color guard met the last rider on the north side of Sturgeon Bay and escorted him to the post office. (next page, top)

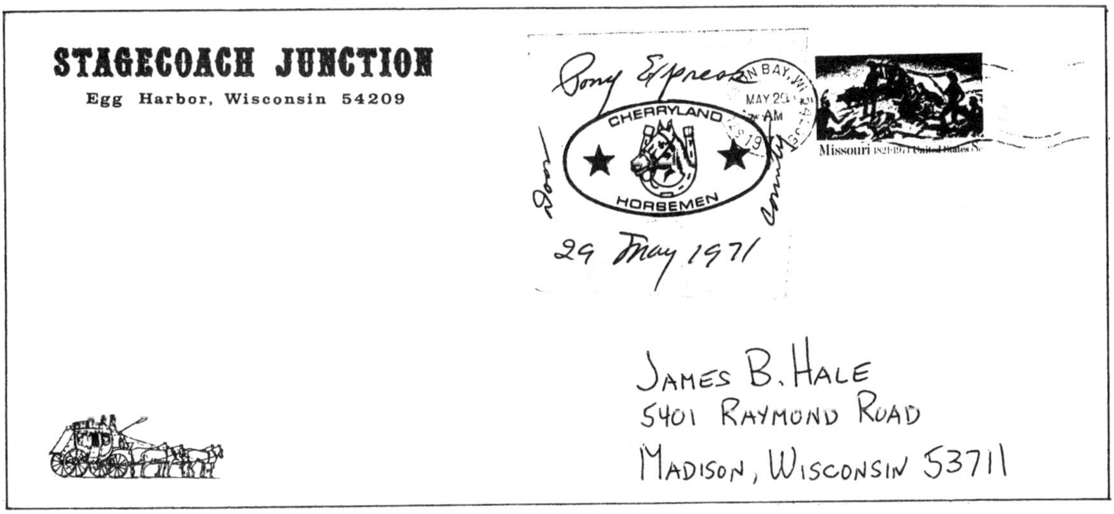

Commemorations

In August, 1930, the Detroit Flying Club of Michigan toured the Great Lakes area in private aircraft. The Club mail cacheted airmail covers such as these from the cities where they made overnight stops, in this case at Sturgeon Bay. Covers probably were sold to raise funds for the Club, as well as to be souvenirs for members.

A cover observing Navy Day in 1948 was mailed at Egg Harbor. This was an effort by an individual collector who apparently chose Egg Harbor because it seemed like a good naval name.

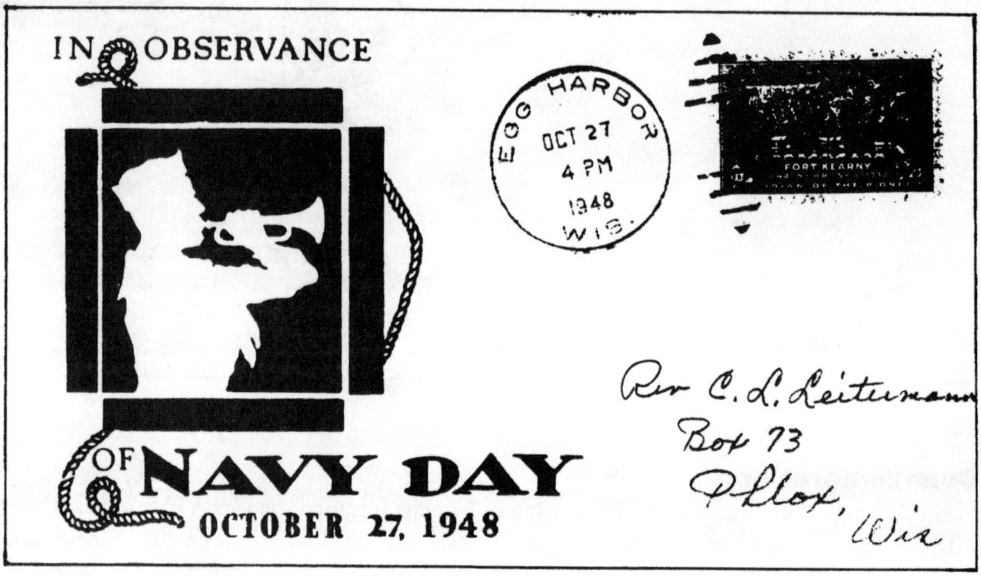

Any post office with Washington in its name was very busy postmarking covers for collectors on February 22, 1932, the 200th anniversary of President George Washington's birth. Washington Island was no exception, as this cover (next page, top) demonstrates.

October 8, 1971, was the 100th anniversary of the great forest fire that swept north up both sides of Green Bay and ravaged all of southern Door County. An example of a privately produced memorial cover is shown here. (next page, bottom)

WASHINGTON ISLAND,
WISC.
1732 = 1932.
GEORGE WASHINGTON
BICENTENNIAL
WASHINGTON ISL
FEB
22
8 AM
1932
WIS.
Mr. Paul J. Arlander
1345 Prospect Place
Brooklyn, N.Y.

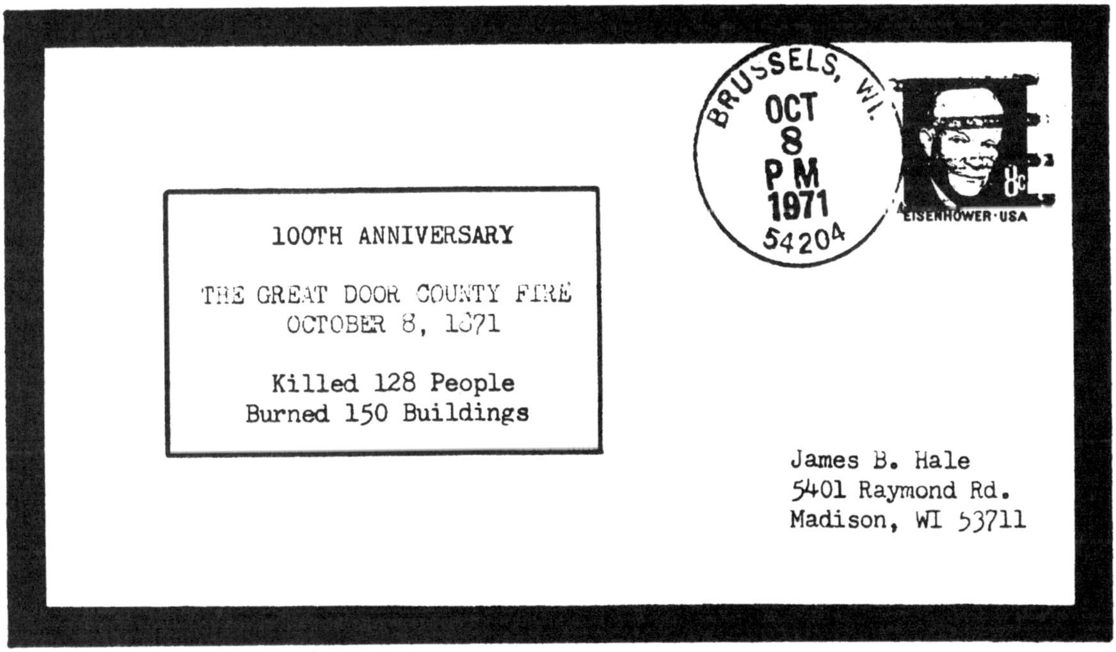
BRUSSELS, WI.
OCT
8
PM
1971
54204
EISENHOWER · USA
100TH ANNIVERSARY
THE GREAT DOOR COUNTY FIRE
OCTOBER 8, 1871
Killed 128 People
Burned 150 Buildings
James B. Hale
5401 Raymond Rd.
Madison, WI 53711

A similar cover-by-collector commemorates the 100th birthday of the establishment of a post office at Ellison Bay.

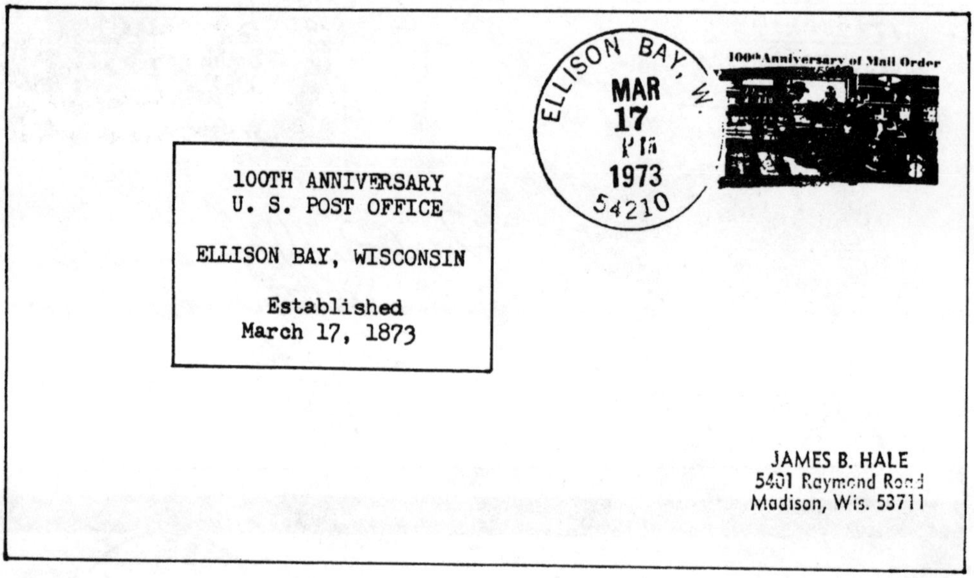

In 1977, a group calling themselves LaSalle Expedition II set out from Montreal, Canada, by canoe to recreate the original explorations of Robert Cavalier Sieur de La Salle, the first white explorer of the Mississippi Valley in 1679. Leaving Montreal, the expedition planned to reach Chicago in December, and then travel on Illinois river systems to the Mississippi River. They ran into more adventure than they expected in crossing Lake Michigan from Pointe Detour, Michigan, to Washington Island. Two of their six handmade canoes swamped in ten-foot waves and gale-force winds on November 5, but they managed to reach the Island safely. The expedition carried mail which was postmarked at many of their overnight stops. Commemorative covers were mailed at Washington Island, Baileys Harbor, and Sturgeon Bay in Door County. (next page)

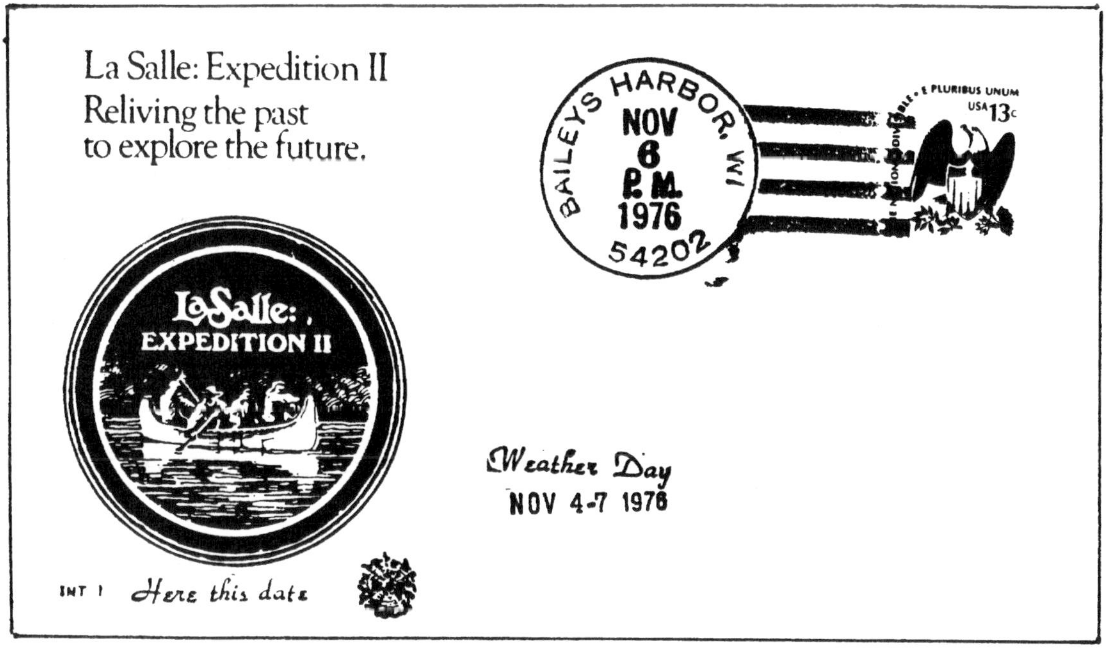
La Salle: Expedition II
Reliving the past
to explore the future.
LaSalle:
EXPEDITION II
BAILEYS HARBOR, WI
NOV
6
P.M.
1976
54202
E PLURIBUS UNUM
USA 13c
Weather Day
NOV 4-7 1976
INT I
Here this date

Bibliography

Anclam, Elsie. 1963. "Childhood at Baileys Harbor." *The Peninsula* 7:24-25.

Anonymous. 1985. *Commemorative Biographical Record of the Counties of Brown, Kewaunee and Door, Wisconsin*. J.H. Beers & Co., Chicago. 779 pp.

Anonymous. 1899. *Illustrated Atlas of Door County*. Randall and Williams, Oshkosh, WI. 54 pp.

Anonymous. 1910. *Washington Island Souvenir Business Directory*. Locally published. 32 unnumbered pages.

Anonymous. 1965. *Centennial Echoes* 1865-1925. Bethel Community Church, Washington Island, WI. 80 pp.

Anonymous. 1977. "LaSalle Expedition Covers." *Stamp Collector*, January 1, 1977.

Anonymous. 1990. *Newport - Out of Wilderness into Wilderness*. Newport State Park, Ellison Bay, WI. 17 pp.

Byfield, Arthur F. 1953. *Ephraim 1853-1953*. Men's Club of Ephraim, WI. 85 pp.

Door County Library, Sturgeon Bay, WI. Microfilmed files of Sturgeon Bay newspapers.

Eaton, Conan Bryant. 1966. *The Naming. A Part of the History of Washington Island*. Published by the author, Washington Island, WI 32 pp.

Eaton, Conan Bryant. 1972. *Washington Island, Wisconsin: 1836-1876*. Published by the author, Washington Island, WI 84 pp.

Eaton, Conan Bryant. 1988. "The Island Mail." Pages 1-4 in Washington Island Insights 1988, L. Gordon, editor.

Foote, Philo A., Edith Doane and James B. Hale. 1972. "A First Report on Wisconsin R.F.D. Cancellations." *Badger Postal History* 11(3):1-5.

Gordon, Lorel, editor. 1988. *Washington Island Insights 1988*. Published by the editor, Washington Island, WI 96 pp.

Grosse, Grace and Lorraine Varnell. 1966. *A Century in God's Country*. Ellison Bay, WI 66 pp. Paperback.

Hagedorn, Bernard (chairman). 1962. *Sister Bay Golden Jubilee 1912-1962*. Published at the Village of Sister Bay. 85 pp.

Hale, James B. 1972. "Evergreen - A Company Post Office." *Badger Postal History* 12(1):4-5. Reprinted in *Stamp Collector*, January 14, 1978.

Hale, James B. 1983. "Early Rural Mail Service in Door County, Wisconsin." *Badger Postal History* 22(3):2-5.

Hale, James B. 1989. "Postmark Typos Revealed." *Badger Postal History* 29(1):7.

Holand, Hjalmar R. 1917. *History of Door County, Wisconsin*. The S.J. Clarke Publishing Co., Chicago. Volume I, 459 pp. Volume II, 480 pp.

Holand, Hjalmar R. 1931. "When The U.S. Mail Came To Door County." *Peninsula Historical Review* 5(1):1-9.

Holand, Hjalmar R. 1972. *Old Peninsula Days*. Reprint of 1925 edition by Wisconsin Horizons, Ltd., Madison, WI 245 pp.

Jacobs, Burleigh E. 1954. "Early Wisconsin Postal History." *Wisconsin Postal History Society Booster* 6(2):8.

Johnson, Katherine. 1969. "An Early Ephraim Settler." *The Peninsula* 8:49-50.

Kahlert, John. 1976. *Early Door County Buildings*. Meadow Lane Publishers, Baileys Harbor, WI 120 pp.

Kellogg, Louise Phelps. 1910. "Organization, Boundaries and Names of Wisconsin Counties." *Proceedings of the State Historical Society of Wisconsin for 1909*:184-231.

Leet, Merwin. 1978. *Railway mail postmarks of Wisconsin and upper Michigan*. Bulletin #12,

Wisconsin Postal History Society, Madison, WI. 107 pp.

Mailer, Stan. 1989. *Green Bay & Western - The First 111 Years*. Hundman Publishing Co., Edmonds, WA. 352 pp.

Martin, Charles I. 1881. *History of Door County, Wisconsin, together with biographies of nearly seven hundred families and mention of 4,000 persons*. Expositor Job Print., Sturgeon Bay, WI. 136 pp.

McDonald, Raymond. 1984. *Four Islands: A History of Detroit, Rock, St. Martins, and Washington Islands*. Published by the author. 172 pp.

National Archives and Records Service. 1980. Post Office Department reports of site locations 1837-1950. Microfilm publication M1126, roll 661. Washington, DC.

Peil, Annie. 1976. *The Way We Were!* Published by the author, Baileys Harbor, WI 52 pp.

Peterson, Leonard. 1991. *Rowleys Bay - Reliving the Heritage of Northern Door County.* Published by the author, Ellison Bay, WI 285 pp.

Powers, Mary Grace. 1959. "Johan Berndt Eliason." *The Peninsula* 4:6-13.

Purinton, Dick. 1990. *Over and Back - A Picture History of Transportation to Washington Island.* Washington Island Ferry Line, Inc., Washington Island, WI 96 pp.

Reynolds, Lucille W. 1960. "The Jacksonport Story." *The Peninsula* 5:1-7.

Richow, Harold. 1985. *Rural Free Delivery Postmarks of Wisconsin.* Bulletin #16, Wisconsin Postal History Society, Madison, WI. 8 pp.

Schreiber, Edward and Lois. 1990. *Fish Creek Voices - An Oral History of a Door County Village.* William Caxton Ltd., Ellison Bay, WI. 278 pp.

Shafer, Joseph (editor). 1924. *Wisconsin Domesday Book - Town Studies.* State Historical Society of Wisconsin, Madison, WI. 168 pp. Town of Sevastopol: pp. 124-128, by Marie A. Kasten.

Stapleton, Grover M. 1948. "The Development of Door County As Shown By Legal

Documents And Records." *The Peninsula* 1:27-36.

State Historical Society of Wisconsin. Card file of post office data in the Society's Library, Madison, WI.

United States Post Office Department. 1907. *U.S. official postal guide.* J.B. Lyon Co., Albany, NY. 940 pp.

United States Post Office Department. 1911. Map of Door County, Wisconsin, showing rural delivery service. Archives of the State Historical Society of Wisconsin, Madison, WI.

United States Post Office Department. 1968a. Records of appointment of postmasters - Wisconsin - 1832-1930. Microfilm of records from the National Archives, Washington, DC, owned by the Wisconsin Postal History Society.

United States Post Office Department. 1968b. Miscellaneous records of the Post Office Department in the National Archives, Washington, DC.

United States Post Office Department. 1969. Records of the Postmasters and Rural Carriers Division, Washington, DC.

United States Postal Service. 1974. Records of the Post Office Department - Registers of Appointments of Postmasters - Wisconsin - 1930-September 30, 1971. Microfilm from the National Archives and Records Service, Washington, DC, owned by the Wisconsin Postal History Society.

Vail, Malcom D. 1956. *Tales of Ephraim Waters.* Privately printed, Chicago. 24 unnumbered pages.

Whitney, Anne T. 1973. *Let's Talk about Washington Island 1850-1950.* Technic Graphics/Graphic Dimensions, Chicago, IL. 108 pp.

Wisconsin Postal History Society. 1967. *Post Offices Past And Present In The Territory And The State of Wisconsin.* Bulletin #8, Madison, WI. 37 pp.

Wisconsin Postal History Society. 1969. Records of postmasters from various reports of the U.S. Post Office Department held by the Society.

Appendix 1

Dates of Establishment - Door County Post Offices

1. Washington Harbor - Jun 22, 1854
2. Sturgeon Bay - Oct 22, 1855
3. Fish Creek - Aug 26, 1858
4. Nasewaupee - Sep 4, 1858
5. Marcus (later Forestville) - Sep 16, 1858
6. Chickatock (later Garnder) - Oct 27, 1858
7. Little Sturgeon - Nov 12, 1860
8. Baileys Harbor - Dec 4, 1860
9. Egg Harbor - Aug 3, 1861
10. Ephraim - Nov 13, 1861
11. Brussels - Nov 14, 1862
12. Duchateau - Dec 12, 1862
13. Clay Banks - Dec 16, 1862
14. Chambers Island - Apr 26, 1866
15. Jacksonport - May 29, 1867
16. North Bay - Feb 25, 1870
17. Williamsonville (later Tornado) - Jan 3, 1871
18. Warren's Corners (later Horn's Pier and Cheeseville) - Aug 11, 1871
19. Foscoro - Aug 14, 1871
20. Namur - Jun 14, 1872
21. Sister Bay - Feb 21, 1873
22. Ellison Bay - Mar 17, 1873
23. Maplewood - Feb 17, 1874
24. Sevastopol - Feb 17, 1874
25. Malakoff - Jun 18, 1874
26. Sawyer - Jul 13, 1874
27. Rowleys Bay (later Rowley) - Jul 1, 1878
28. Lily Bay - May 6, 1879
29. Leccia - Apr 15, 1880
30. Fagerwick - Jan 25, 1881
31. Salona - Aug 1, 1881
32. Voseville - Sep 27, 1881
33. Stevenson's Pier - Jan 30, 1882
34. Minor - Jul 31, 1882

35. Newport - Oct 17, 1882
36. Stokes - Jan 4, 1883
37. Hedge Hog (later Gills Rock) - Apr 16, 1883
38. Evergreen - Nov 16, 1885
39. Fetzer - Jan 11, 1887
40. Carnot - Jun 23, 1891
41. Vignes - Nov 10, 1891
42. Detroit Harbor (later Washington Island) - May 3, 1892
43. Institute - Dec 24, 1892
44. Kolberg - Jan 12, 1895
45. Hainesville - Sep 22, 1896
46. Graceport - Jan 4, 1898
47. Valmy - July 1, 1899
48. Hastings - Jan 4, 1902

Appendix 2

Dates of Closing - Door County Post Offices

Nasewaupee - Jan 29, 1862
Chambers Island - Aug 13, 1868
North Bay - May 19, 1873
Duchateau - Nov 13, 1873
Malakoff - Dec 22, 1881
Minor - Oct 3, 1882
Lily Bay - Oct 5, 1882
Fagerwick - Oct 23, 1882
Leccia - Dec 9, 1885
Fetzer - Jul 18, 1888
Warren's Corners/Horn's Pier/Cheeseville - Aug 4, 1893
Evergreen - Sep 23, 1898
Sevastopol - Oct 15, 1902
Voseville - Oct 31, 1902
Foscoro - Nov 15, 1902
Hainesville - Nov 15, 1902
Clay Banks - Feb 28, 1903
Stokes - Jul 14, 1903
Valmy - Dec 31, 1903
Salona - Jan 30, 1904
Vignes - Jan 30, 1904
Graceport - Apr 30, 1904
Hastings - Apr 30, 1904
Newport - Apr 30, 1904
Rowley/Rowleys Bay - Apr 30, 1904
Hedge Hog/Gills Rock - Jul 30, 1904
Chickatock/Garnder - Jan 14, 1905
Little Sturgeon - Apr 29, 1905
Namur - Apr 29, 1905
Stevenson's Pier - Apr 29, 1905
Institute - Apr 30, 1906
Kolberg - Feb 15, 1907
Williamsonville/Tornado - Feb 28, 1907
Carnot - Mar 15, 1907
Washington Harbor - Jan 31, 1916
Sawyer - Apr 30, 1938
Jacksonport - May 15, 1970

Appendix 3

Door County Post Offices By Township

Washington
Detroit Harbor/Washington Island
Fagerwick
Washington Harbor

Liberty Grove
Ellison Bay
Hedge Hog/Gills Rock
Newport
Rowley/Rowleys Bay
North Bay
Sister Bay

Gibraltar
Chambers Island
Ephraim
Fish Creek

Bailey's Harbor
Baileys Harbor

Egg Harbor
Egg Harbor
Fetzer
Graceport
Hastings

Jacksonport
Jacksonport

Sevastopol
Sevastopol
Institute
Malakoff
Lily Bay

Valmy
Voseville

Sturgeon Bay
Evergreen
Nasewaupee
Sawyer
Sturgeon Bay

Nasewaupee
Hainesville
Stokes

Gardner
Chickatock/Gardner
Little Sturgeon
Stevenson's Pier
Williamsonville/Tornado

Union
Duchateau
Namur

Brussels
Brussels
Kolberg
Leccia
Minor

Forestville
Carnot
Maplewood
Marcus/Forestville

Clay Banks
Clay Banks
Foscoro
Salona
Vignes
Warren's Corners/Horn's Pier/Cheeseville

Appendix 4

Door County's Nineteenth Century Women Postmasters

1878-1891 Matilda Tostenson, Ellison Bay
1884-1892 Harriet Watson, Tornado
1891-1892 Catherine Duwe, Forestville
1892 (July-December) August Wohltman, Baileys Harbor
1892-1897 Clementine Braunroth, Institute
1893 (May-September) Anna B. Dickson, Sister Bay
1894-1898 Flora C. Pinney, Evergreen
1895-1898 Mary L. Batchelder, Sevastopol
1895-1897 Anna Soukop, Stokes
1896-1902 Stena Torgerson, Hainesville
1898-1902 Anna M. Bassford, Sevastopol
1899-1903 Caroline Ludwick, Stokes
1899-1900 Ella Simon, Valmy

Appendix 5

Door County Postmasters with Most Years of Service

Fred Erskine, Jacksonport - 1915-1958 - 43 years
Jules G. Pierre, Brussels - 1906-1947 - 41 years
Samuel M. Hogenson, Ephraim - 1915-1951 - 36 years
Veronica Russell, Maplewood - 1949-1984 - 35 years
Magnus Magnusson, Washington Island - 1924-1958 - 34 years
Hans P. Jacobs, Ephraim - 1861-1894 - 33 years
Francois Pierre, Brussels - 1870-1902 - 32 years
Bert E. Thorp, Ephriam - 1951-1983 - 32 years
Charles L. Fellows, Foscoro - 1872-1902 - 30 years
Walter H. Severson, Ellison Bay - 1942-1972 - 30 years

Appendix 6 - Post Office Site Document

All post offices were periodically required by the U.S. Post Office Department to supply information on geographic locations and other data.

C

Post Office Department,
TOPOGRAPHER'S OFFICE,
Washington, Aug. 6, 1878.

Sir:

To enable the Topographer of this Department to determine, with as much accuracy as possible, the relative positions of Post Offices, so that they may be correctly delineated on its maps, the Postmaster General requests you to fill up the spaces and answer the questions below, and return the same, verified by your signature and dated, under cover to this Office.

Respectfully, &c.,

E.L.V.
Topographer P. O. Dept.

To Postmaster at Clay Banks,
Door Co.
Wiss

The (P. O. Dept.) name of my Office is Clay Banks
*Its *local name* is Clay Banks
It is situated in the North west quarter of *Section No.* 28, in *Township* 26 (north or south), *Range* 26 (east or west), *County* of Door, *State* of Wisconsin

The name of the most prominent *river* near it is Ahnapee
The name of the nearest *creek* is Bear Creek
This Office is 9 miles from said *river*, on the North side of it, and is [illegible] ~~miles from~~ said ~~nearest~~ *creek*, on the South side of it.

The name of the nearest Office on route No. 25 395 is Horn's Pier, and its distance is 5 miles, by the traveled road, in a Northerly direction from this my Office.
The name of the nearest Office, *on the same route*, on the other side, is Forestville
and its distance is 3 miles in a Southerly direction from this my Office.

The name of the nearest Office *off the route* is [illegible]ville, [illegible] Co, and its distance by the most direct road is 7½ miles in a [illegible] direction from this my Office.
This Office is at a distance of 47 miles from the [illegible] Station of the Lake Shore Railroad, on the North side of the railroad.

State, under this, the names of all other Offices near your Office, in different directions from it, and their distances from it by the most direct roads.

*If the town, village, or site of the Post Office, be known by *another name than that of the Post Office*, state that other name here, that it may be identified on the map of the State (or Territory).

☞ A *diagram* of the township and sections (or, where the land is not so divided, a sketch map,) showing the precise location of your Office, together with the adjoining Post Offices, towns, or villages, the roads, *railroads*, and larger streams or creeks, in addition to the above, will be useful, and is desired.—(*See diagram blank* accompanying this, to be filled up.)

(*Signature of Postmaster.*) Theodore Pieplow

(*Date.*) August 17th 1878

Diagram *showing the site of the* Clay Banks *Post Office in Township* 26 *Range* 26 *of* Clay Banks *Principal Meridian, County of* Door*, State of* Wisconsin*, with the adjacent Townships and Post Offices.*

Clay Banks,
Door Co.
Wis.

It is requested that the exact site of the proposed, or existing Post Office, as also the roads to the adjoining Offices, and the larger streams or rivers, be marked on this diagram, to be returned as soon as possible to the Post Office Department. If on, or near a railroad, mark the railroad and adjacent Station accurately.

(NORTH.)

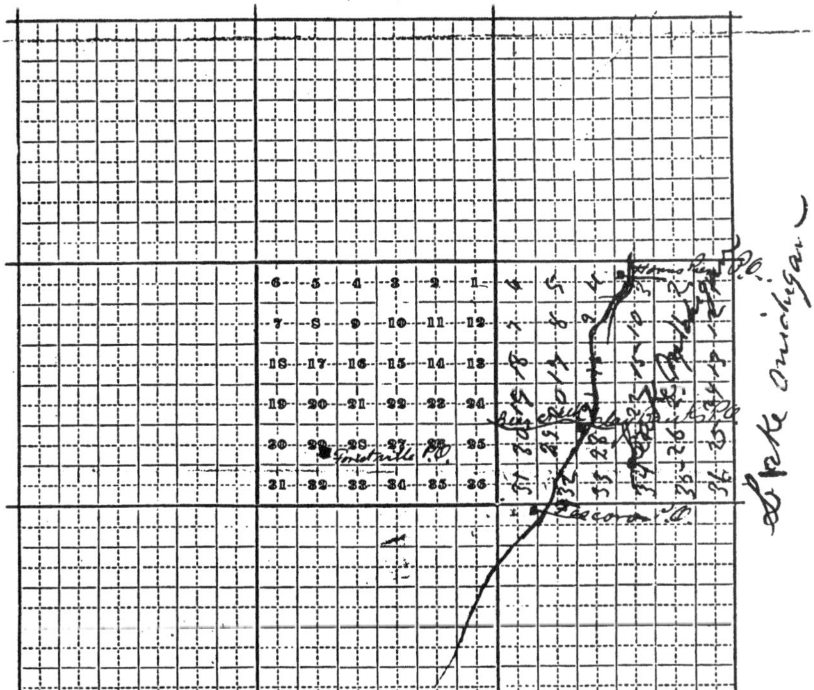

Scale ½ inch to the mile.

(SOUTH.)

Photo Credits

Annie Peil: 97, 147
Author's collection: 52, 54, 56, 77, 94, 112, 122-123, 144, 149, 161-162, 165-166, 168, 181- 182
Door County Advocate: 87-88, 156, 158, 170, 176
Gibraltar Historical Society (Wm. Guenzel collection): 67, 70-72, 74
Orville Schopf: 138-139, 141
Wisconsin Dept. of Natural Resources: 128-129